I0792984

IMAGES
of Rail

Railroads of Fort Bend County

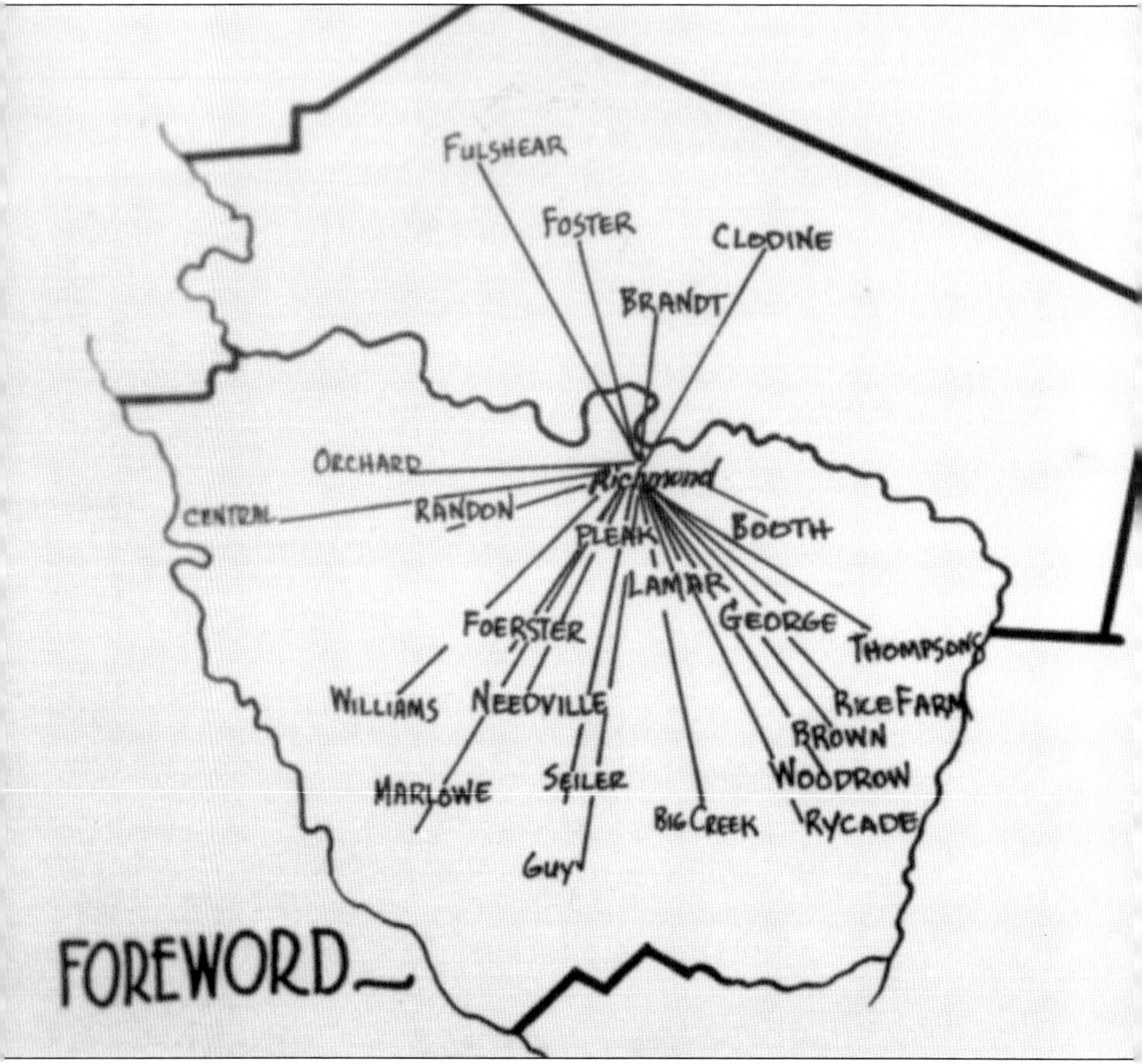

This early map of Fort Bend County, Texas, shows the locations of many of the major towns of the county in the late 1890s. Many of these towns were serviced by at least one of the eight railroad companies built in Fort Bend County. Many of these same towns are still serviced by rail. (Courtesy of the Fort Bend County Libraries, Genealogy and Local History Department.)

On the Cover: A San Antonio and Aransas Pass passenger train from Houston is arriving at the Flushear depot as waiting passengers get ready for departure to their next destination. This is a typical scene that is repeated daily throughout Fort Bend County. (Courtesy of the Fort Bend County Libraries, Genealogy and Local History Department.)

IMAGES
of Rail

RAILROADS OF FORT BEND COUNTY

Jim Vollmar and
the Rosenberg Railroad Museum

ARCADIA
PUBLISHING

ISBN 978-0-7385-7901-6

Published by Arcadia Publishing
Charleston, South Carolina

Printed in the United States of America

Library of Congress Control Number: 2010923098

For all general information contact Arcadia Publishing at:
Telephone 843-853-2070
Fax 843-853-0044
E-mail sales@arcadiapublishing.com
For customer service and orders:
Toll-Free 1-888-313-2665

Visit us on the Internet at www.arcadiapublishing.com

This book is dedicated to all of the faithful volunteers and supporters of the Rosenberg Railroad Museum, whose hard work and dedication have made the museum an environment where all can visit, learn, and enjoy the rich railroad history of Fort Bend County.

Contents

ACKNOWLEDGMENTS

The photographs used to illustrate this book have been selected from the archives of the Fort Bend County Libraries, Genealogy and Local History Department; the Rosenberg Railroad Museum; and from the personal collection of my very good friend, Ken Stavinoha, historian for the Rosenberg Railroad Museum. Unless otherwise noted, all images appearing in this book were graciously provided by the Fort Bend County Libraries, Genealogy and Local History Department.

There are several people who I wish to thank for their assistance and encouragement with this, my first book project. I am deeply indebted to my wife, Pam, and family for allowing me the time to pursue my passion of railroading and for their encouragement and support in my first book endeavor.

Also, Jana H. Smith, executive director of the Rosenberg Railroad Museum, for her expert guidance and assisting me in arranging the photographs for each chapter.

Special thanks goes to my very good friend Ken Stavinoha for his inspiration that fostered my interest in local history (I hated history as a kid in school). His expert knowledge of the railroad history of Fort Bend County and of railroads in Texas was absolutely invaluable.

I would also like to thank my editor at Arcadia Publishing, Ms. Hannah Carney, for her patience, expert guidance, and encouragement.

—Jim Vollmar

INTRODUCTION

Establishing a dependable mode of transportation is vital to the economic growth and prosperity of any community. Having a reliable means of moving people in and out of the community as well as transporting products to market and having access to major shipping hubs and ports proved to be paramount in the early years of Fort Bend County and the nation. It has been said that this country owes more to its railroads, as an agency in increasing its wealth and population, then to all of the other agencies combined. Through the railroads, the vast wealth of our prairies, forests, and mines has been unearthed and their products placed into the markets of the world. In the early 1900s, it was stated that no other invention of that time has contributed so much to the prosperity and happiness of mankind as the railroad.

Fort Bend County was formed in the early 1820s by members of Stephen F. Austin's "Old Three Hundred." Initially steamships operated up and down the Brazos River to transport goods to market before the railroads came along and linked the county to some of the largest and busiest ports in the nation. In 1854, a general act was passed to encourage the construction of railroads in Texas by means of donations of public lands. The first railroads chartered carried the donation of up to eight sections of 640 acres for each mile of rail completed. In addition, a 200-foot right-of-way across public land was also granted, which allowed additional grounds for constructing depots and terminals as necessary.

The effects of the Civil War were felt by the railroads more than any other enterprise, and the financial depression extended from 1862 to 1869, when construction practically came to a complete halt. Only 204 miles of track were completed in a 10-year period from the end of 1860 to December 1870.

In towns throughout the United States, the railroad depot was the center of activity for the community. The same can be said for towns throughout Fort Bend County; the railroad depot was considered the hub of activity for the community. People and freight were on the move, and the railroad depot was the center of all the action. A unique aspect to the depot was found in the city of Rosenberg, Texas, where the Galveston, Harrisburg, and San Antonio (GH&SA) and Gulf, Colorado, and Santa Fe (GC&SF) Railroads shared common structures for their passenger and freight service. This was due to the close proximity of these two rail lines with one another through town. Some depots along the Southern Pacific route had beautifully manicured parks on their grounds treating their visitors to a wonderful sight upon their arrival.

The county developed economic diversity with the continued growth of agriculture commodities such as cotton, rice, sugar, corn, livestock, and hides. Later with the discovery of oil and development of sulfur mines, the cities and towns throughout the county continued to flourish and grow.

As many as eight separate railroad companies were chartered in and operated through Fort Bend County, including the very first rail line to be constructed in the state of Texas. Today four Class 1 railroads operate in Fort Bend County, making it a diverse economic center of South Texas.

One

The Buffalo Bayou, Brazos, and Colorado Railroad

The pioneer of Texas railroading was the Buffalo Bayou, Brazos, and Colorado (BBB&C) Railroad. Chartered on February 11, 1850, it was the first railroad built in Texas. It was designed to develop and secure trade of the fertile Brazos and Colorado Valleys down to the seaports of Galveston. Construction started at Buffalo Bayou in Harrisburg in 1851. The first 20-mile segment reached Stafford's Point in Fort Bend County in 1853. By 1855, the BBB&C had reached the eastern bank of the Brazos River in Richmond, Texas. Bridging the Brazos proved to be a serious problem for the railroad. Early attempts to span the river utilized a floating pontoon bridge, which was constructed at river level and could be swung out of the way to allow boat traffic to pass. Because of the steep grade involved, passengers were offered a choice to walk or take the daredevil ride across the river. On occasion, the train would have to be fished out of the river. By 1860, the BBB&C had been completed west to Alleyton, Texas, but progress halted due to the start of the Civil War. In December 1870, a new charter was obtained under the name of Galveston, Harrisburg, and San Antonio Railroad and was to be built to San Antonio. During this time, the railroad became known as the "Sunset Route," because the trains traveled west toward the setting sun. On June 30, 1889, the GH&SA Railroad was leased to the Southern Pacific Company but operated as its own organization. In 1918, the GH&SA built a branch line from Rosenberg through Needville and Guy to Damon, Texas. This line was abandoned in sections beginning in the 1950s through the 1980s. On March 1, 1927, the GH&SA was leased to the Texas and New Orleans (T&NO) Railroad Company. The company merged with T&NO Railroad on June 30, 1934, and on November 1, 1961, the T&NO was merged into the Southern Pacific Railroad. In December 1996, the Union Pacific Railroad (UP) purchased the Southern Pacific, making Union Pacific the largest railroad company in North America.

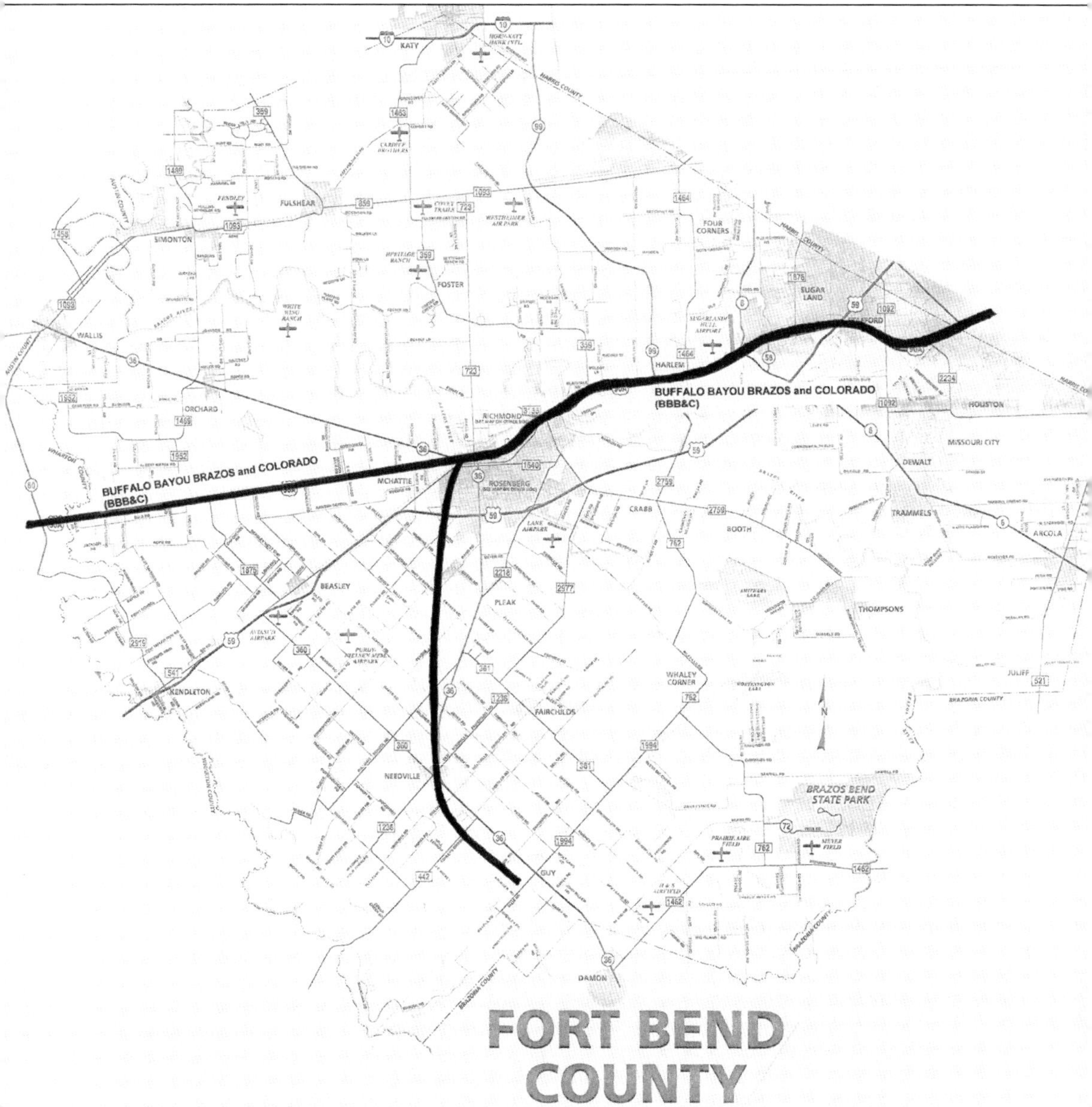

This map of Fort Bend County reflects the route of the Buffalo Bayou, Brazos, and Colorado Railroad. This was the first railroad to start construction in Texas. Its original 20-mile segment started in Harrisburg and ran to Stafford's Point. Towns along this route through Fort Bend County include Missouri City, Stafford, Sugar Land, Richmond, and Rosenberg, Texas.

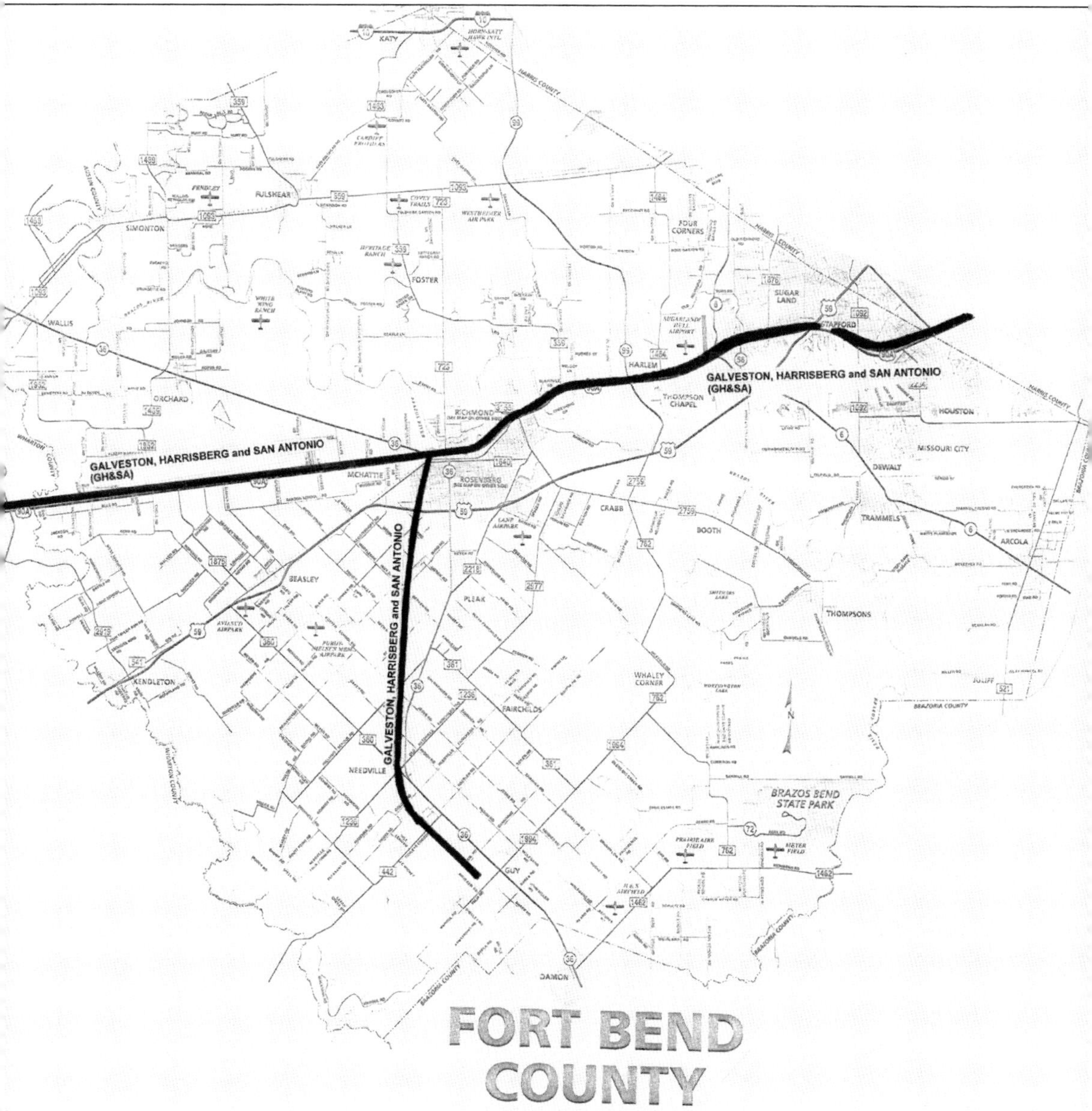

This map of Fort Bend County reflects the route of the Galveston, Harrisburg, and San Antonio Railroad. Originally known as the Buffalo Bayou, Brazos, and Colorado Railroad, a new charter was obtained in December 1870, and the line became know as the Galveston, Harrisburg, and San Antonio Railroad.

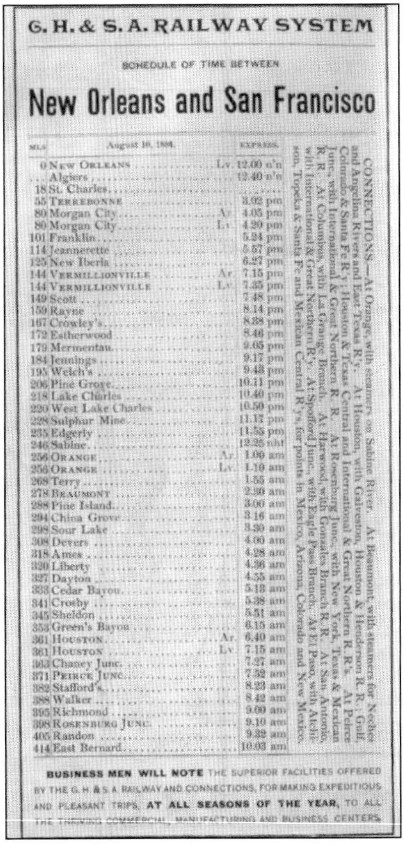

G. H. & S. A. RAILWAY SYSTEM

SCHEDULE OF TIME BETWEEN

New Orleans and San Francisco

MLS	August 10, 1884.		EXPRESS.
0	NEW ORLEANS	Lv.	12.00 n'n
...	Algiers		12.40 n'n
18	St. Charles		
55	TERREBONNE		3.02 pm
80	Morgan City	Ar.	4.05 pm
80	Morgan City	Lv.	4.20 pm
101	Franklin		5.24 pm
114	Jeannerette		5.57 pm
125	New Iberia		6.27 pm
144	VERMILLIONVILLE	Ar.	7.15 pm
144	VERMILLIONVILLE	Lv.	7.35 pm
149	Scott		7.48 pm
159	Rayne		8.14 pm
167	Crowley's		8.28 pm
172	Estherwood		8.46 pm
179	Mermentau		9.05 pm
184	Jennings		9.17 pm
195	Welch's		9.48 pm
206	Pine Grove		10.11 pm
218	Lake Charles		10.40 pm
220	West Lake Charles		10.50 pm
228	Sulphur Mine		11.17 pm
235	Edgerly		11.55 pm
246	Sabine		12.25 nht
256	ORANGE	Ar.	1.00 am
256	ORANGE	Lv.	1.10 am
268	Terry		1.55 am
278	BEAUMONT		2.30 am
288	Pine Island		3.00 am
294	China Grove		3.16 am
298	Sour Lake		3.30 am
308	Devers		4.00 am
318	Ames		4.28 am
320	Liberty		4.36 am
327	Dayton		4.55 am
333	Cedar Bayou		5.13 am
341	Crosby		5.38 am
345	Sheldon		5.51 am
353	Green's Bayou		6.15 am
361	HOUSTON	Ar.	6.40 am
361	HOUSTON	Lv.	7.15 am
363	Chaney Junc.		7.27 am
371	PEIRCE JUNC.		7.52 am
382	Stafford's		8.23 am
388	Walker		8.42 am
395	Richmond		9.00 am
398	ROSENBURG JUNC.		9.10 am
405	Randon		9.32 am
414	East Bernard		10.03 am

CONNECTIONS.—At Orange, with steamers on Sabine River. At Beaumont, with steamers for Neches and Angelina Rivers and East Texas R'y. At Houston, with Galveston, Houston & Henderson R. R.; Gulf, Colorado & Santa Fe R'y; Houston & Texas Central and International & Great Northern R. R's. At Peirce Junc., with International & Great Northern R. R. At Rosenburg Junc., with New York, Texas & Mexican R. R. At Columbus, with La Grange Branch. At Harwood, with Gonzales Branch R. R. At San Antonio, with International & Great Northern R'y. At Spofford Junc., with Eagle Pass Branch. At El Paso, with Atchison, Topeka & Santa Fe and Mexican Central R'ys, for points in Mexico, Arizona, Colorado and New Mexico.

BUSINESS MEN WILL NOTE THE SUPERIOR FACILITIES OFFERED BY THE G. H. & S. A. RAILWAY AND CONNECTIONS, FOR MAKING EXPEDITIOUS AND PLEASANT TRIPS, **AT ALL SEASONS OF THE YEAR,** TO ALL THE THRIVING COMMERCIAL, MANUFACTURING AND BUSINESS CENTERS.

An employee timetable from August 10, 1884, for the Galveston, Harrisburg, and San Antonio Railroad system provides the arrival and departure times at the stations between New Orleans and San Francisco. Towns along the line in Fort Bend County are Stafford's Point, Walker, Richmond, Rosenberg Junction, and Randon. (Courtesy of the Ken E. Stavinoha Collection.)

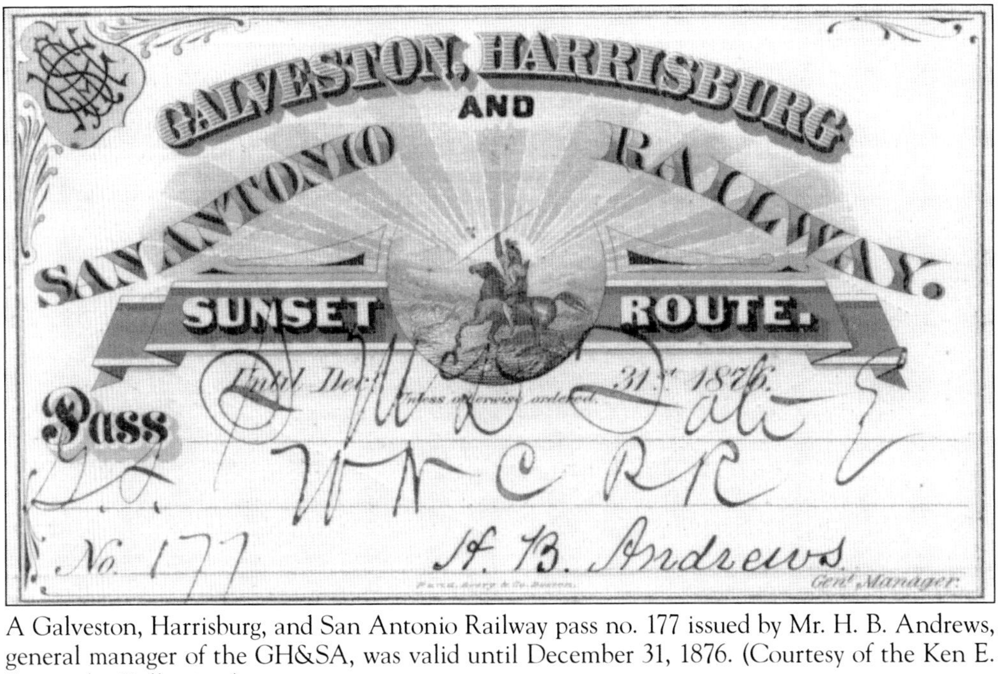

A Galveston, Harrisburg, and San Antonio Railway pass no. 177 issued by Mr. H. B. Andrews, general manager of the GH&SA, was valid until December 31, 1876. (Courtesy of the Ken E. Stavinoha Collection.)

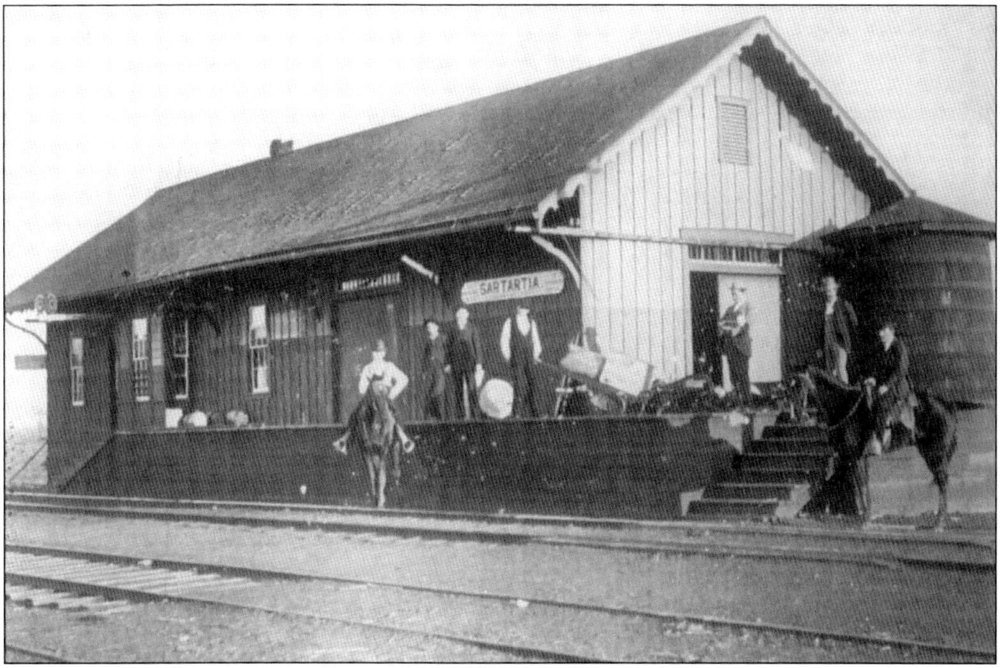

This late 1890s photograph gives a view of the Sartartia depot. Passengers' baggage and various freight items sit on the platform to be loaded onto their trains upon arrival at the depot. (Courtesy of the Ken E. Stavinoha Collection.)

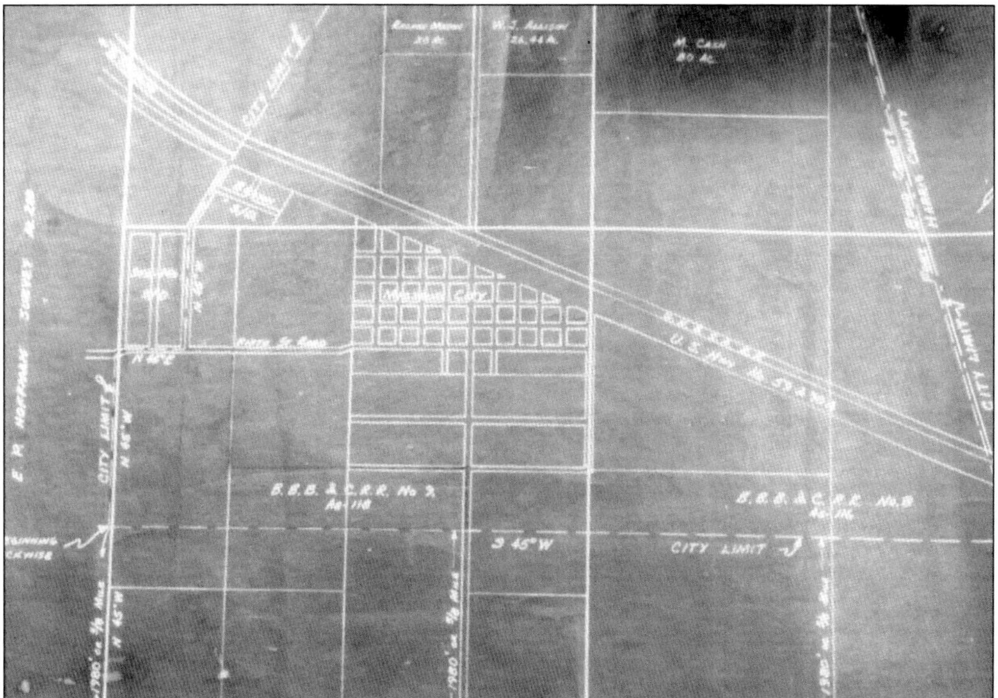

This survey map by E. P. Hoffman of Missouri City, Texas, shows the Galveston, Harrisburg, and San Antonio Railroad traveling through the city.

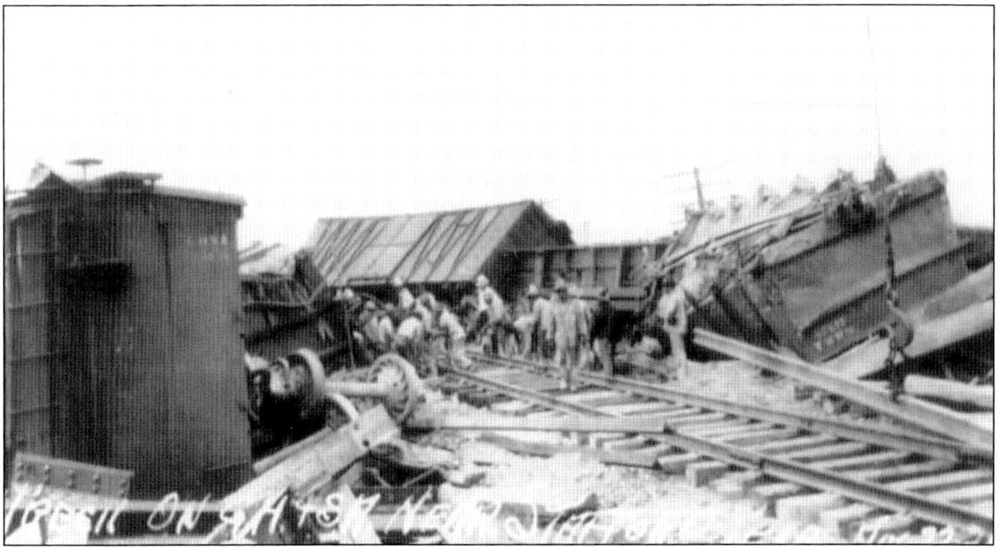

A scene dreaded by railroads anywhere, here is a major wreck on the Galveston, Harrisburg, and San Antonio just outside Stafford, Texas. Cleanup is underway using the railroad crane known as the "Big Hook," so the trains can get going once again.

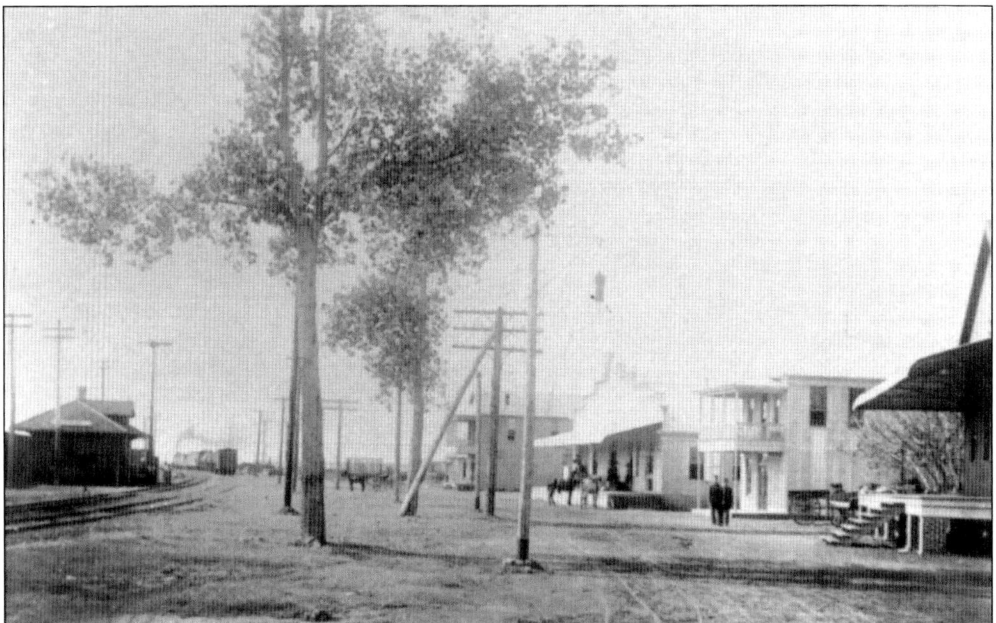

A westbound GH&SA mixed-freight train leaves Sugar Land and the GH&SA freight depot. The next stop is Richmond, Texas.

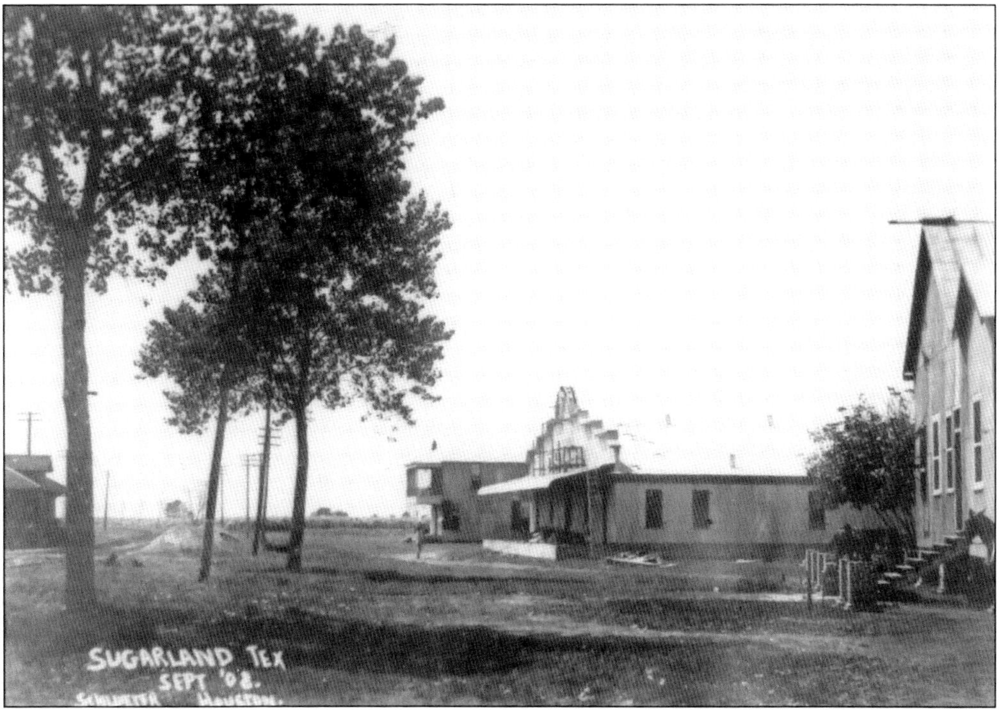

Taken in September 1909, this photograph gives a view of the Galveston, Harrisburg, and San Antonio freight depot and businesses in downtown Sugar Land, Texas.

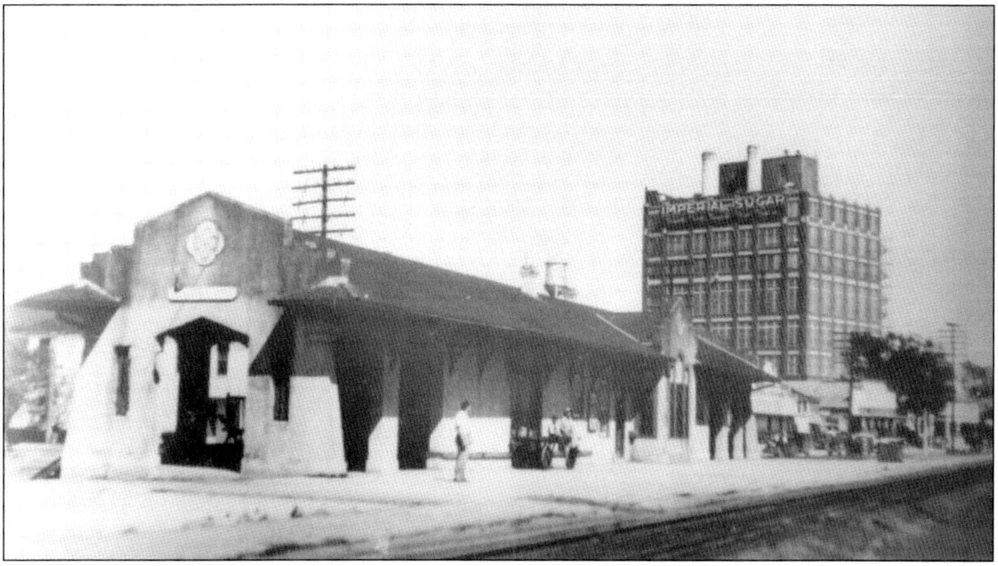

Pictured here is a view of the Galveston, Harrisburg, and San Antonio depot in downtown Sugar Land. The Imperial Sugar Factory Char House can be seen in the background.

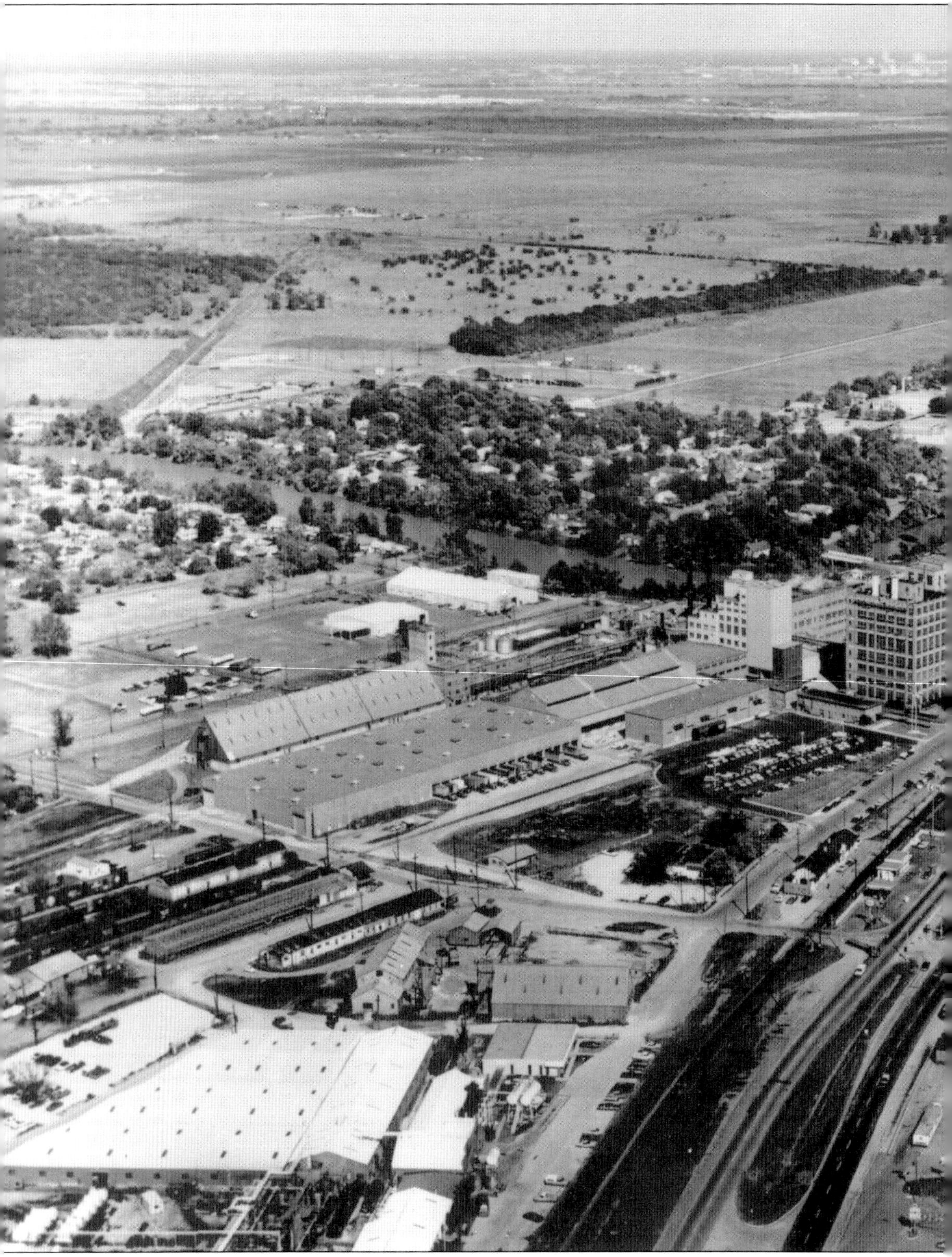

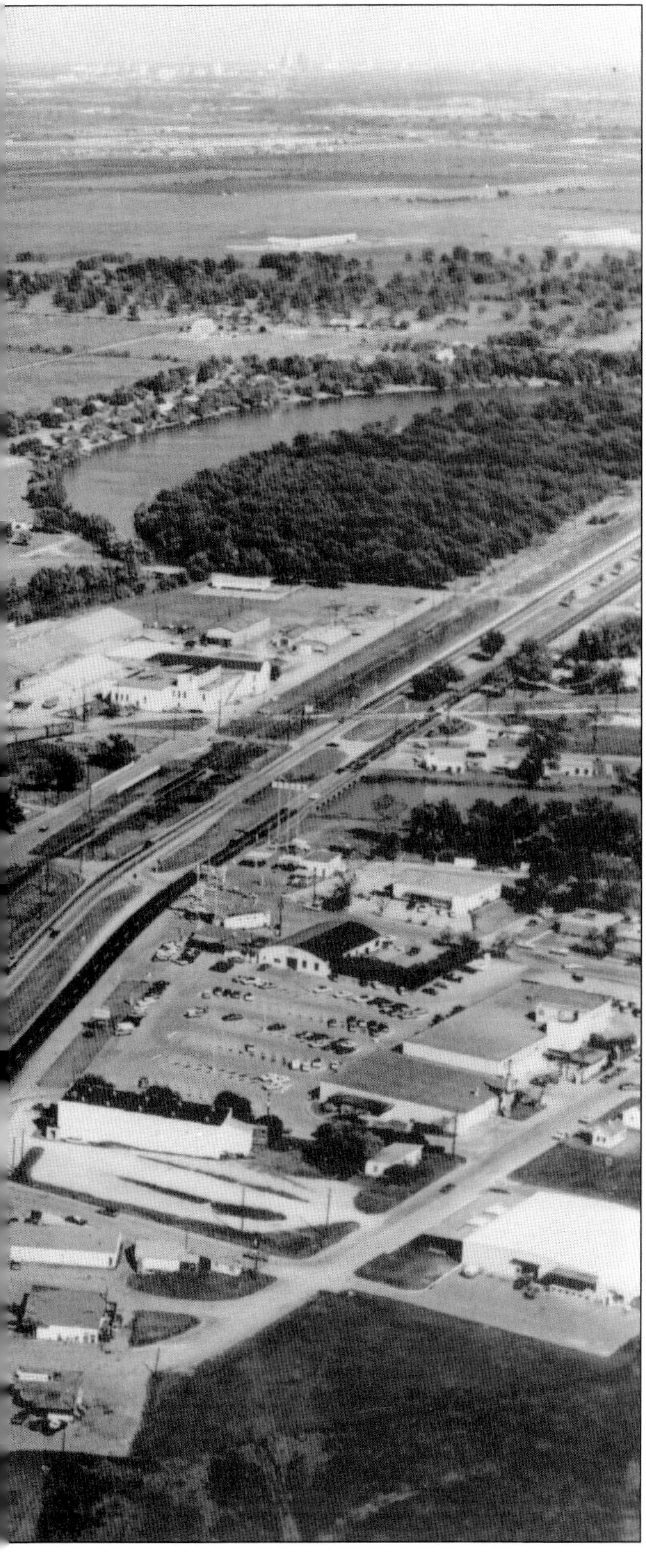

This is an aerial view of the Imperial Sugar Refinery in the late 1950s. The GH&SA depot and rail yard facilities are in plain view in this photograph. Today many of the structures of this facility are still standing; however, the refinery has been shut down since 2005.

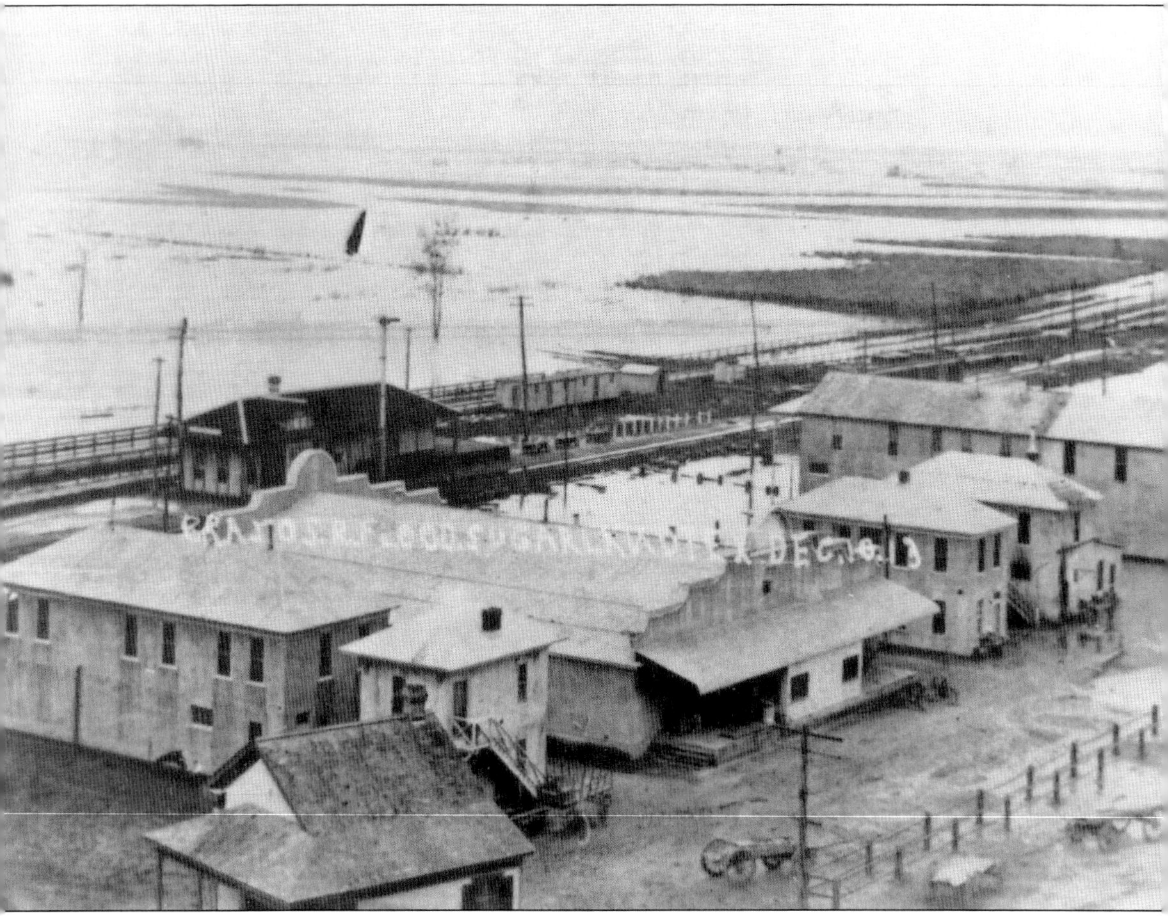

A 1913 aerial view shows the Galveston, Harrisburg, and San Antonio depot in Sugar Land, Texas, during the 1913 flood of the Brazos River.

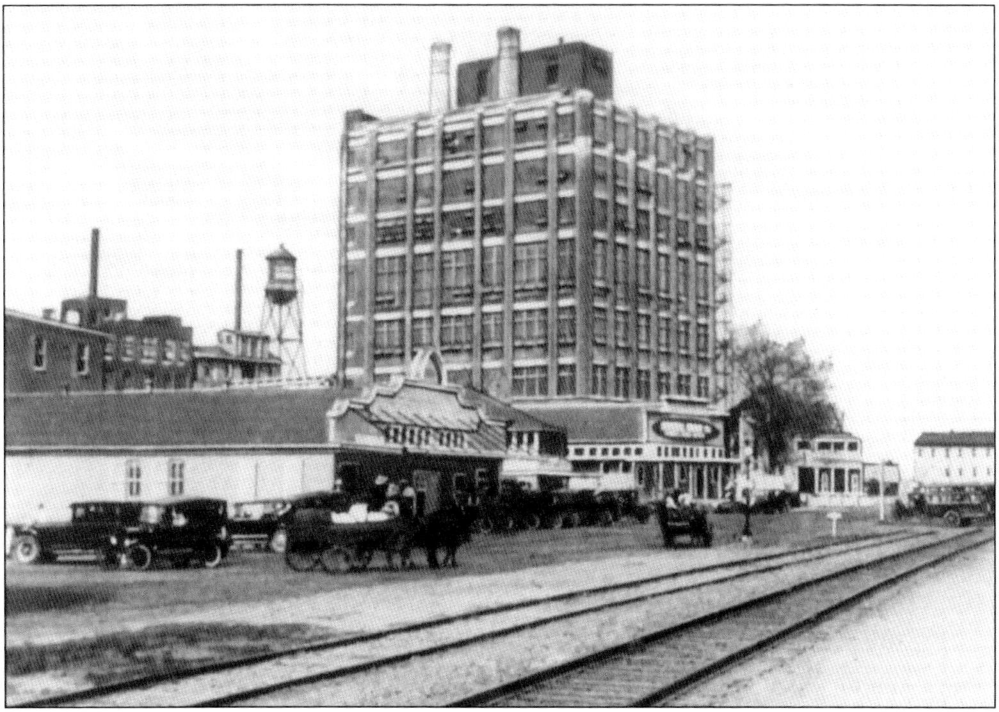

This late-1920s photograph gives a view of the Imperial Sugar General Mercantile store as seen from the GH&SA depot with the Imperial Sugar Factory Char House in the background.

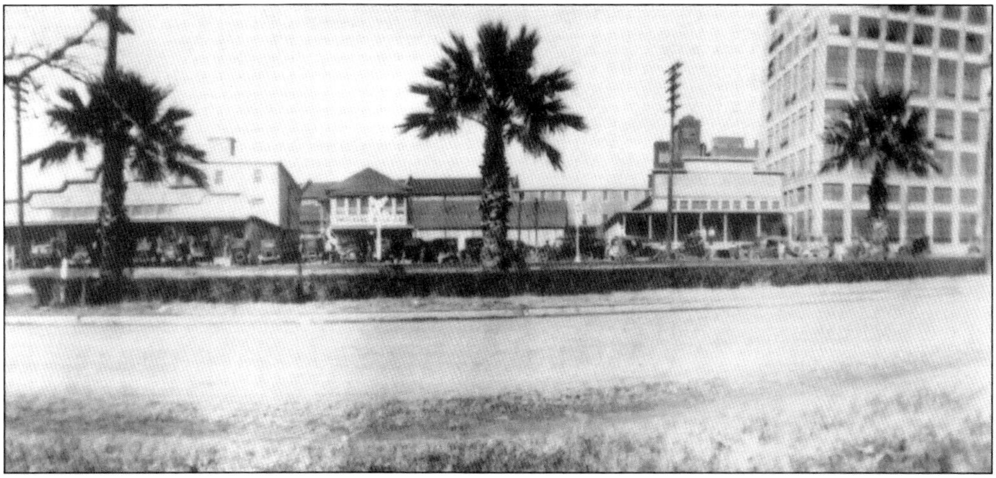

Another late-1920s view of some of the downtown businesses in Sugar Land includes the Imperial Drug Company and the Imperial Sugar General Mercantile.

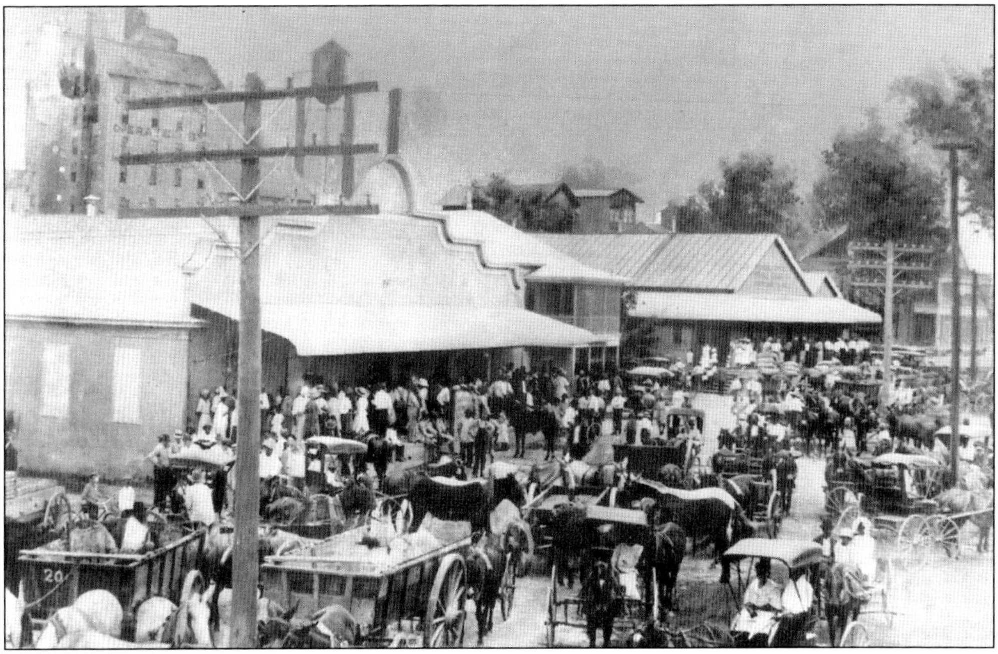

This busy Saturday morning in downtown Sugar Land, Texas, in 1912 features crowds of people from nearby farms coming to shop and visit at the Imperial Sugar General Mercantile and the general offices of the Imperial Sugar Company.

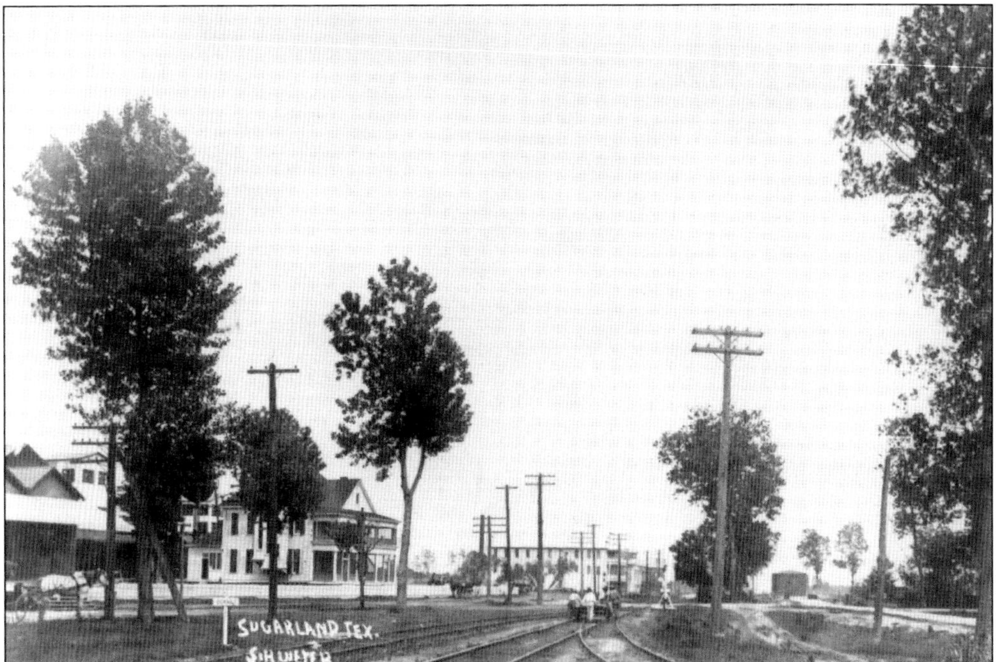

Maintenance work on the railroad is an activity that continues even with railroading today. This late-1900s photograph shows a track gang inspecting the GH&SA main line through Sugar Land.

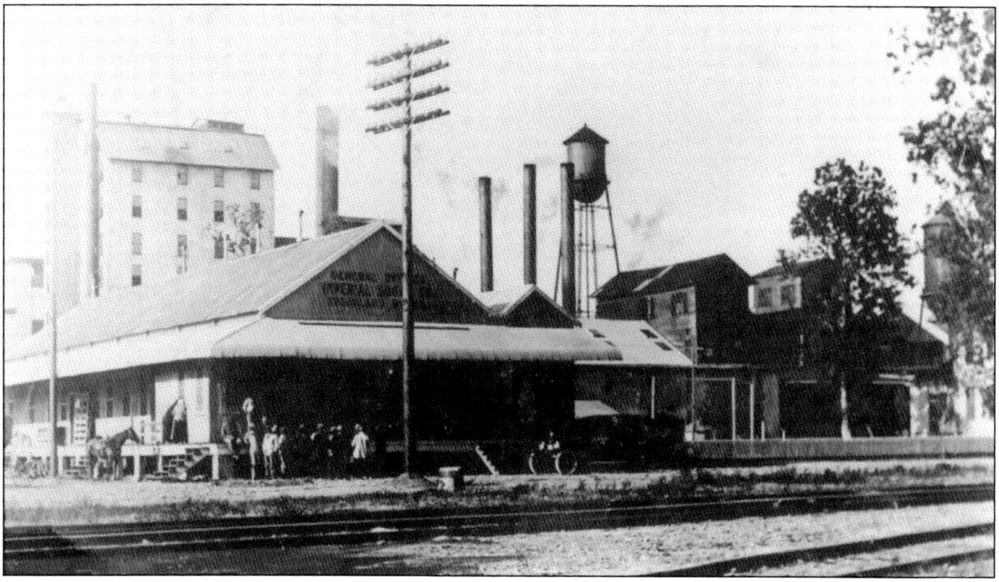

Townspeople gather outside the general offices of the Imperial Sugar Company waiting for the start of another business day. On the porch, two women are seen peeking in the window probably wondering when the doors will open.

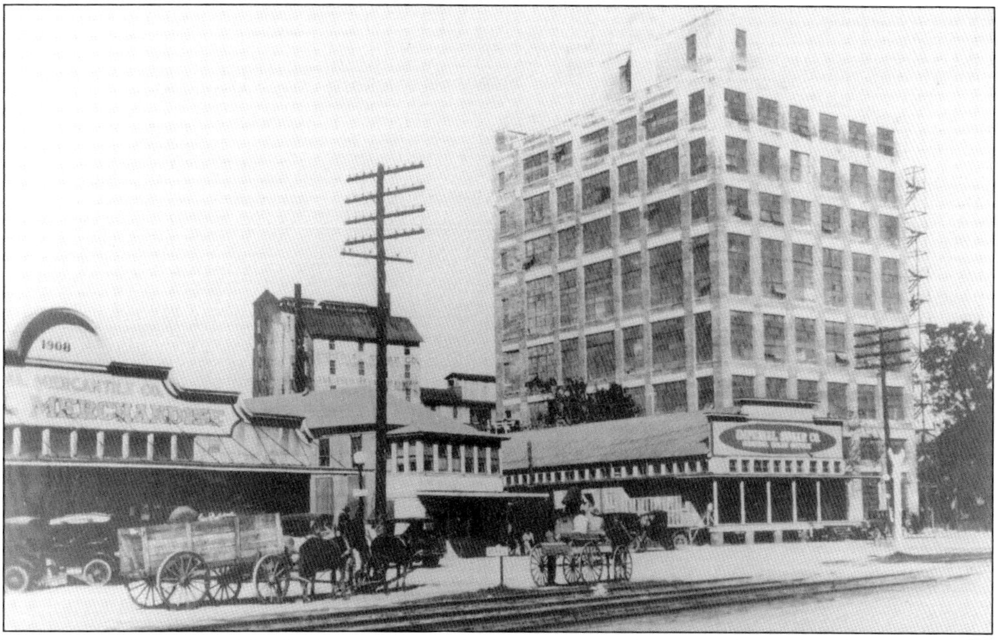

Downtown Sugar Land in the late 1900s finds the townspeople going about their business at the Imperial Sugar General Mercantile store. The Imperial Sugar Refinery buildings make up the skyline of Fort Bend County. The lettering on the building in the background states, "Imperial Sugar Company, the Only Texas Refinery."

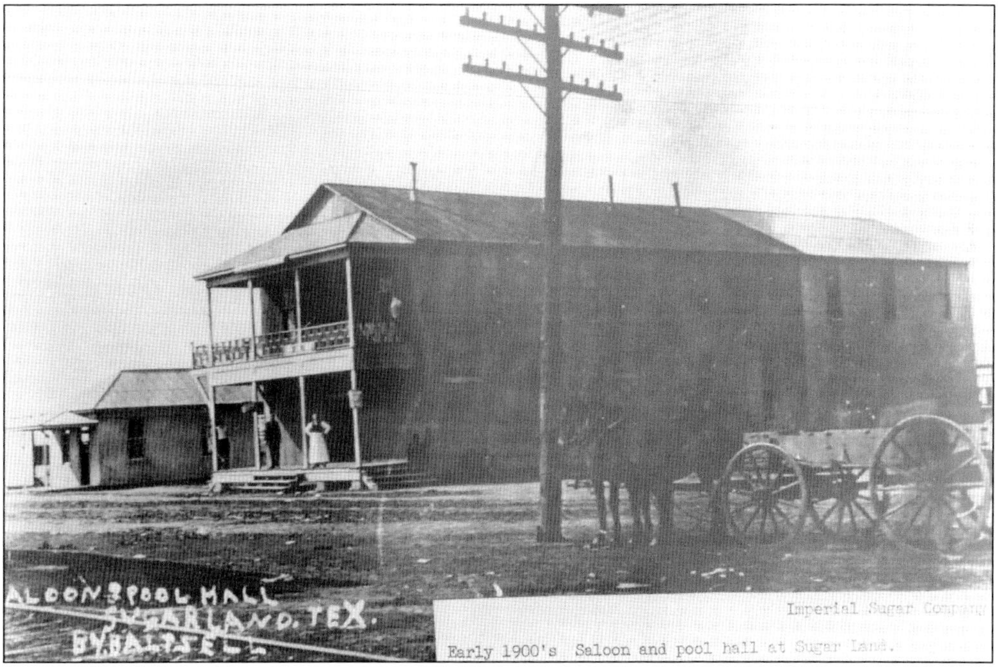

This early 1900s view of a downtown Sugar Land saloon and pool hall also includes the GH&SA tracks out front.

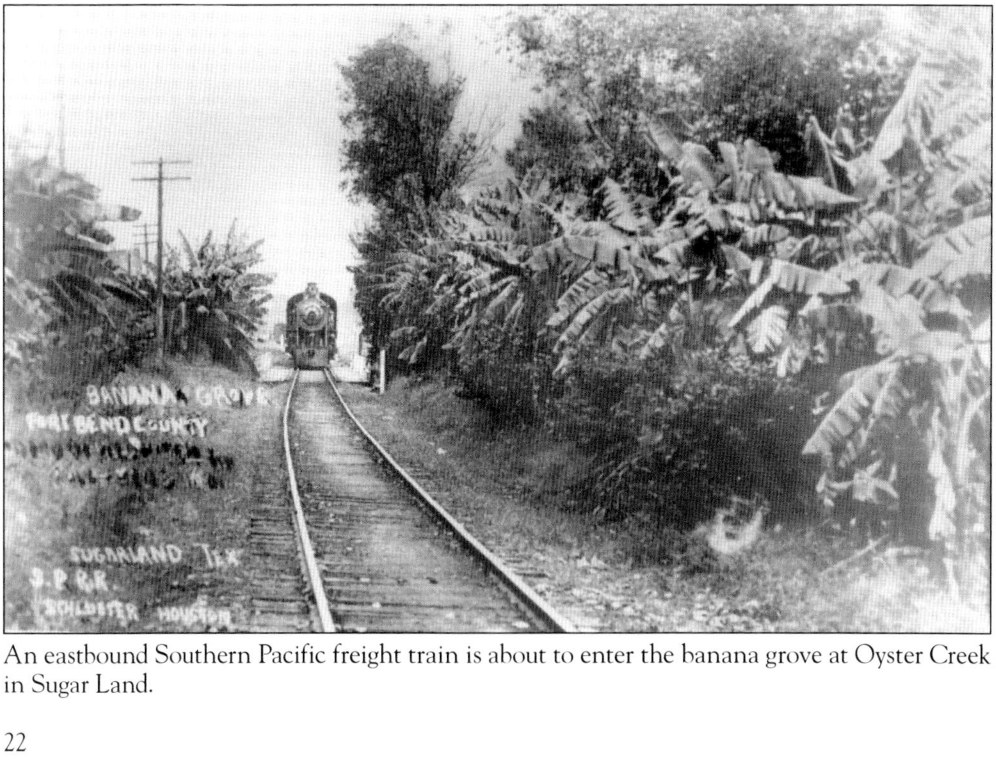

An eastbound Southern Pacific freight train is about to enter the banana grove at Oyster Creek in Sugar Land.

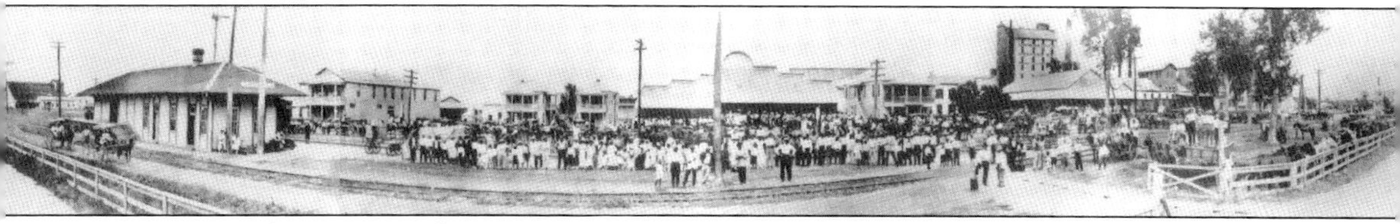

Sugar Land residents pose in this panoramic view of downtown Sugar Land, Texas. The Galveston, Harrisburg, and San Antonio depot is seen at the left.

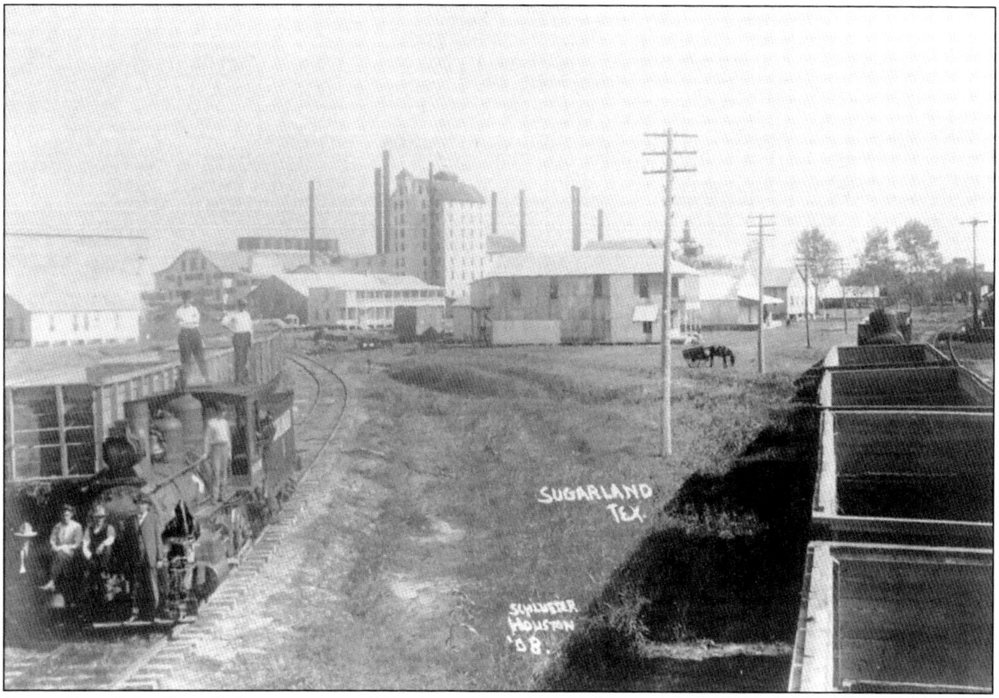

Sugar Land Railroad's Locomotive No. 1 and its crew take a moment from switching duties to take a picture in the rail yards in Sugar Land, Texas.

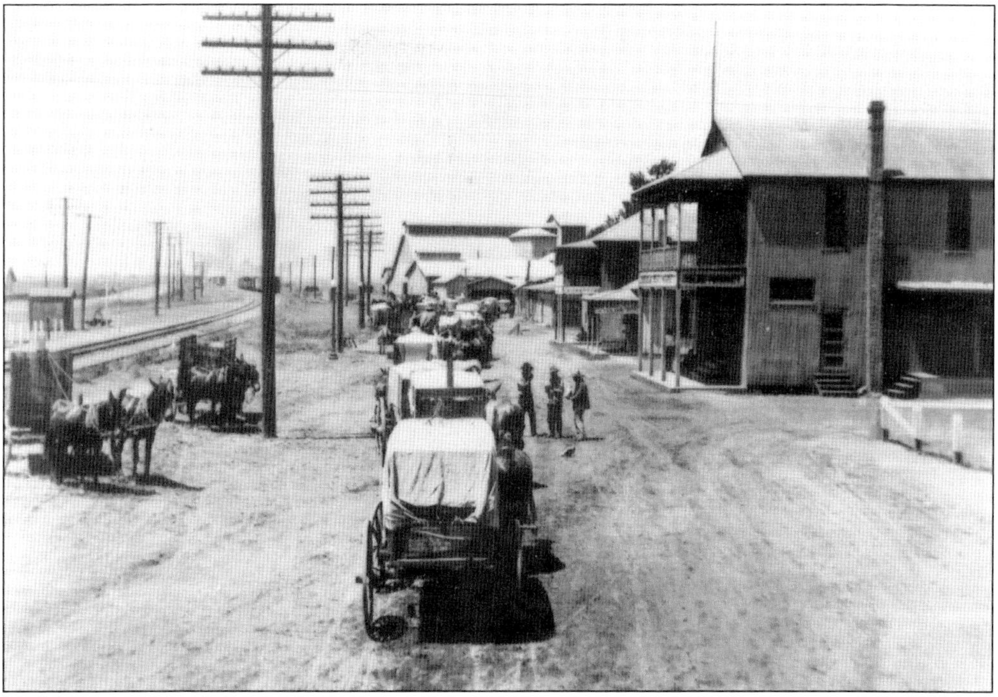

Farmers are lining up their teams for their turn at the seed mill in Sugar Land, Texas. Two GH&SA trains can be seen in the distance heading west.

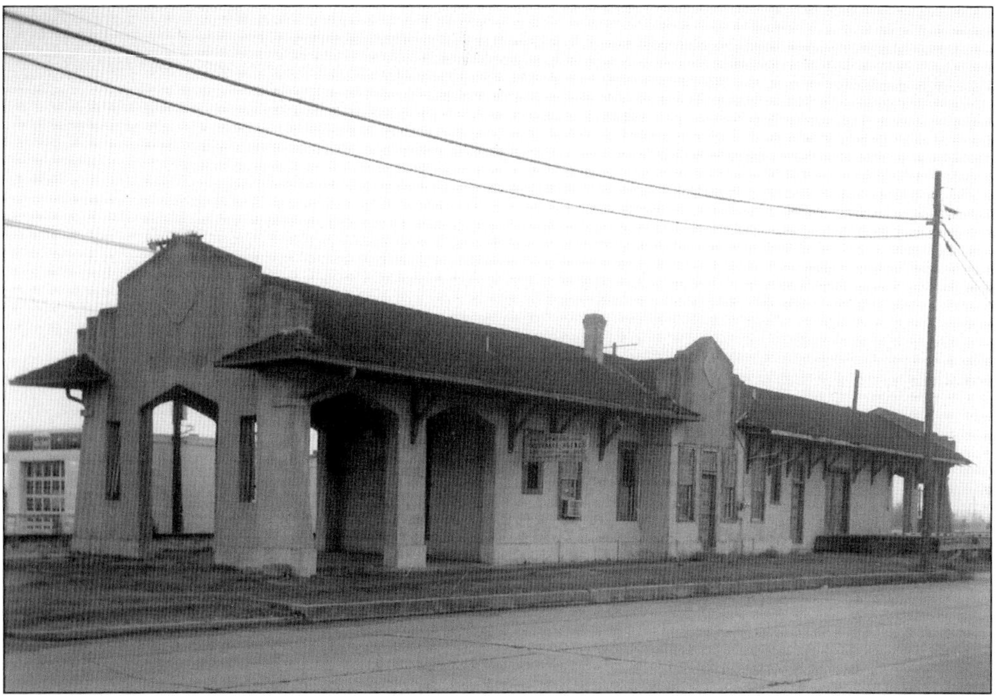

Pictured here is the Galveston, Harrisburg, and San Antonio depot in downtown Sugar Land, Texas. After the railroad vacated the depot, the City of Sugar Land had the depot moved and restored. Today it is the home for the Fort Bend Chamber of Commerce.

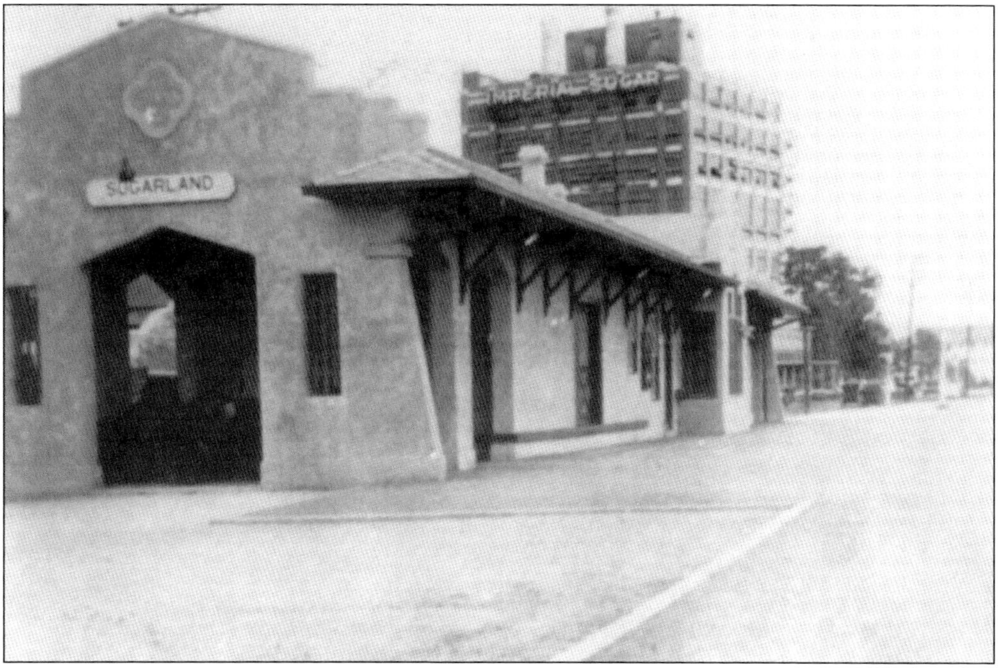

A close-up of the GH&SA depot provides a great view of the architectural details of the structure. The Imperial Sugar Refinery is seen in the background.

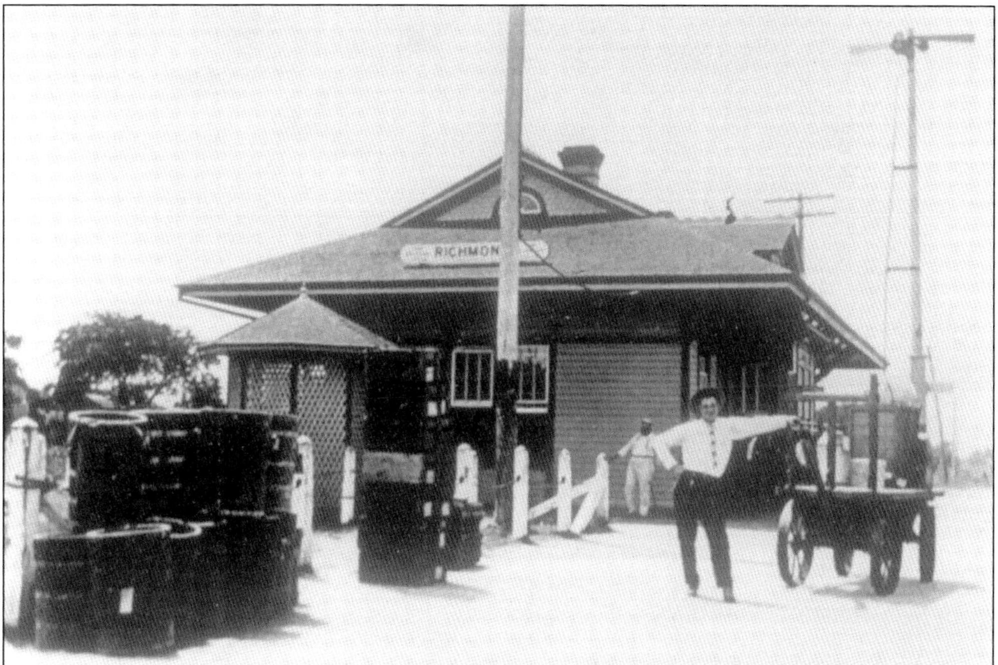

Freight and baggage have been loaded onto the baggage cart waiting to be loaded onto the next train into Richmond, Texas. (Courtesy of the Rosenberg Railroad Museum Collection.)

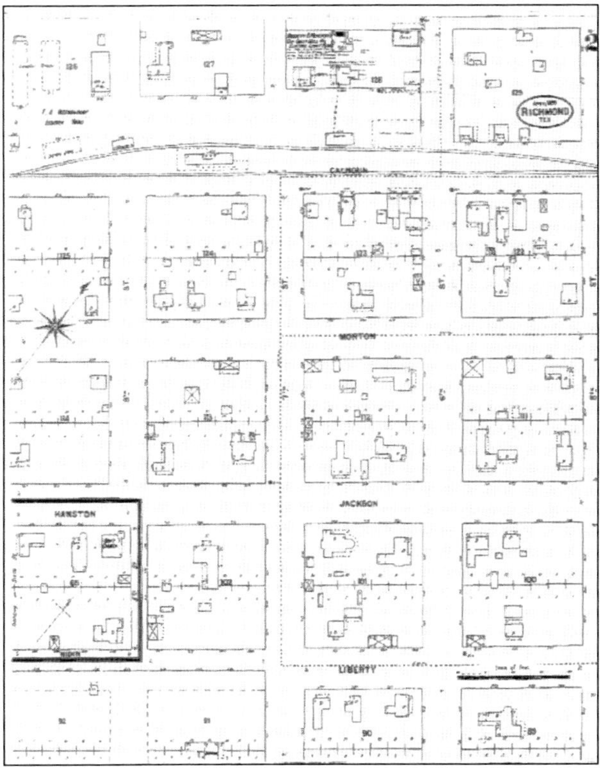

An 1899 Sanborn Fire Insurance map of downtown Richmond provides a layout of the town. The GH&SA depot and track arrangement are also shown.

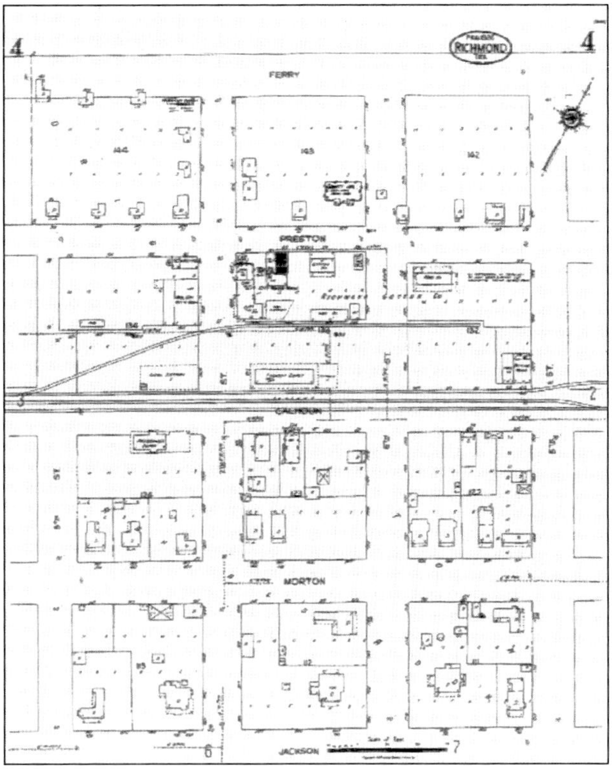

This 1936 Sanborn Fire Insurance map of downtown Richmond shows the changes in the GH&SA track arrangement around the depot. Also some new structures along Morton Street can be seen.

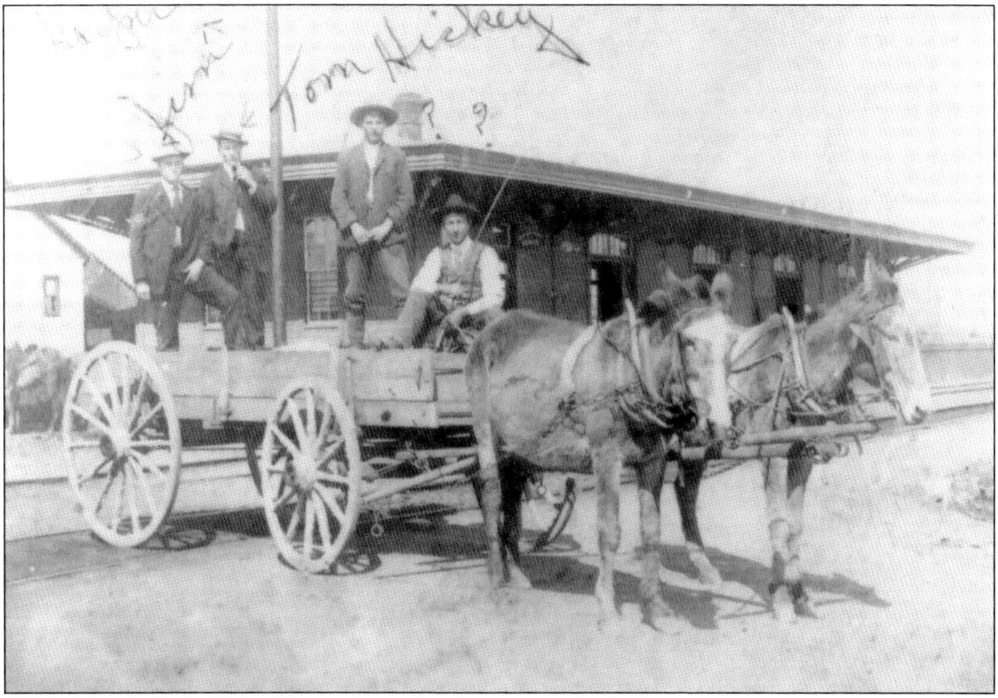

Tom Hickey and Jim Harper bring the wagon to the Galveston, Harrisburg, and San Antonio depot in downtown Richmond, Texas.

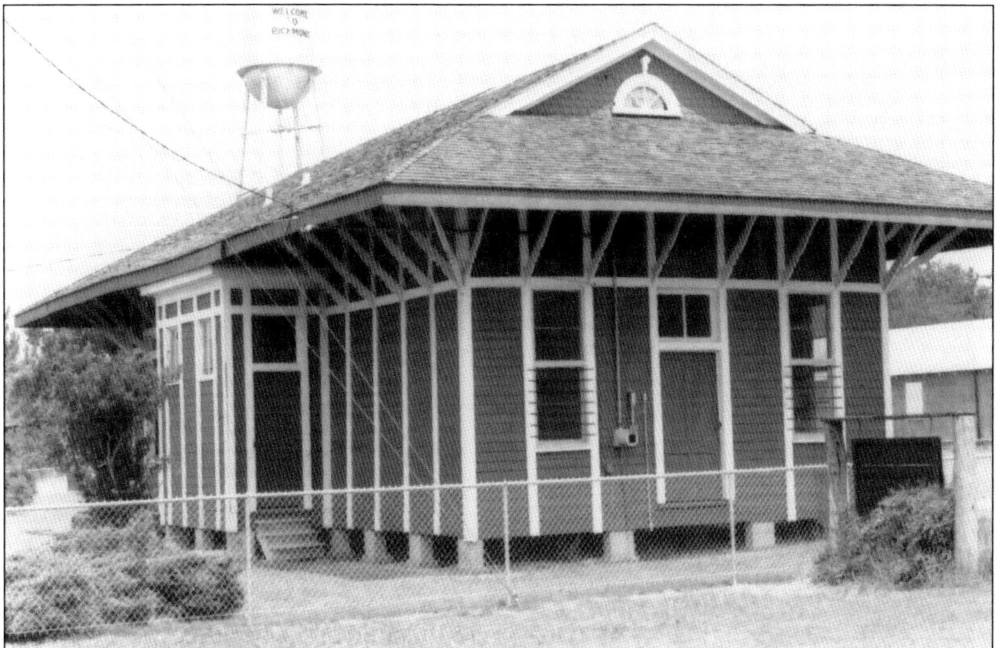

The Galveston, Harrisburg, and San Antonio depot sits in downtown Richmond awaiting restoration. Richmond has had many of its historic buildings restored, and they are open to the public to capture the flavor of lifestyle in early Fort Bend County.

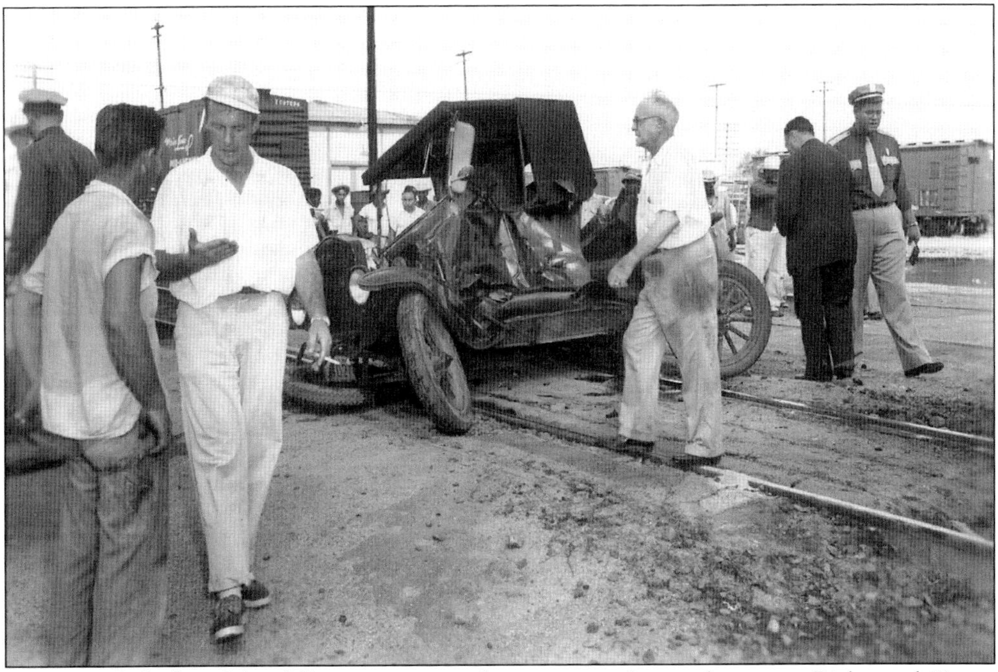

A vintage flatbed truck has fallen victim to a rail-crossing accident in downtown Richmond, Texas. These early crossings were not protected with crossing signals or gates like today's crossings.

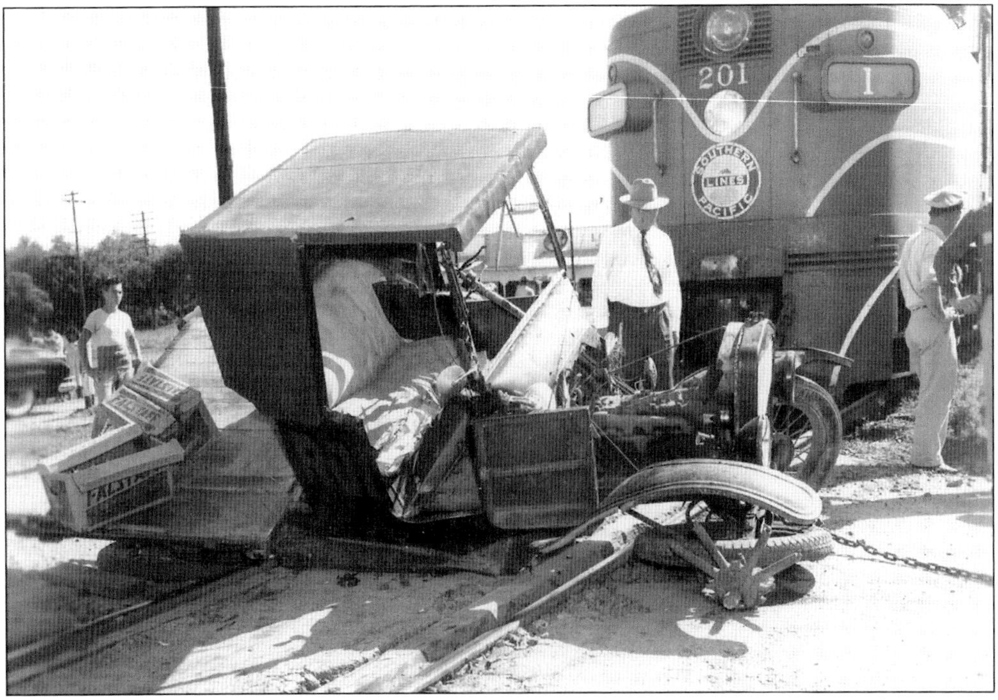

A closer look at the crossing accident shows that the Southern Pacific Sunset Limited Train No. 1 was involved in this accident. It appears that the Sunset Limited was just pulling out from the depot when the accident occurred because the impact did not even knock the cases of Falstaff Beer from the truck bed.

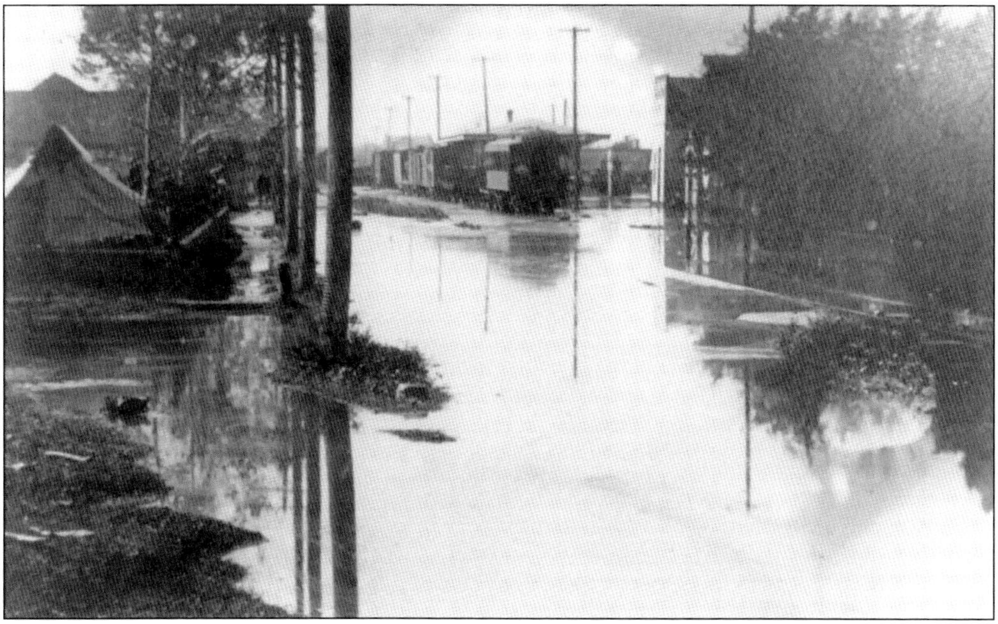

A view of Calhoun Street gives an idea of what the 1913 flood looked like. The Galveston, Harrisburg, and San Antonio depot and railcars can be seen in the distance just barely above water.

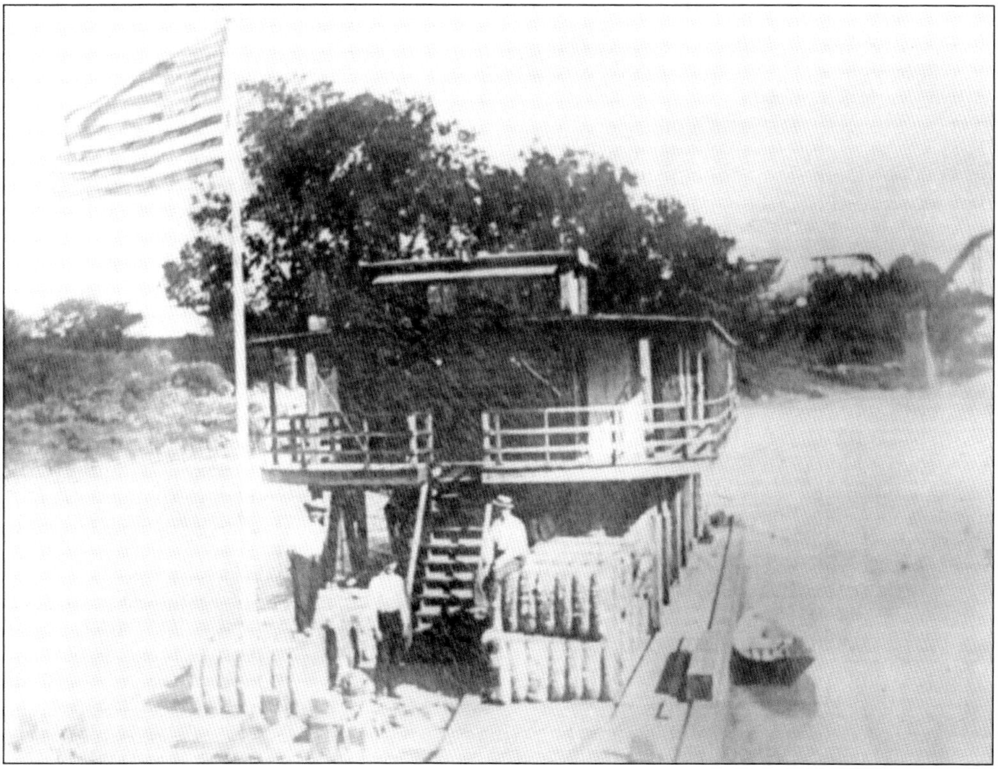

Early means of transporting goods to market included steamships and boats traveling up and down the Brazos River. Here is a view of a ferryboat bringing bales of cotton to port in Richmond, Texas. The GH&SA Railroad Bridge can be seen in the background.

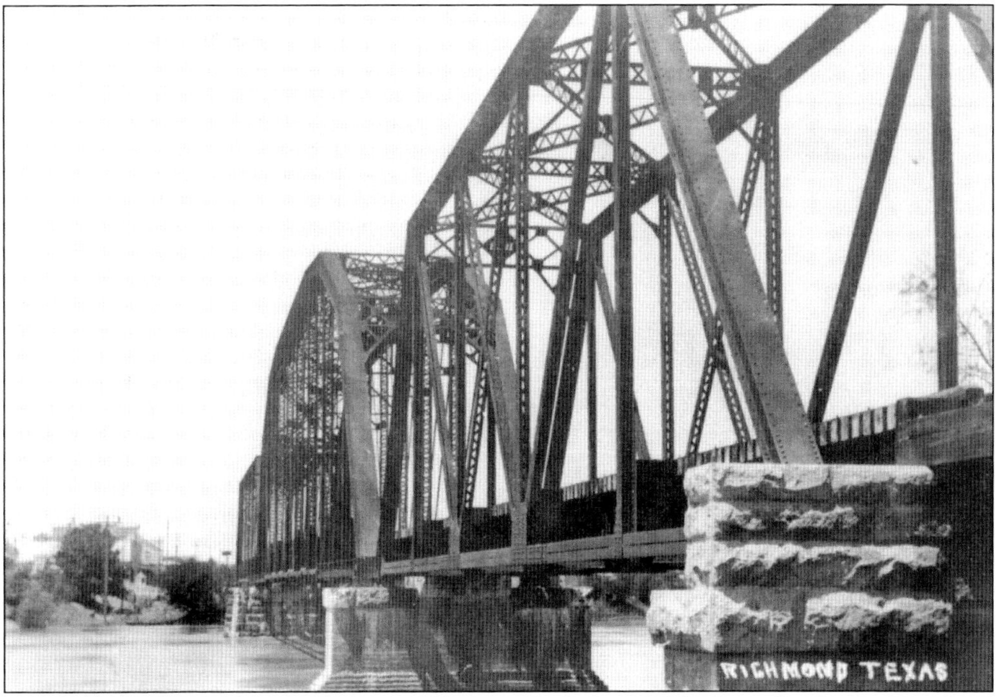

A view of the GH&SA bridge, believed to be around the time of the 1913 flood, was taken from the eastern bank of the Brazos River. The city of Richmond can be seen in the distance.

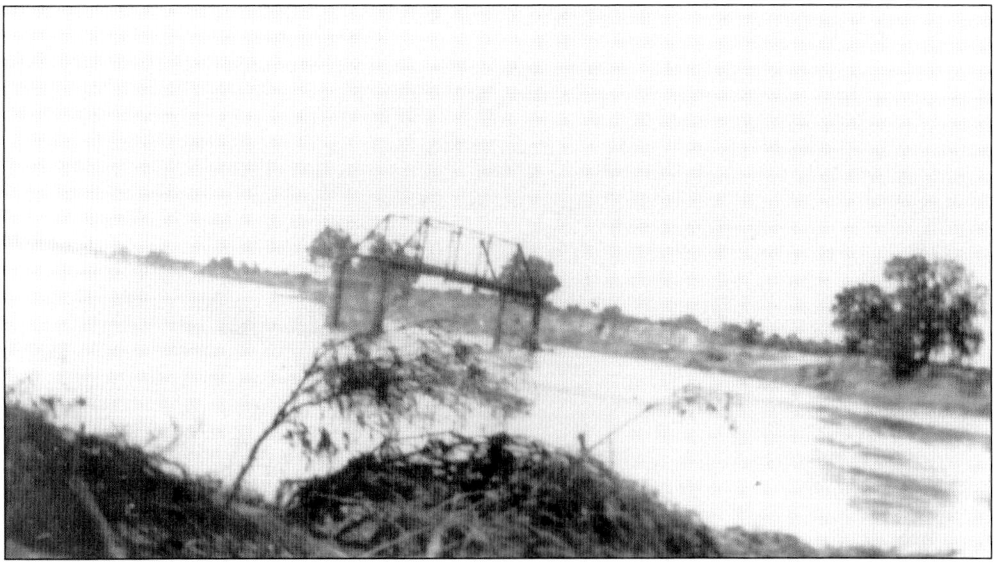

A single span of the highway bridge crossing the Brazos River remains to remind observers of how difficult it was for the river to be spanned by both highway and railway.

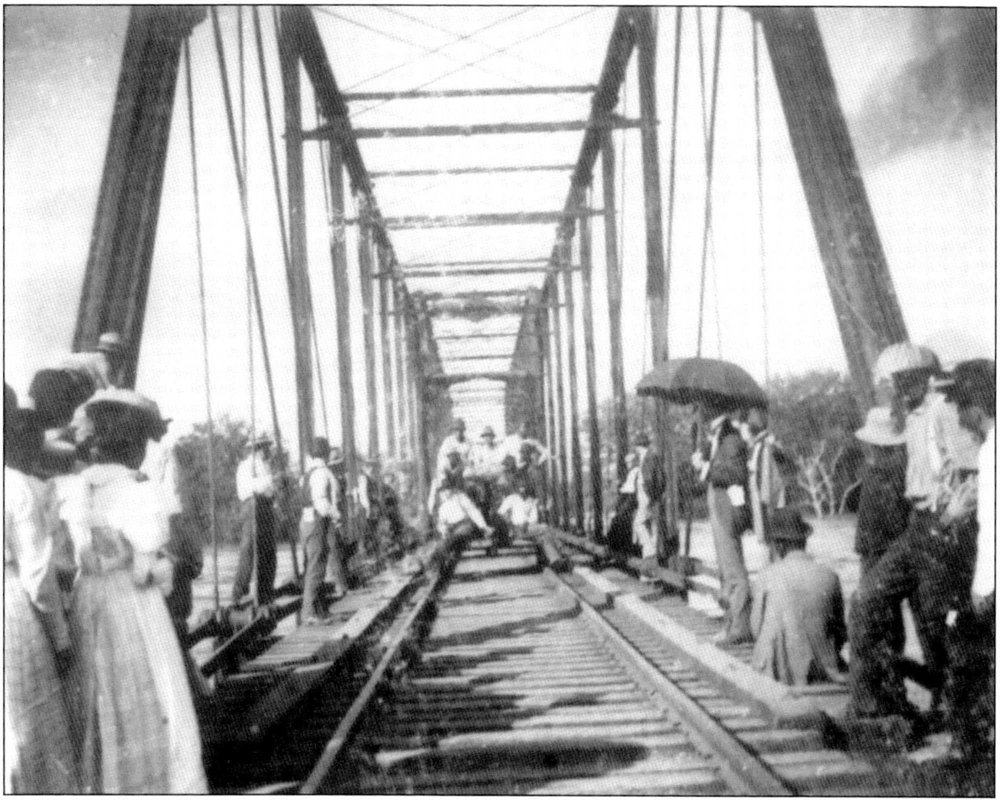

Richmond locals gather on the GH&SA railroad bridge to have a look at the floodwaters of the Brazos River during the flood of 1899. Flooding along the Brazos continues to be a problem, which created the need to develop a system of levy districts along its banks to protect developments in the area from the rising floodwaters when they occur.

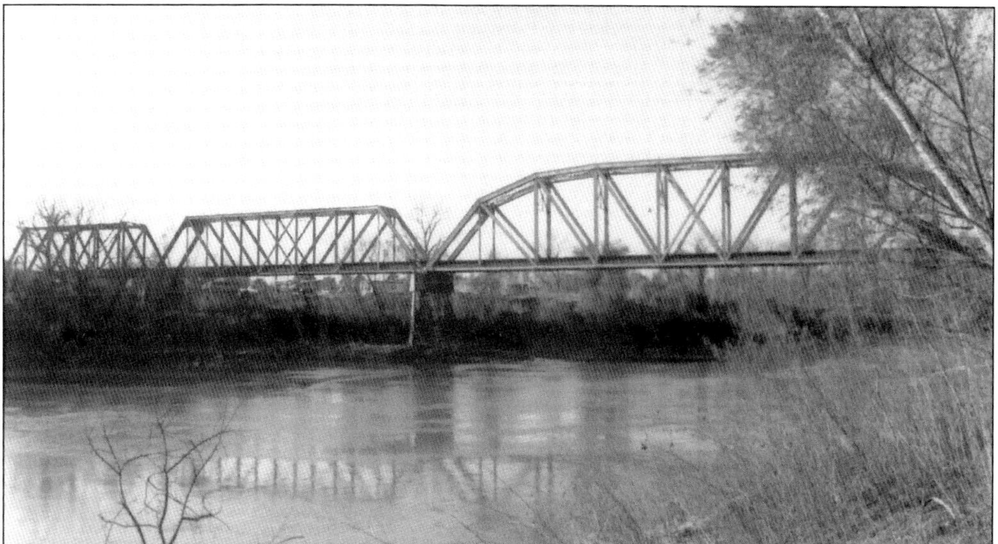

Pictured sometime around the 1913 flood is the Galveston, Harrisburg, and San Antonio railroad bridge across the Brazos River in Richmond, Texas, as floodwaters recede.

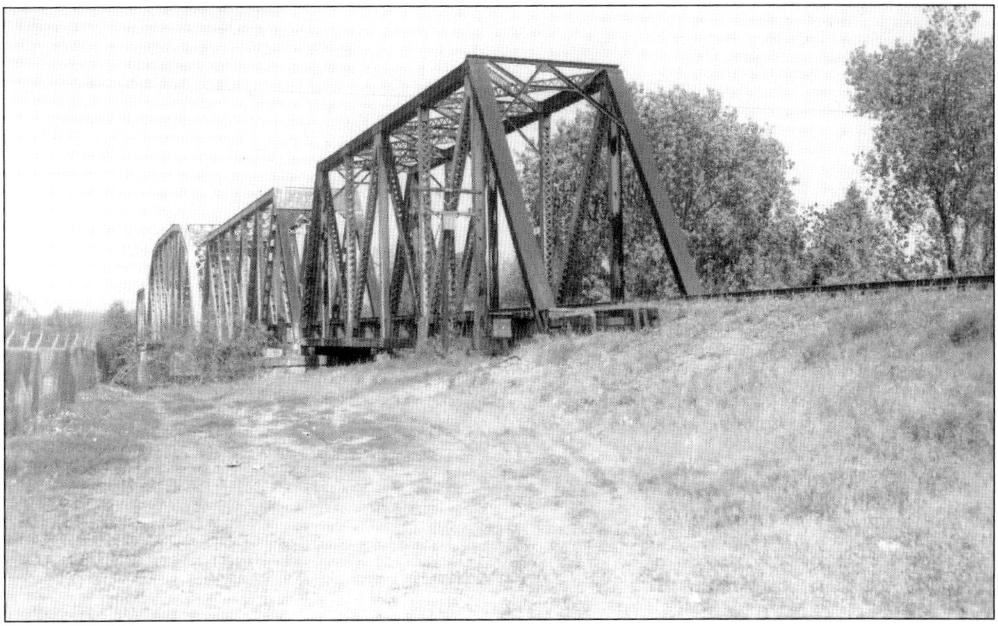

Here is a 1980s view of the GH&SA railroad bridge on the eastern bank of the Brazos River. The eastern side of the Brazos and its low banks remains mostly undeveloped due to occasional flooding.

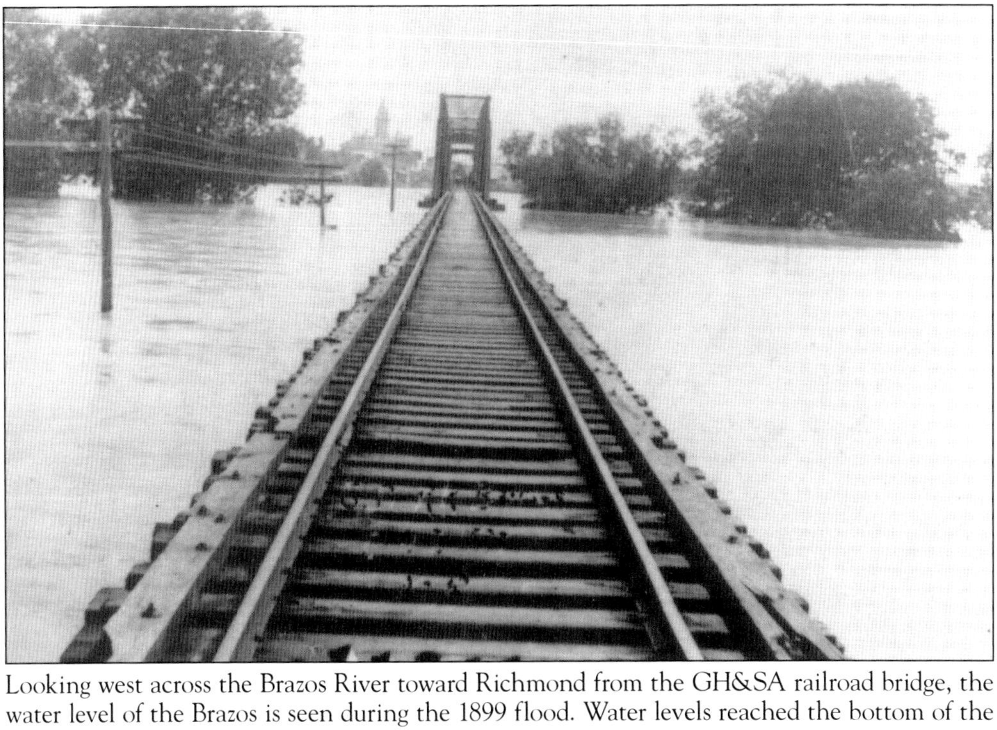

Looking west across the Brazos River toward Richmond from the GH&SA railroad bridge, the water level of the Brazos is seen during the 1899 flood. Water levels reached the bottom of the bridge structure.

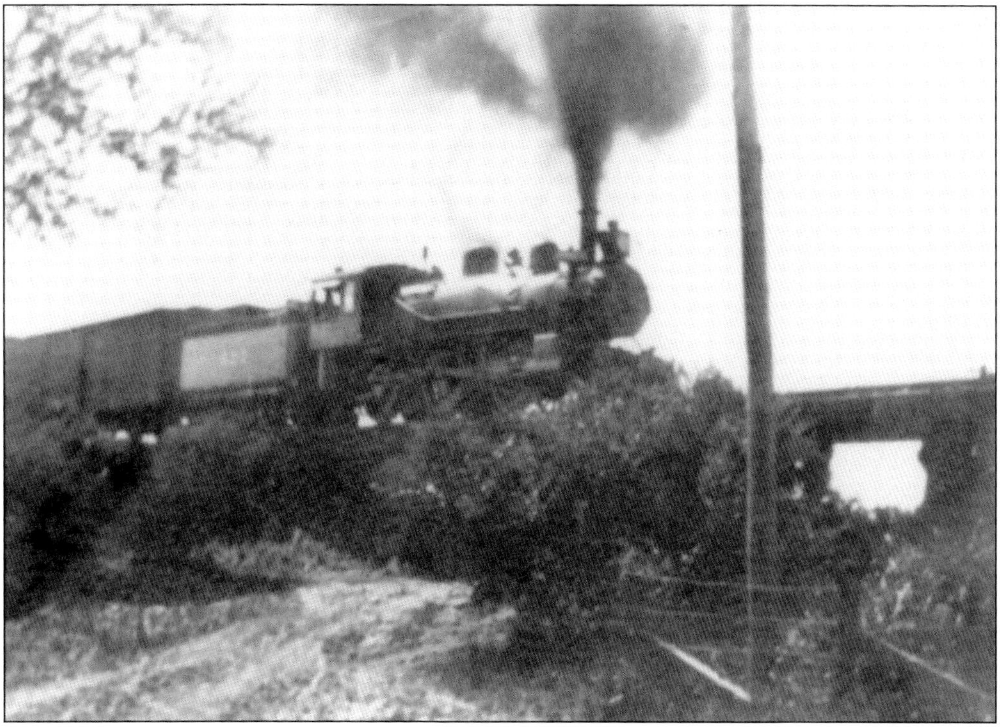

GH&SA Locomotive 422 and its freight train start across the Brazos River heading west into Richmond, Texas.

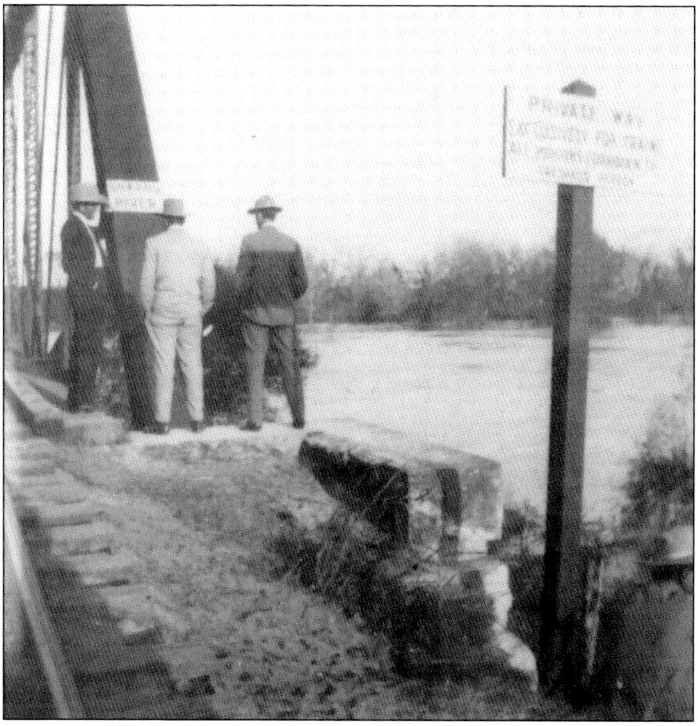

Ignoring the posted "No Trespassing" sign, three men must have a look at the water level of the Brazos River at the GH&SA railroad bridge.

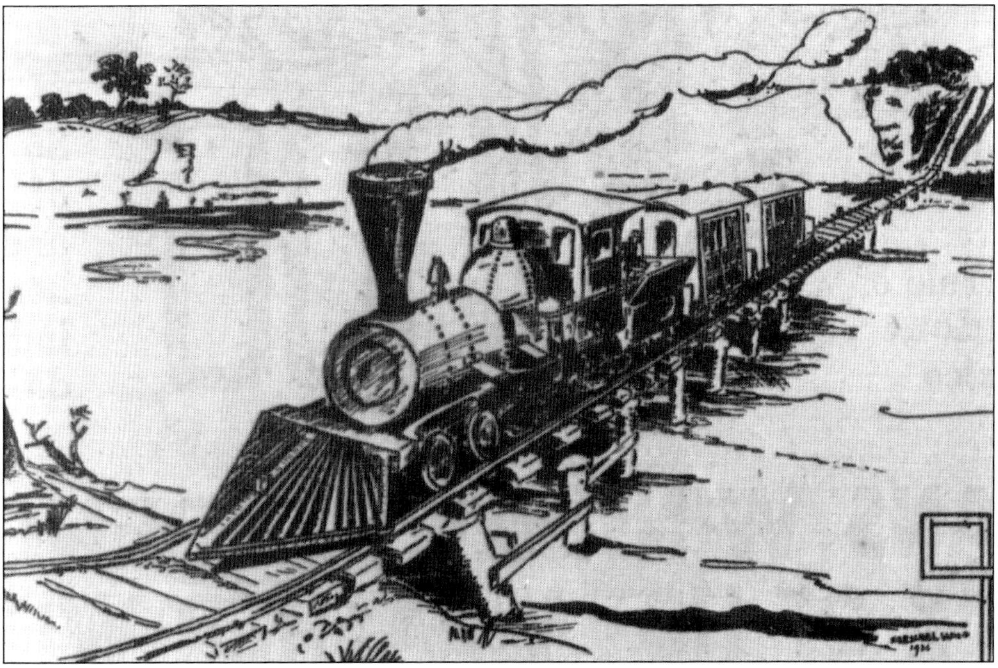

An early drawing depicts the daredevil ride offered by the railroad across the Brazos River before the railroad bridge across the river was constructed.

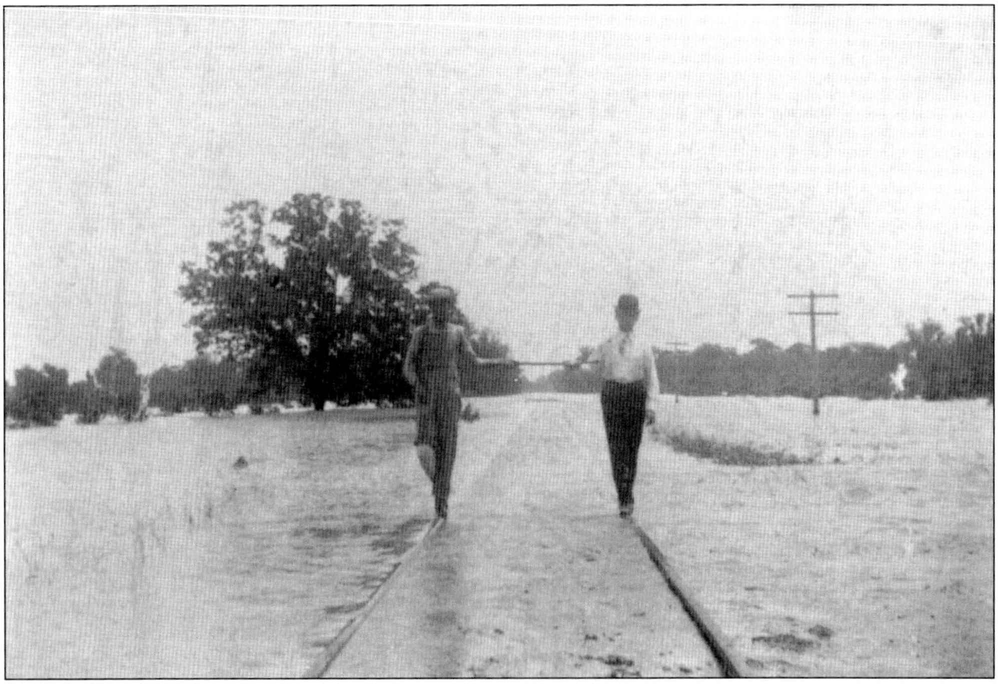

Two young boys walk along the GH&SA railroad tracks during the 1899 flood of the Brazos River in Richmond, Texas.

This track chart shows the Southern Pacific Railroads main line and yard tracks in Rosenberg, Texas. The Southern Pacific manned the Interlocking Tower 17 twenty-four hours a day, seven days a week for over 100 years. The tower operators controlled train movements across the diamond originally known as Rosenberg Junction.

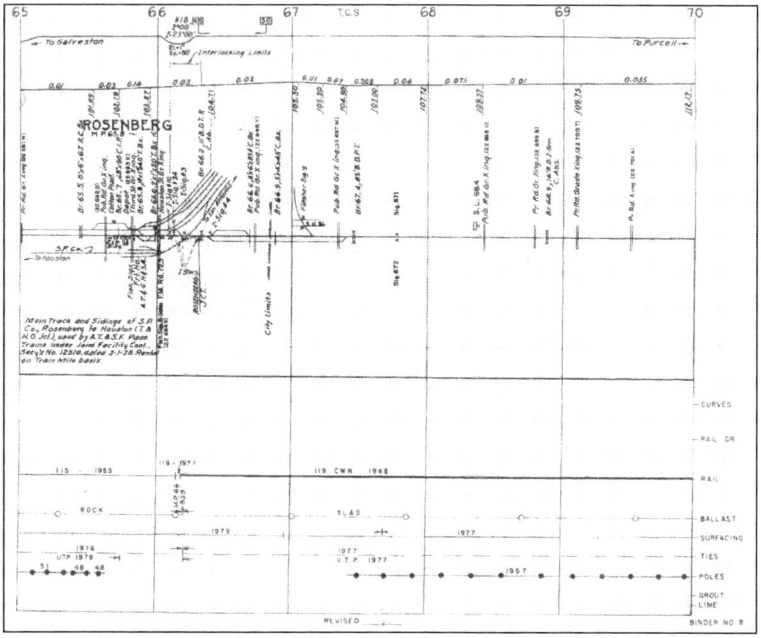

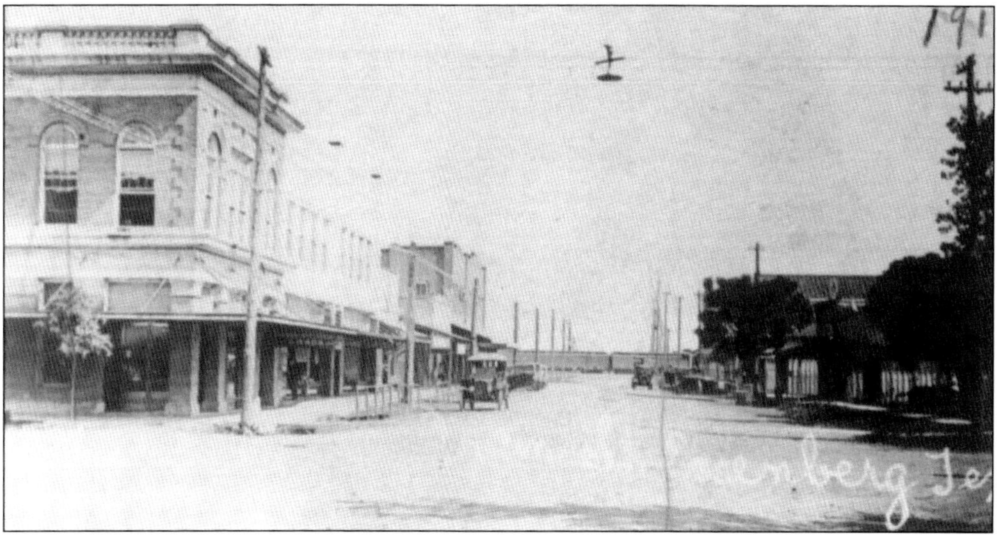

In this 1914 photograph looking down Third Street, a Santa Fe passenger train is at the Rosenberg Union Station.

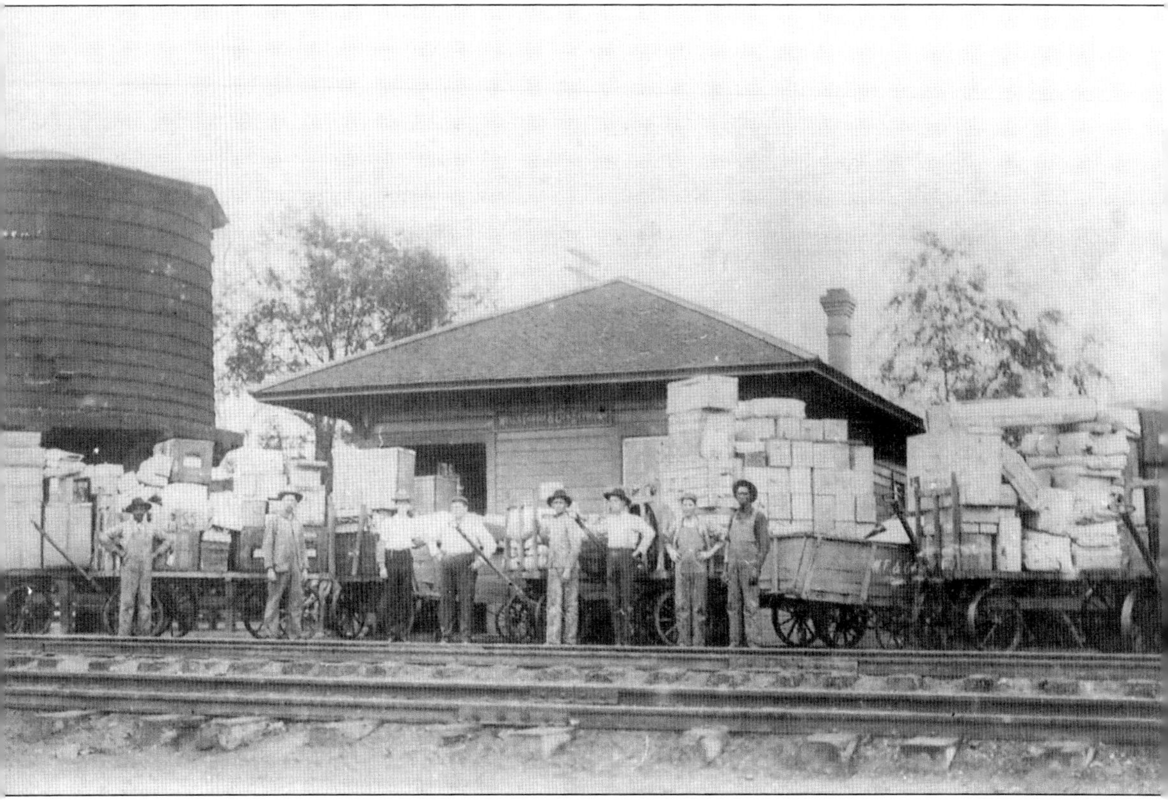

Stacks of freight await the next train in Rosenberg, Texas, at the Wells Fargo Express Building. The Wells Fargo Express was a separate structure from the railroad freight depots.

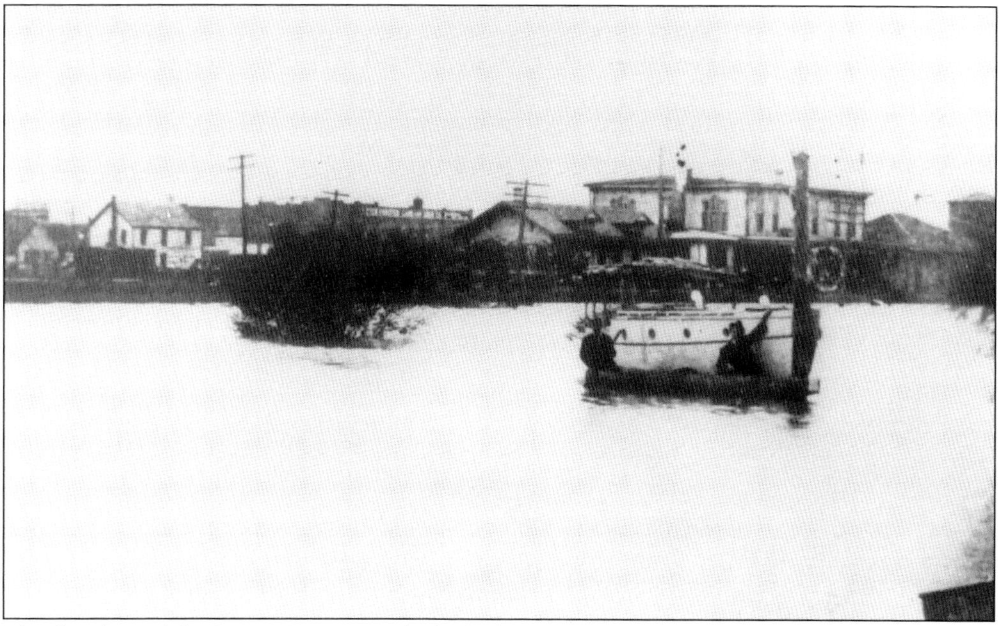

The flooding of the Brazos River must be bad when there is a boat in downtown Rosenberg. The Union Station and Fred Harvey House restaurant are seen in the background.

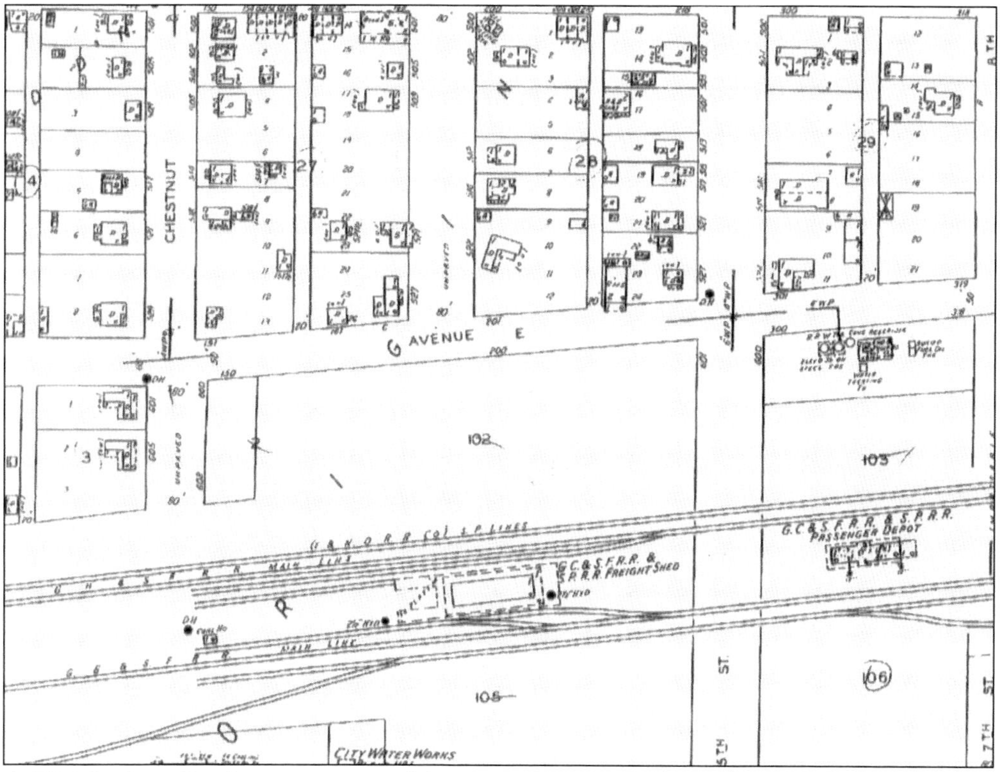

A 1926 Sanborn Fire Insurance map of downtown Rosenberg shows the rail yard tracks as well as the freight and passenger depots.

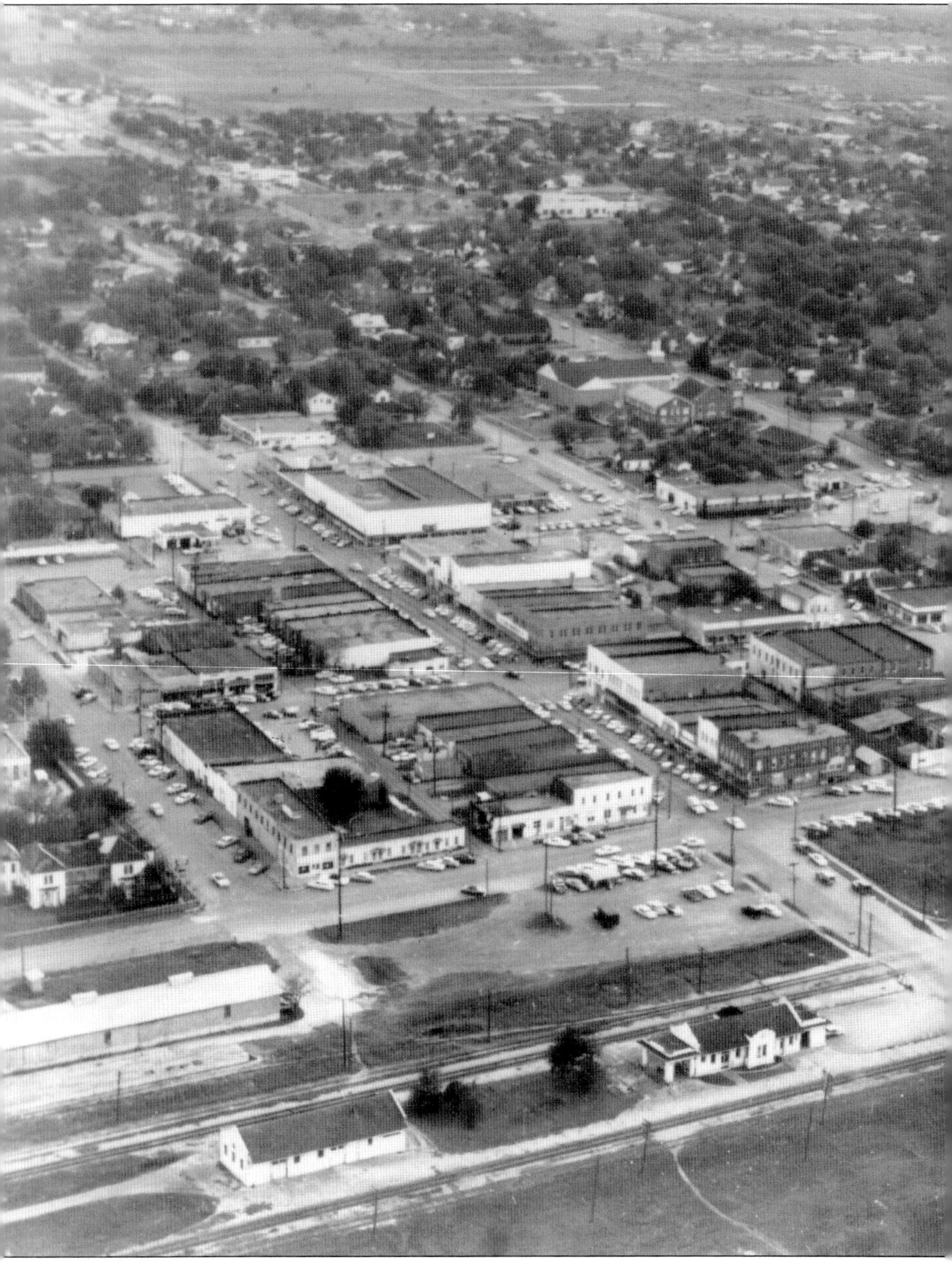

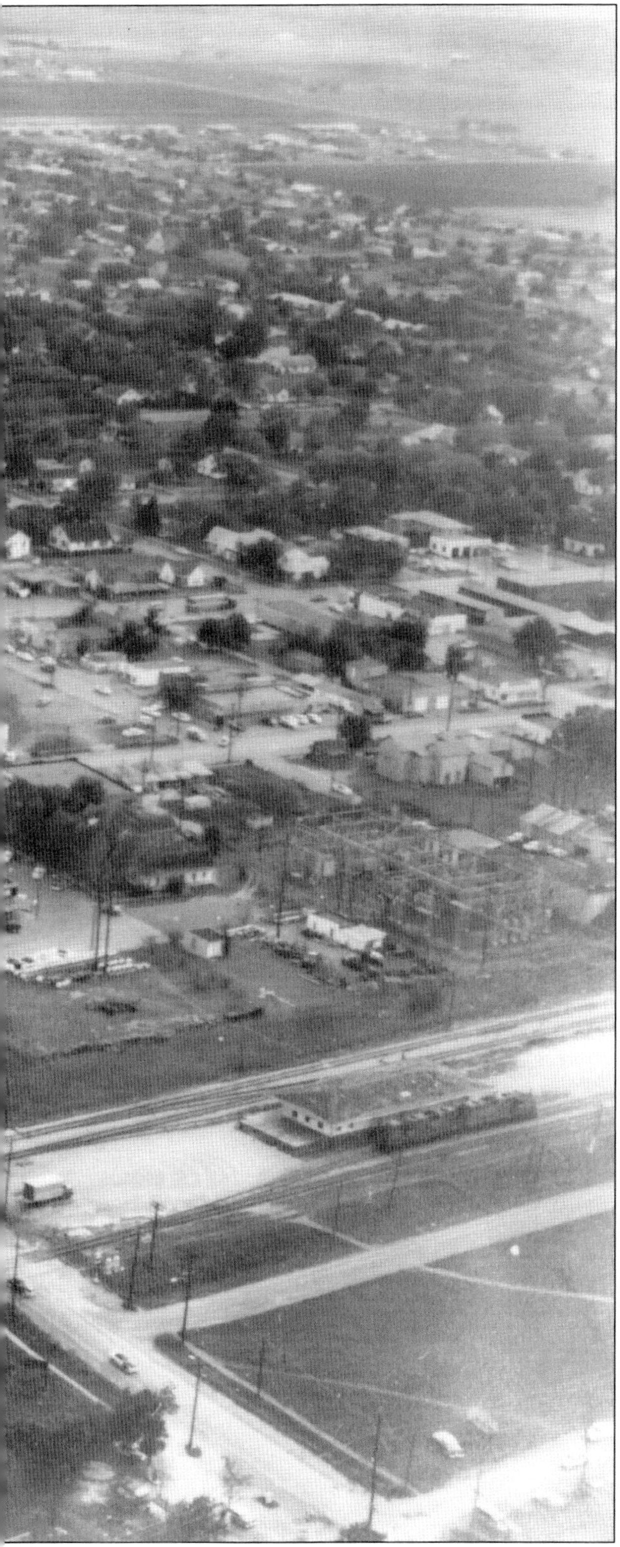

Two SD9 locomotives sit on the freight depots' team track in the lower right of this aerial view of downtown Rosenberg. The passenger depot is also visible in the lower center of this view.

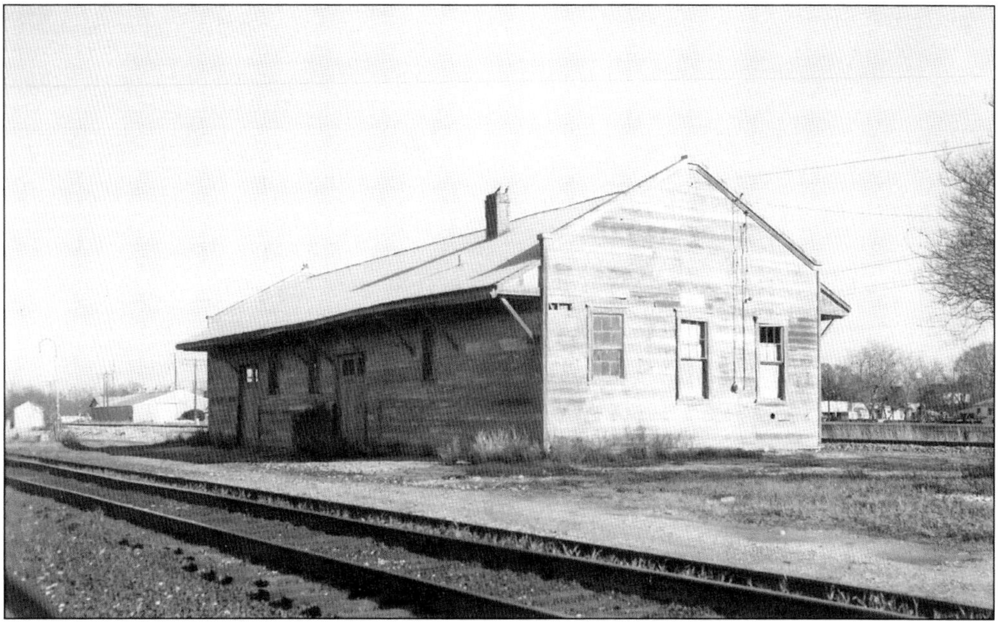

Here is a 1980s up-close look at the GH&SA and GC&SF joint railway express building just east of Third Street in Rosenberg.

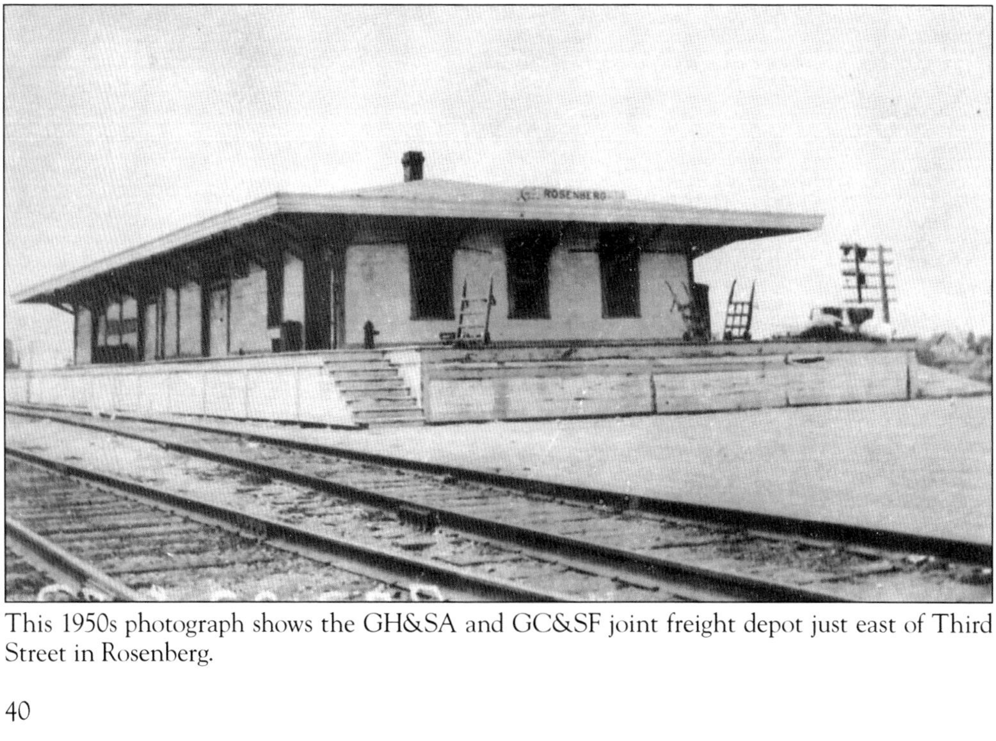

This 1950s photograph shows the GH&SA and GC&SF joint freight depot just east of Third Street in Rosenberg.

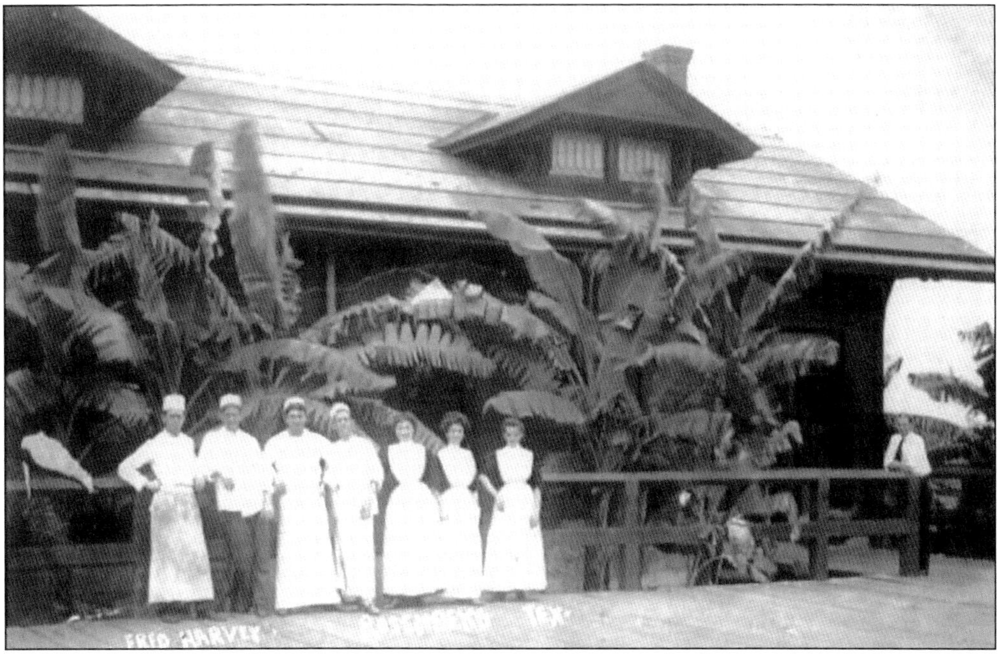

The staff of the Fred Harvey House restaurant, along with Fred Harvey himself, pose for a photograph outside the restaurant at Union Station in Rosenberg, Texas.

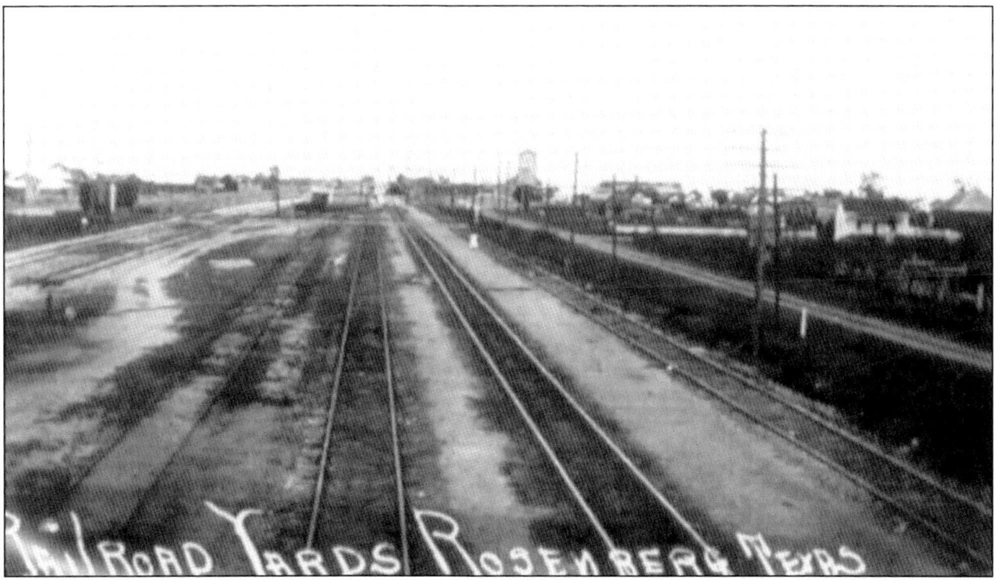

In a view looking west down the Galveston, Harrisburg, and San Antonio main line, there is a Gulf, Colorado, and Santa Fe train crossing the diamond at Tower 17 in Rosenberg, Texas.

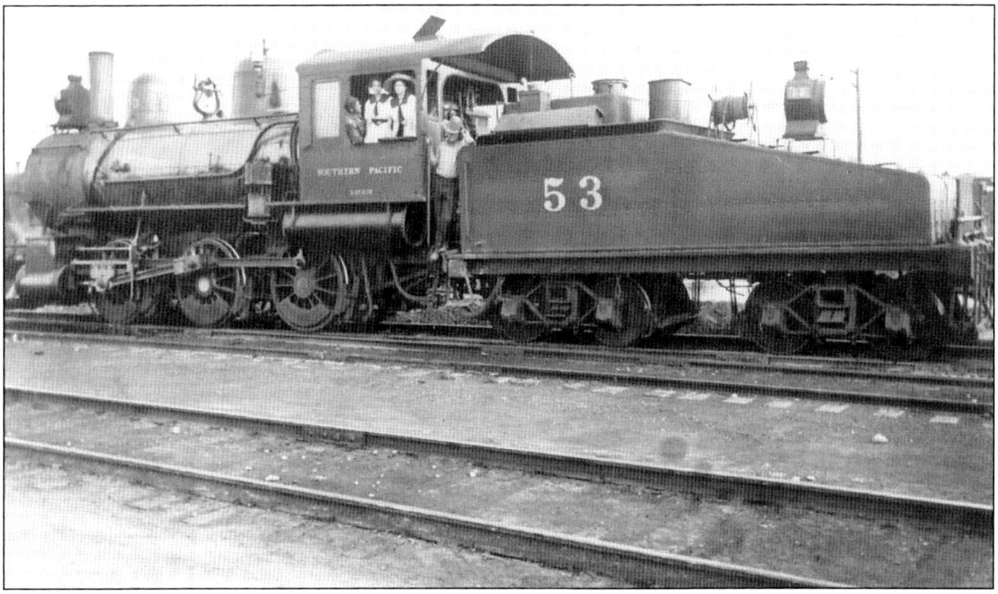

"All Aboard!" is fitting here as a couple of young ladies get a rare opportunity to climb aboard Southern Pacific Locomotive No. 53 with the fireman and engineer looking on.

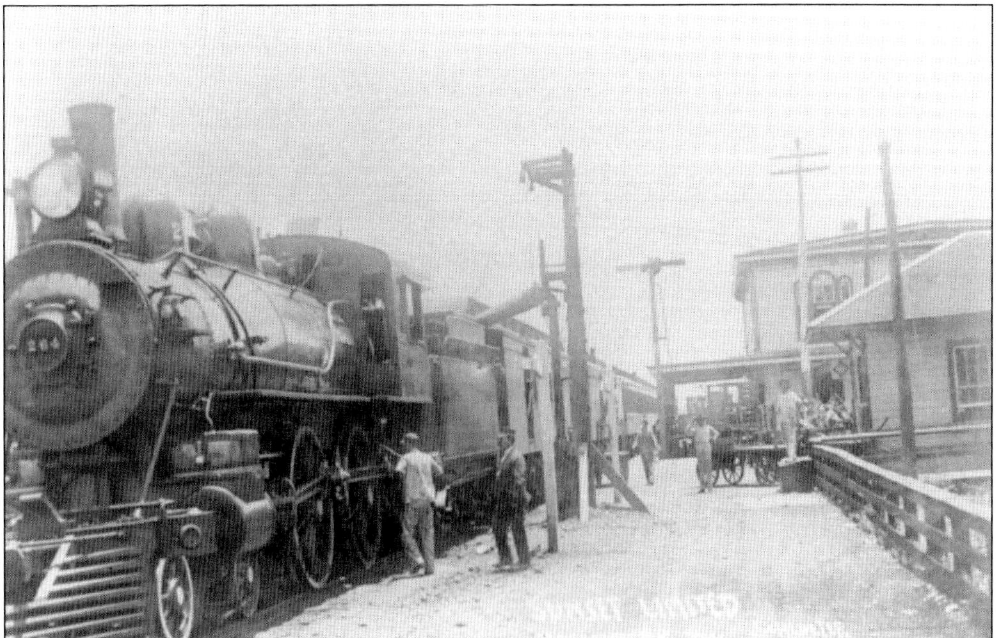

The Sunset Limited takes on water at the Rosenberg Union Station water column before departing for points west.

The night crew gets ready to get to work at the yards in Rosenberg, Texas. The locomotive is stopped just east of the interchange track, which connects the GH&SA with the GC&SF railroad. This interchange track remains in place and sees many Burlington Northern Santa Fe trains hop onto the Union Pacific Glidden Subdivision under trackage rights observed by both railroads.

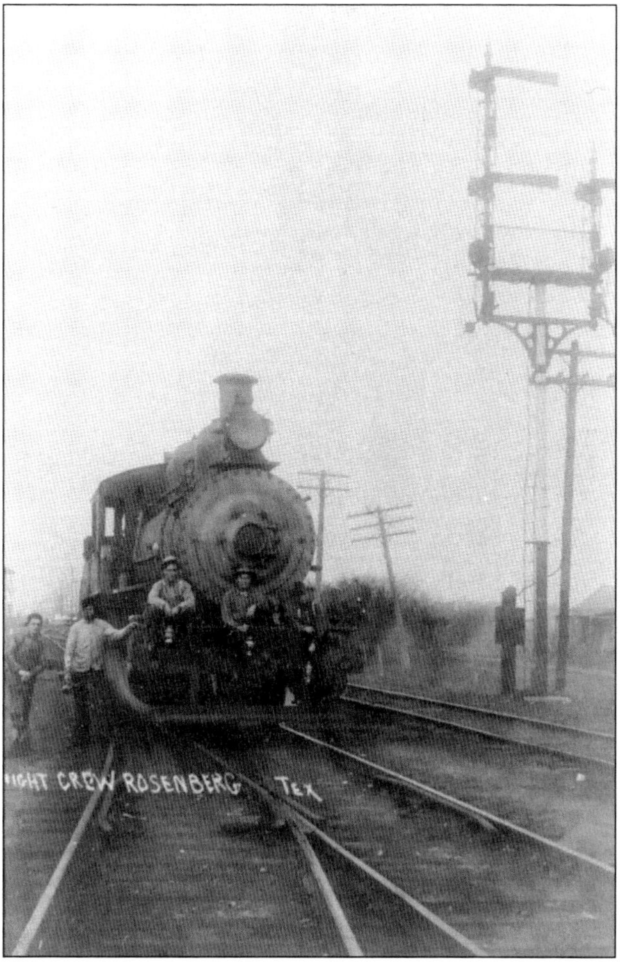

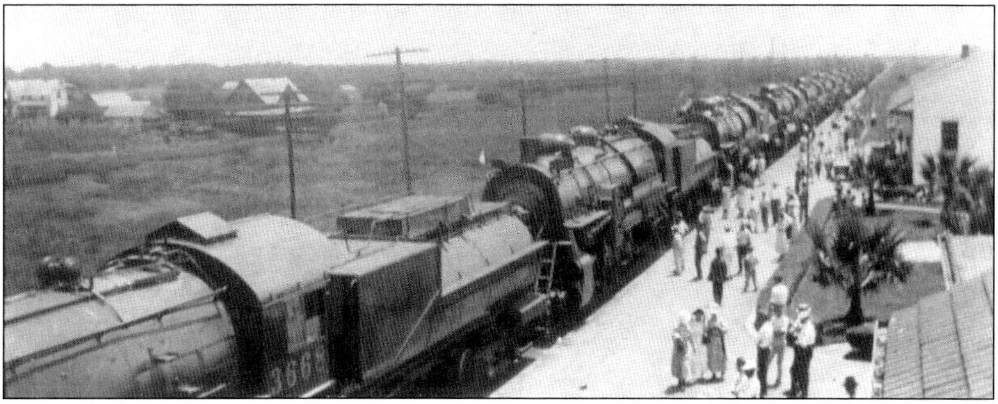

Crowds form at the Rosenberg passenger station to see the Southern Pacific Prosperity Special. Over one dozen steam locomotives are seen in the power set-up of this rare train.

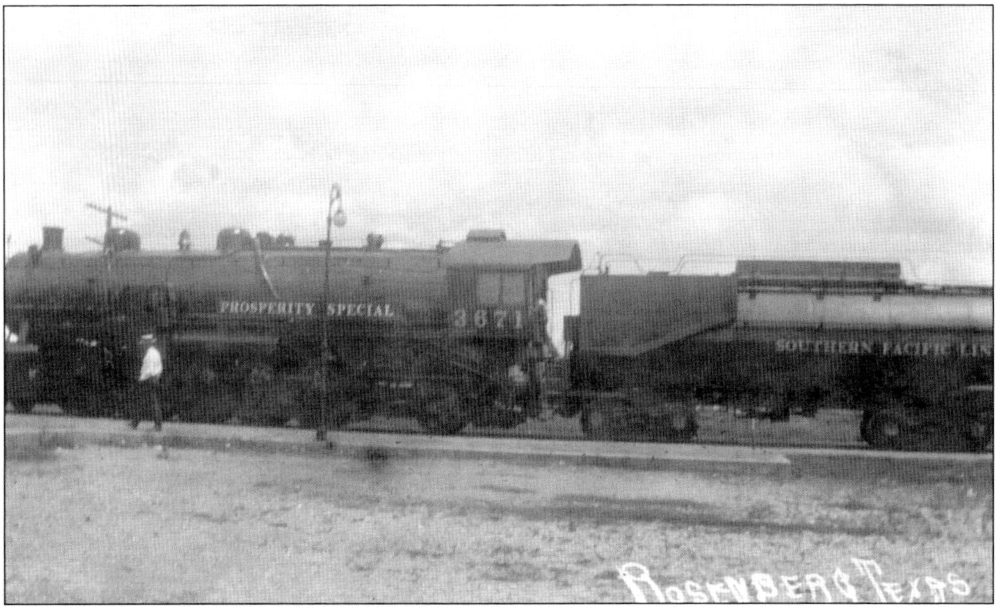

Southern Pacific 3671 leads the Prosperity Special out of the station in Rosenberg, Texas. (Courtesy of the Ken E. Stavinoha Collection.)

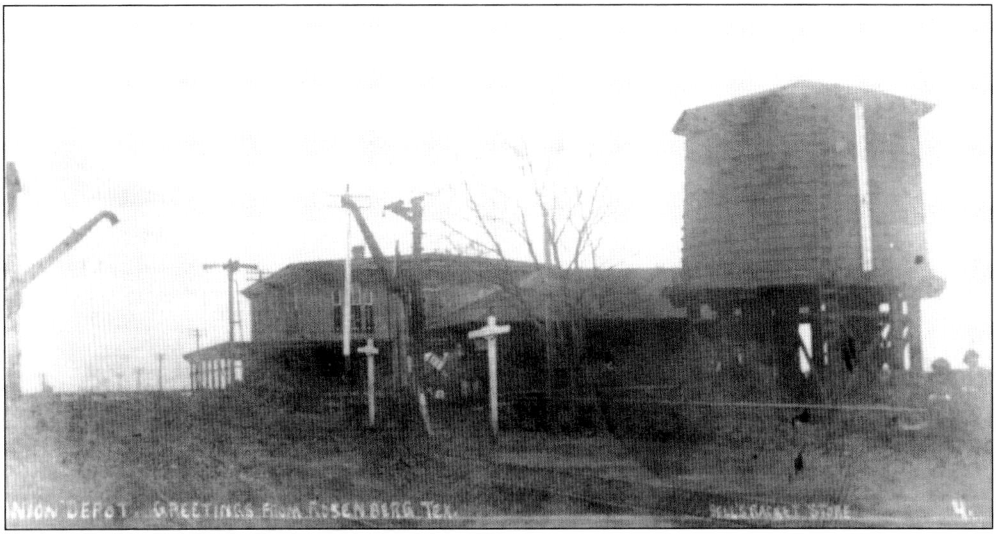

"Greetings from Rosenberg" is the title of this 1907 postcard photograph showing the Union Station, Fred Harvey House restaurant, and water tower waiting for trains to arrive.

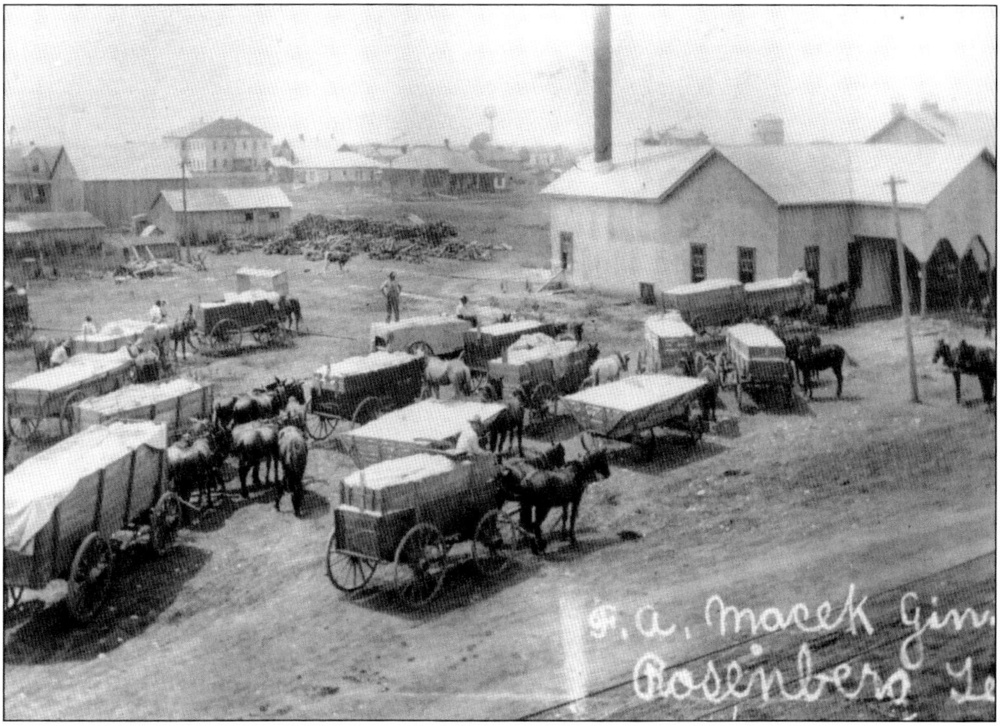

Farmers line up with their loads of cotton at the F. A. Macek gin in Rosenberg, Texas.

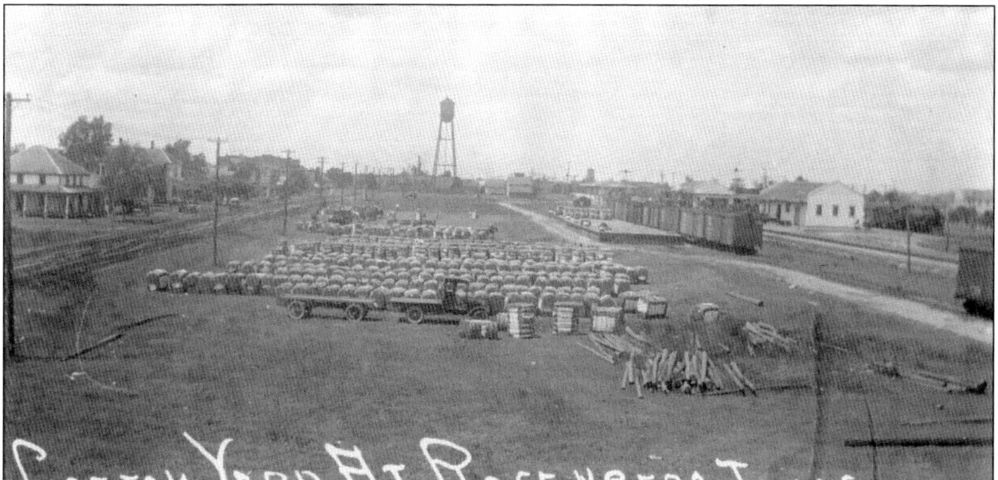

A view of the Rosenberg cotton yards includes the Gulf, Colorado, and Santa Fe tracks to the right and the Galveston, Harrisburg, and San Antonio tracks to the left.

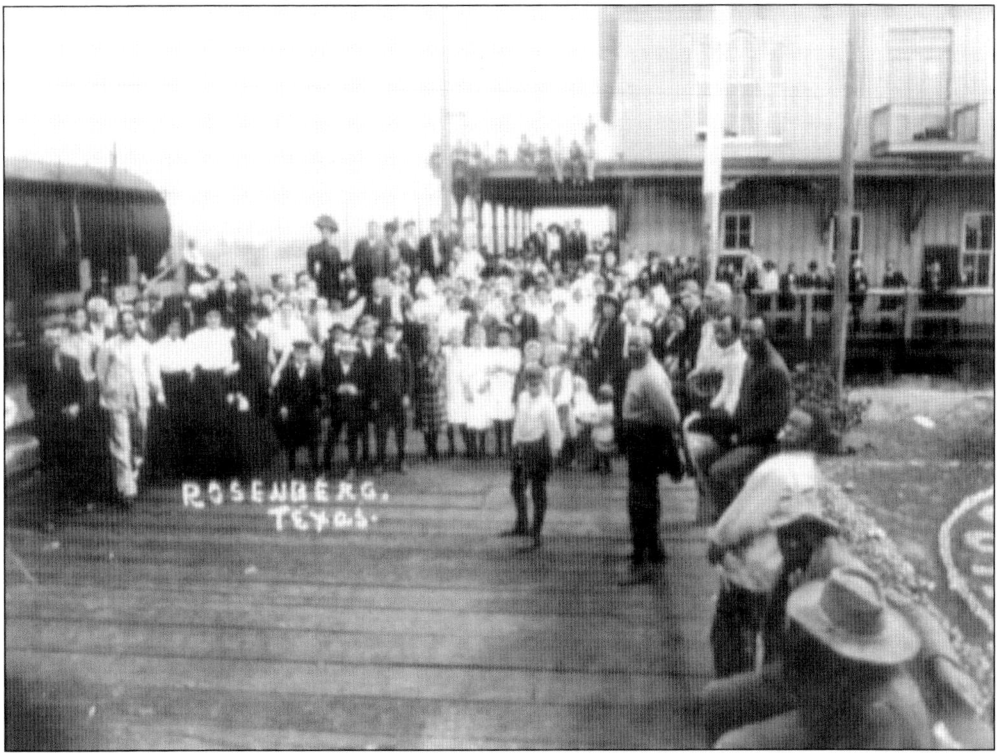

Residents and travelers alike gather at Union Station in Rosenberg, Texas. The depot was a central hub of activity for the town as seen in this photograph.

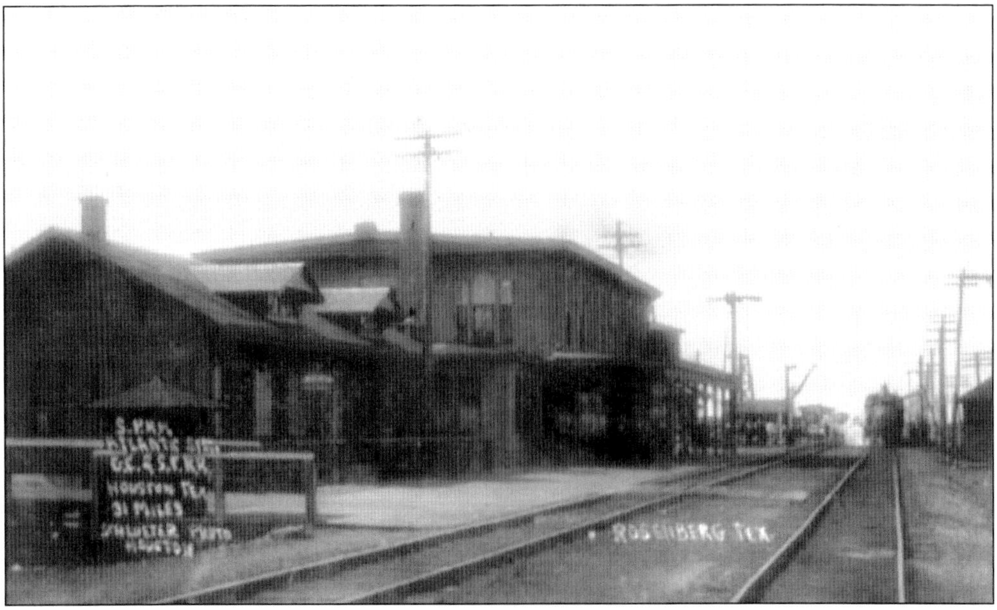

Passengers prepare to board the Sunset Limited just east of Union Station as the locomotive takes on water for the trip into Houston.

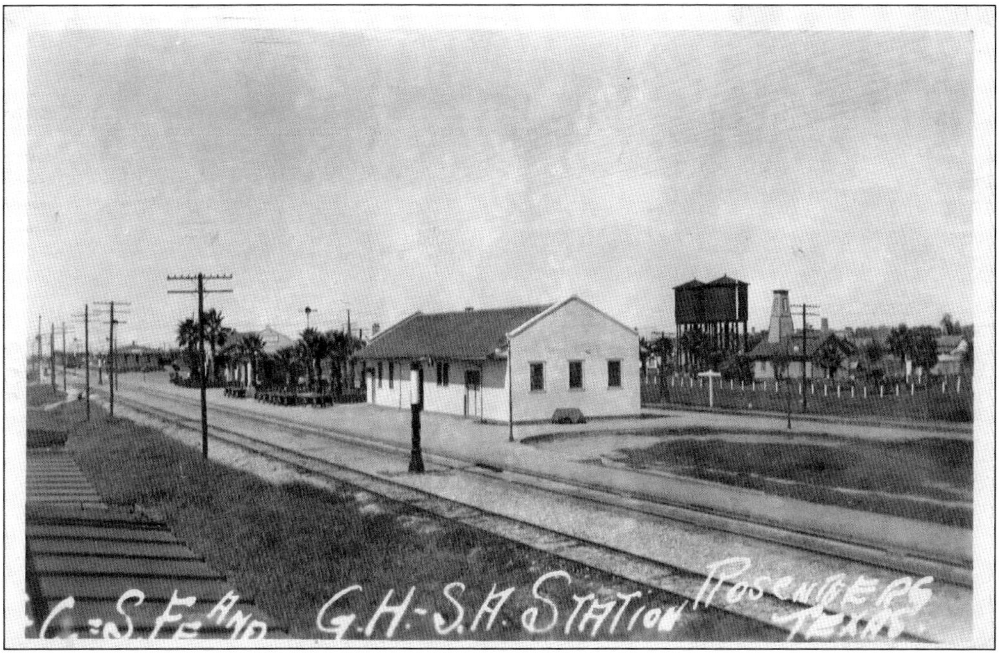

Pictured here are the joint GH&SA and GC&SF railroad freight and passenger depots in downtown Rosenberg, Texas. (Courtesy of the Ken E. Stavinoha Collection.)

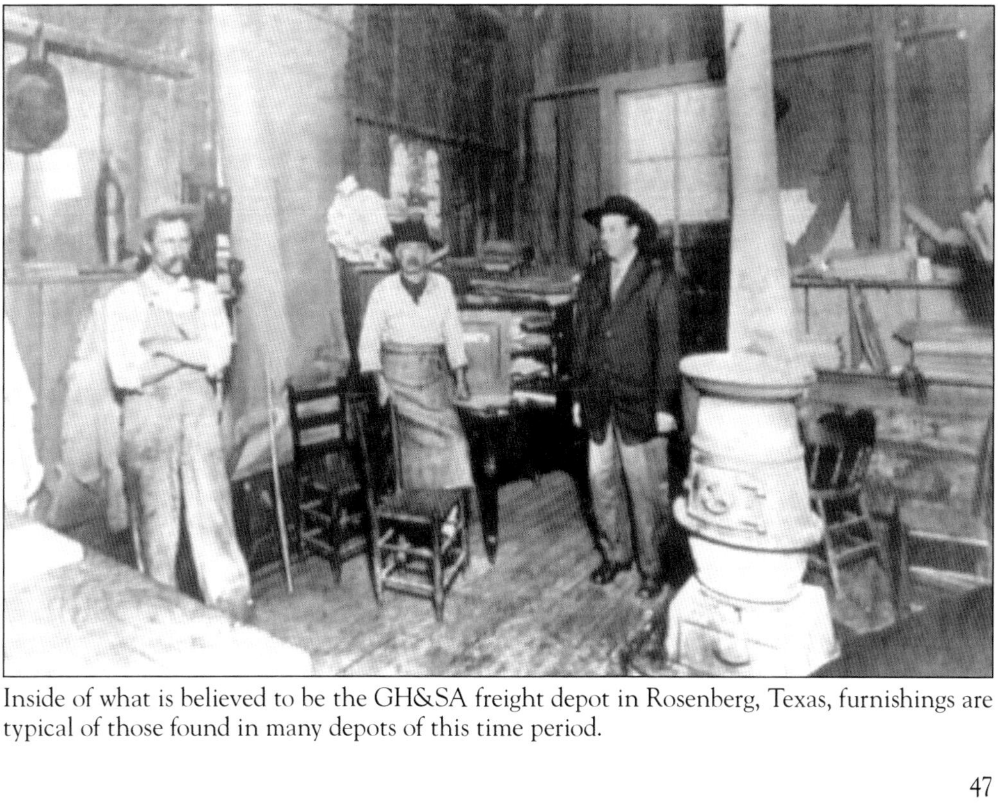

Inside of what is believed to be the GH&SA freight depot in Rosenberg, Texas, furnishings are typical of those found in many depots of this time period.

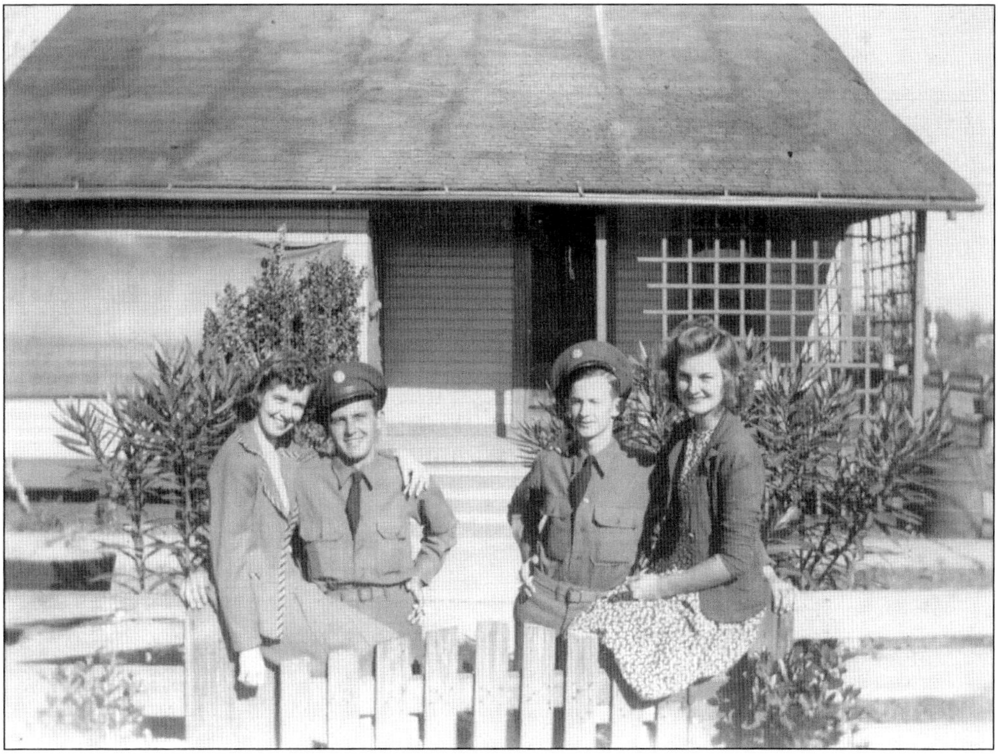

Fred and Katie Walger (left) and an unidentified couple are pictured in front of their railroad section house in Rosenberg, Texas. (Courtesy of the Rosenberg Railroad Museum.)

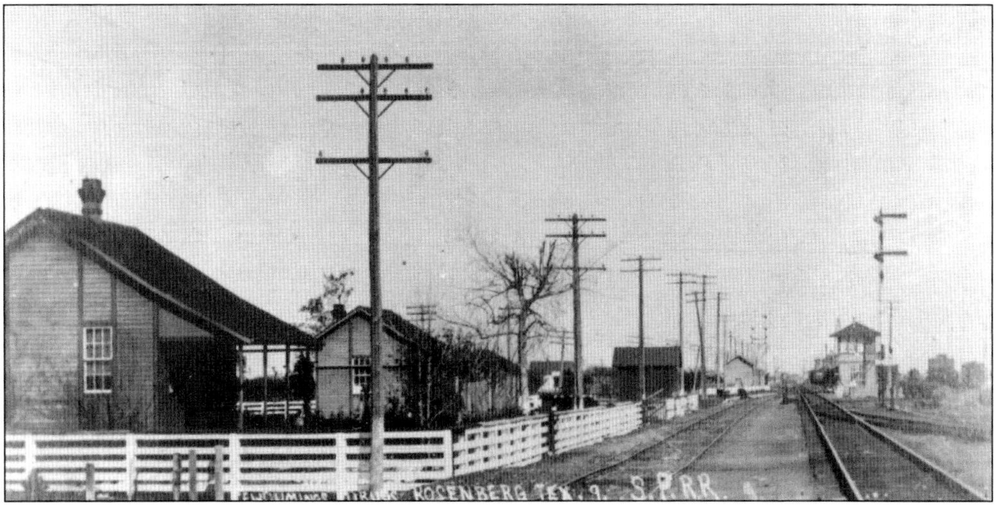

Looking east along the Southern Pacific main line are the section foremen houses on the left and Tower 17 on the right. The houses were removed in the 1950s, but the tower remained in service until February 10, 2004.

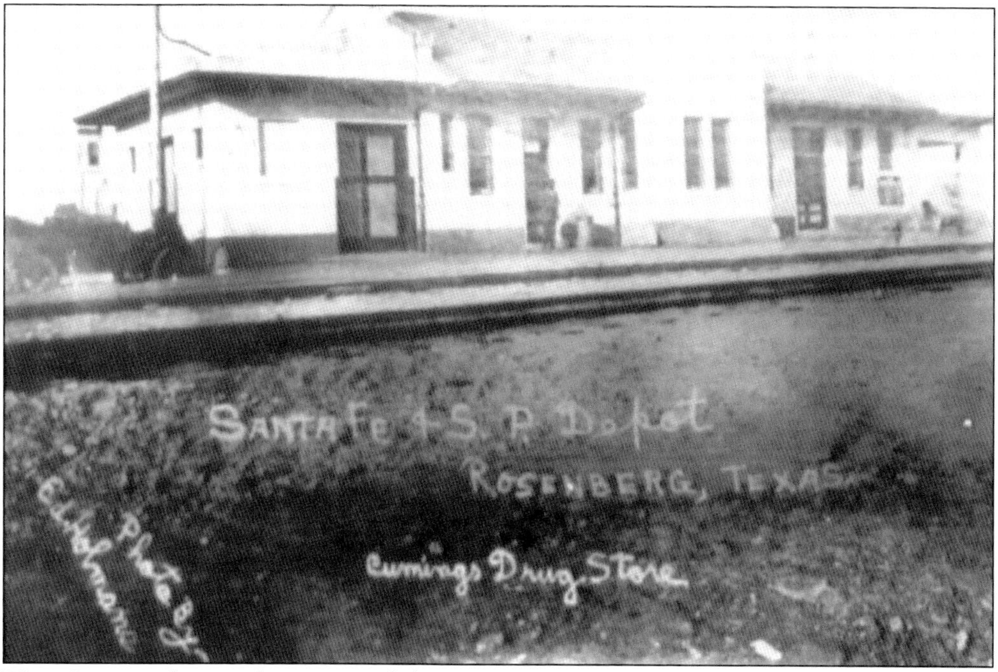

This photograph provides a view of the Santa Fe and Southern Pacific passenger depot in Rosenberg, Texas.

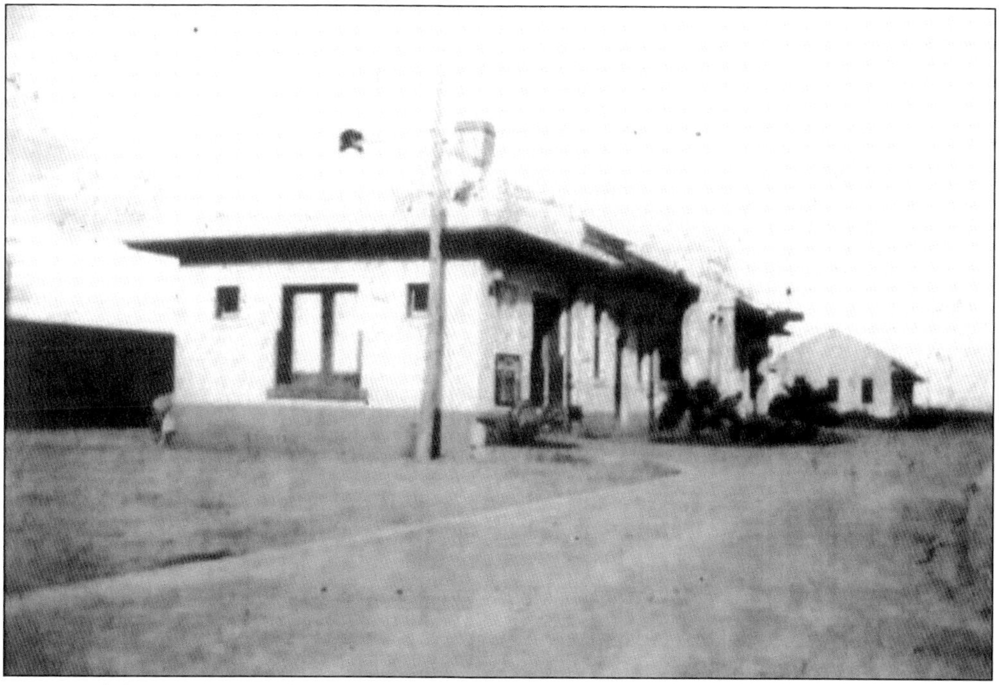
A view of the Santa Fe and Southern Pacific passenger depot also features the railway express building in the background in Rosenberg, Texas.

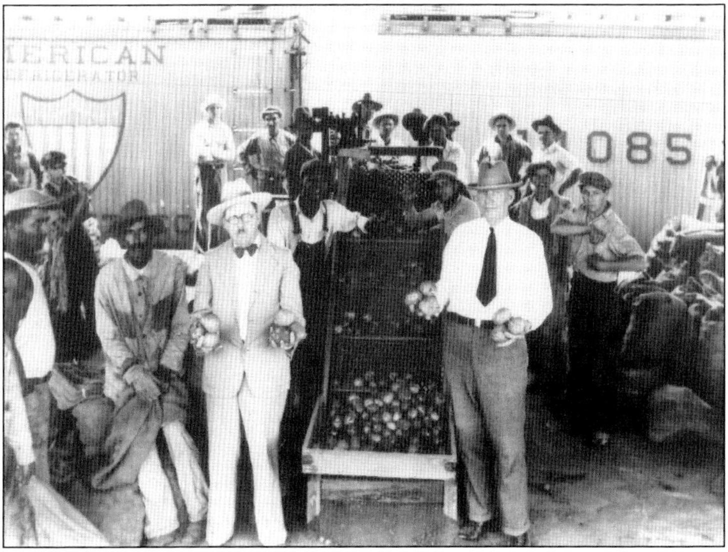

Fresh produce is heading to market via the GH&SA Railroad in ice-filled refrigerator railcars. Local produce inspectors approve the produce for shipment.

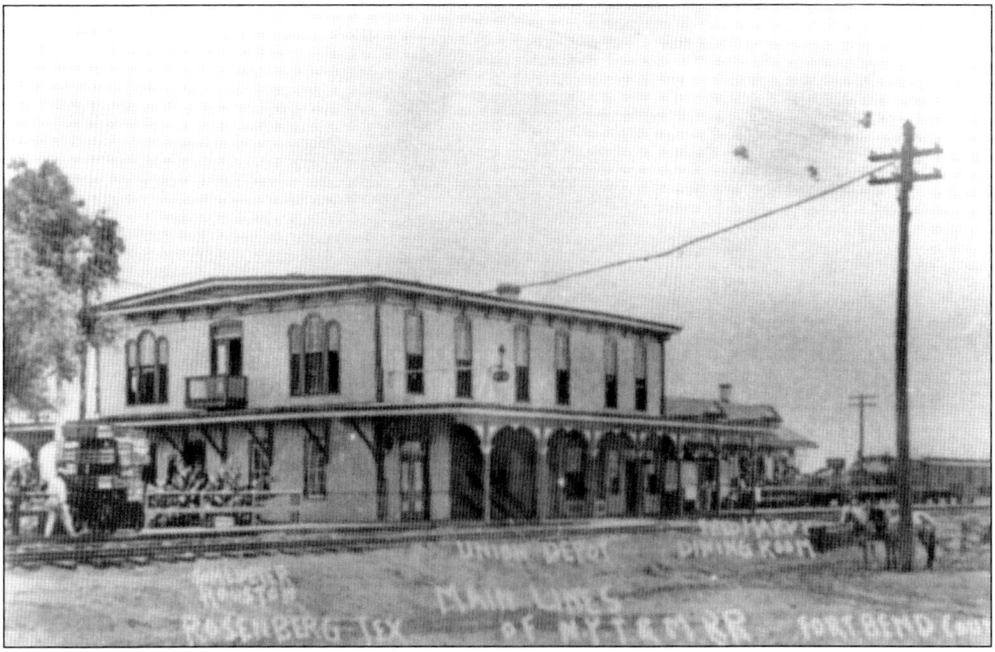

The Sunset Limited Train No. 1 arrives at Union Station in Rosenberg, Texas. The Fred Harvey House is to the right of the depot.

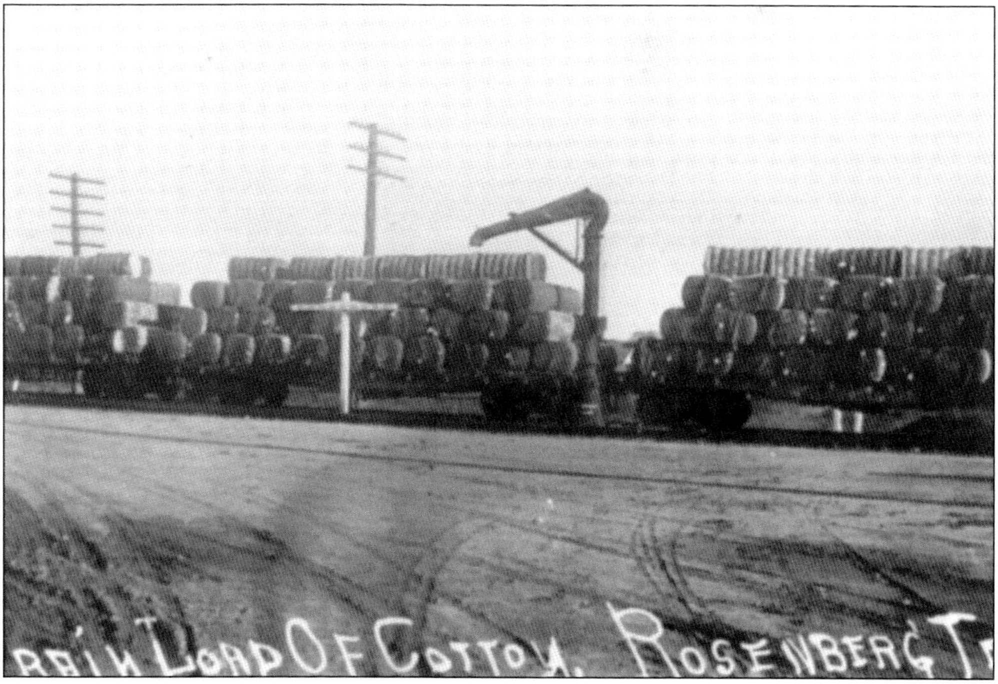

Flatcars loaded with cotton in the Southern Pacific rail yard in Rosenberg wait to be shipped out to market.

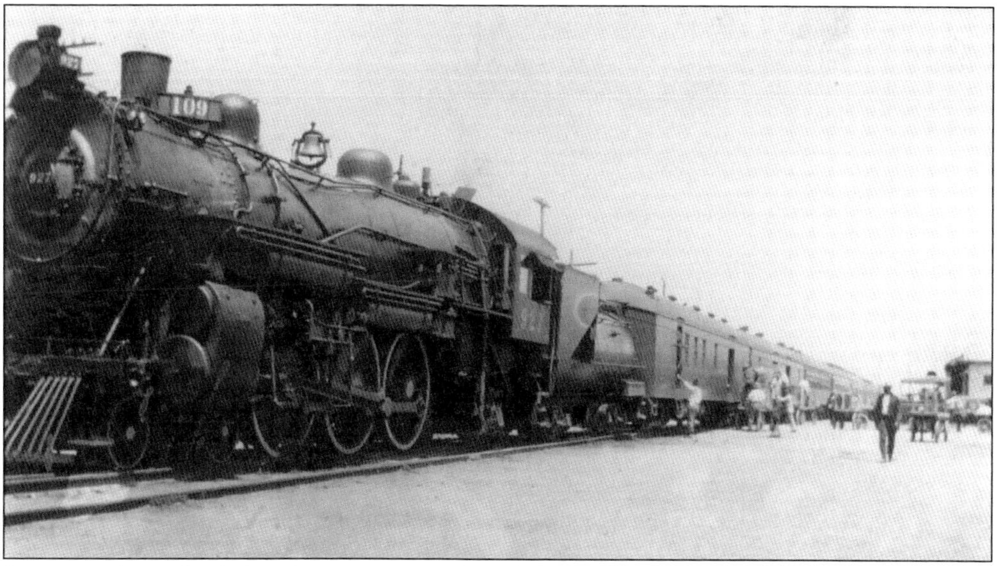

Baggage is being loaded and passengers are boarding the Sunset Limited Train No. 1 at Union Station in Rosenberg, Texas. (Courtesy of the Ken E. Stavinoha Collection.)

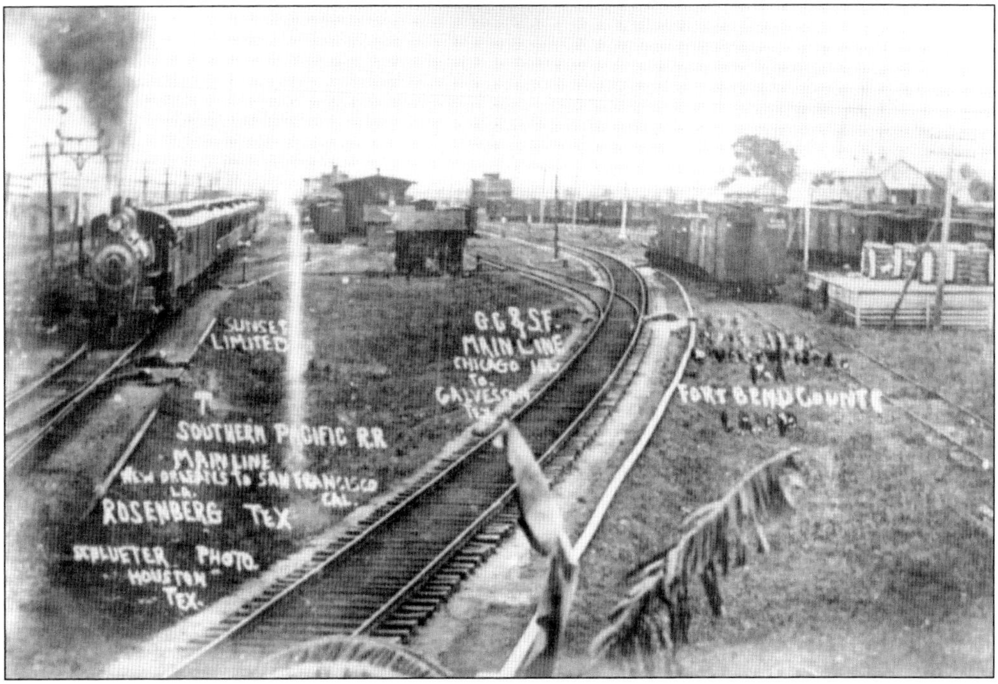

The Sunset Limited Train No. 1 is lined up for a straight shot through the Tower 17 interlocker while the Rosenberg rail yards are busy with activity.

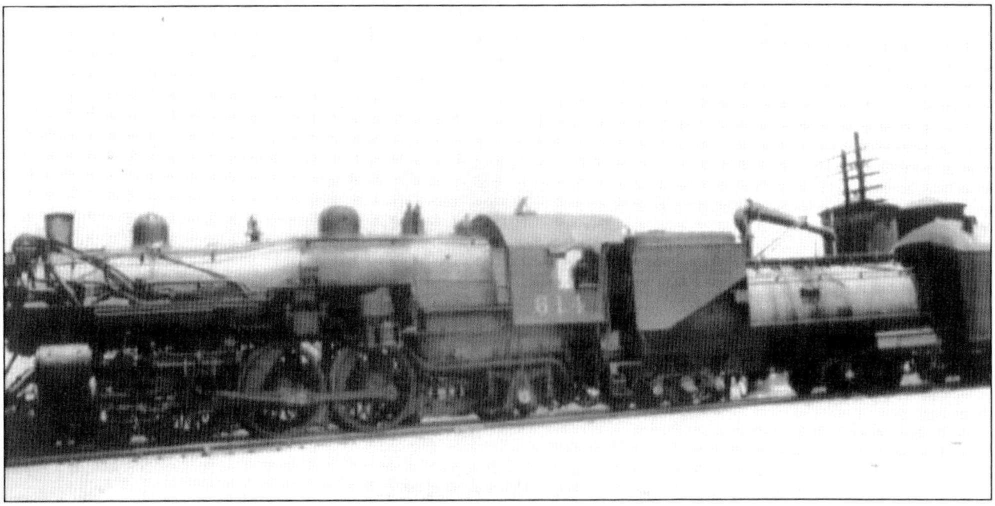

Southern Pacific Locomotive No. 614 has the lead duties on the Sunset Limited out of Rosenberg, Texas. (Courtesy of the Ken E. Stavinoha Collection.)

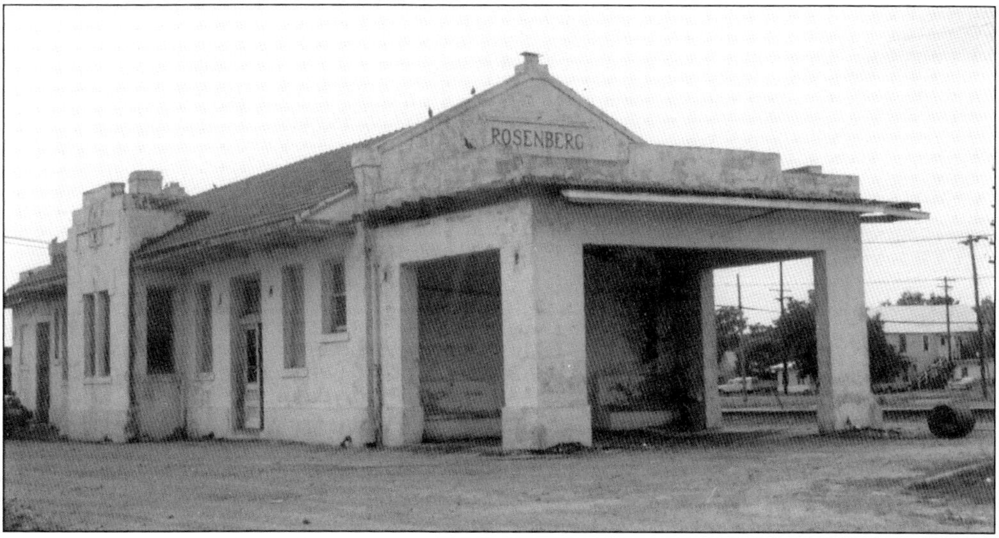

These were the final days of the GH&SA and GC&SF passenger station. Railroad operations had already ceased at the time this photograph was taken in the late 1970s.

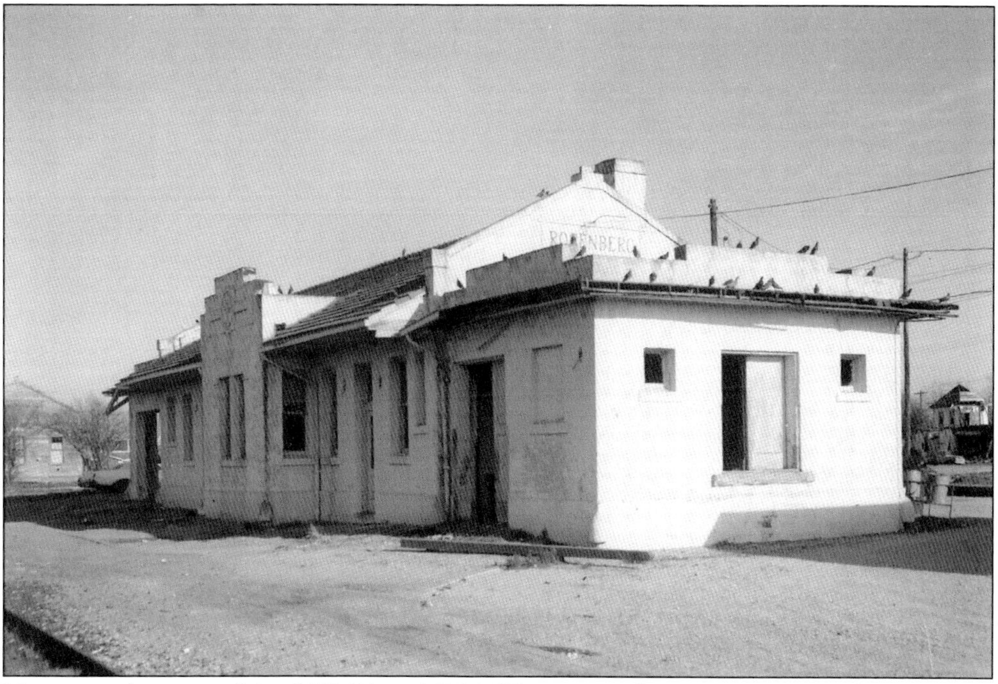

Here is another view of the GH&SA and GC&SF passenger depot. Long past are the days of the beautiful depot parks and grounds that once were part of this unique structure.

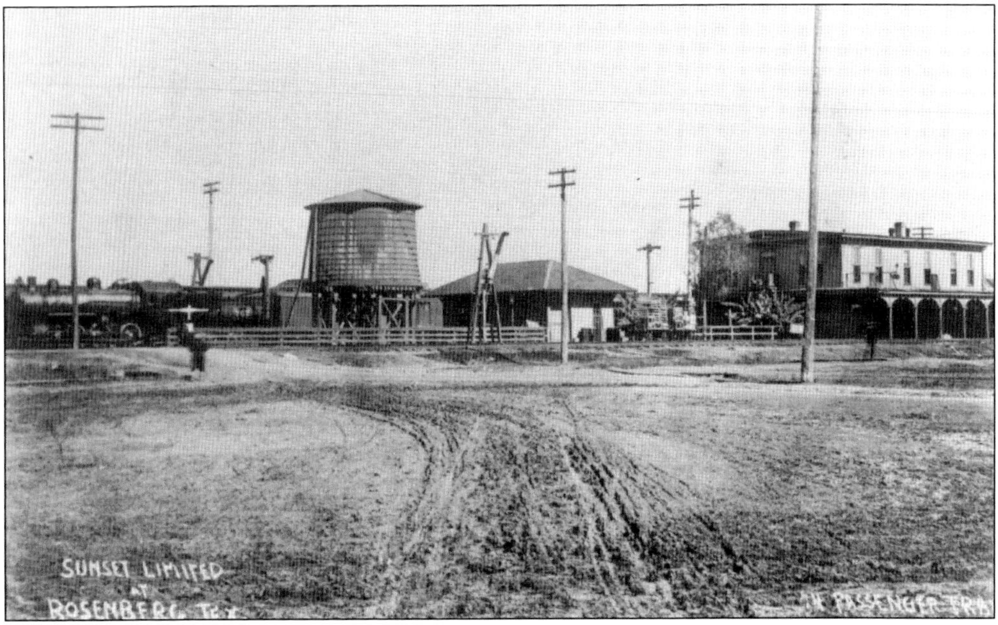

The Sunset Limited stands at Union Station in Rosenberg. Also in view are the railroad's water tower and Wells Fargo Building.

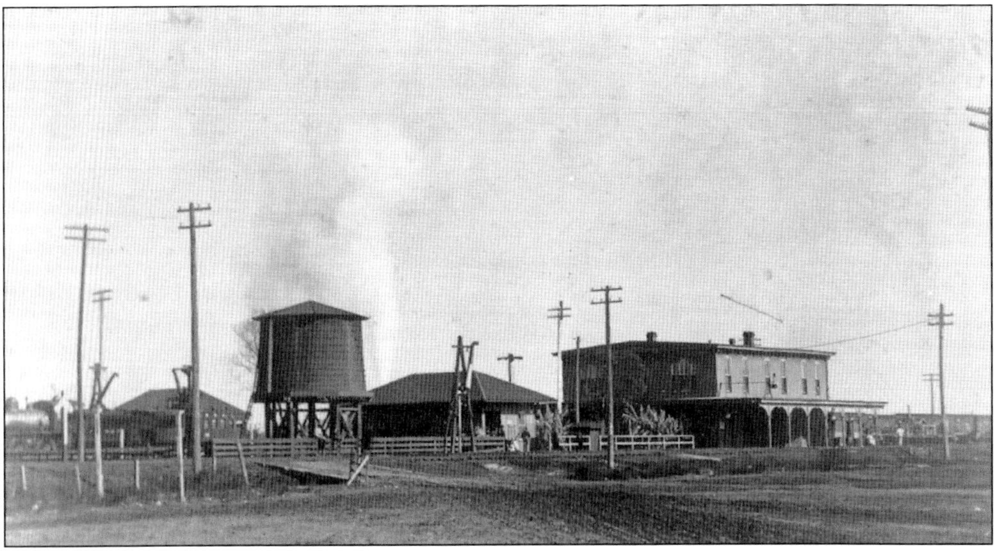

A local switching locomotive waits for its next assignment in the Rosenberg yard. Steam can be seen rising from behind the Wells Fargo Building as another train leaves the Rosenberg Union Station.

Tower 17 operator Mr. C. C. Harris stands in front of Tower 17 in this 1907 photograph. Mr. Harris was one of the first operators of this Rosenberg landmark that still stands today at the Rosenberg Railroad Museum as an interactive exhibit. (Courtesy of the Rosenberg Railroad Museum Collection.)

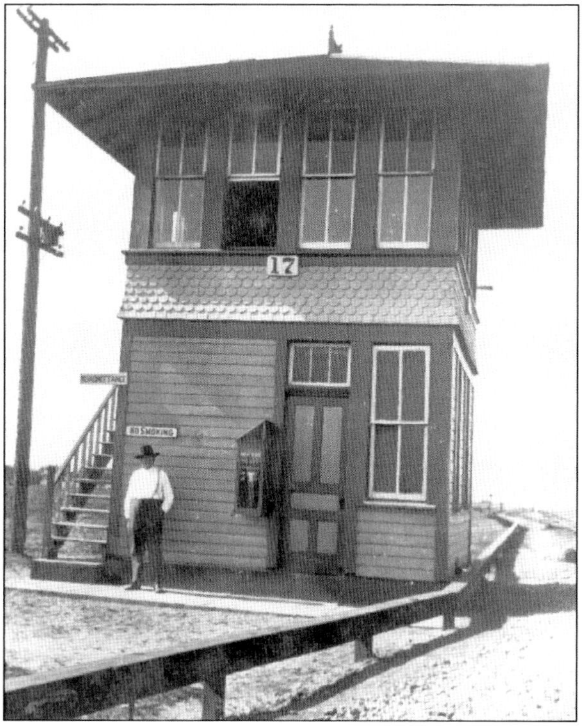

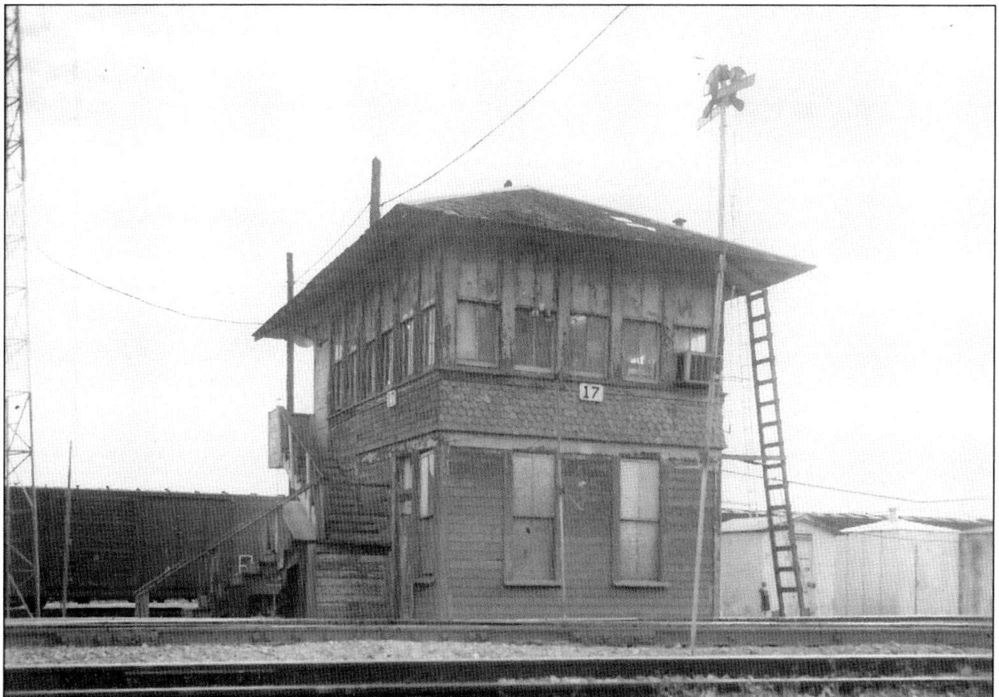

Tower 17 as seen in this 1980s photograph shows the addition made to the tower during the mid-1950s, when the station agent relocated to the second floor. Additional storage space was also added to the first floor during this modification to the building.

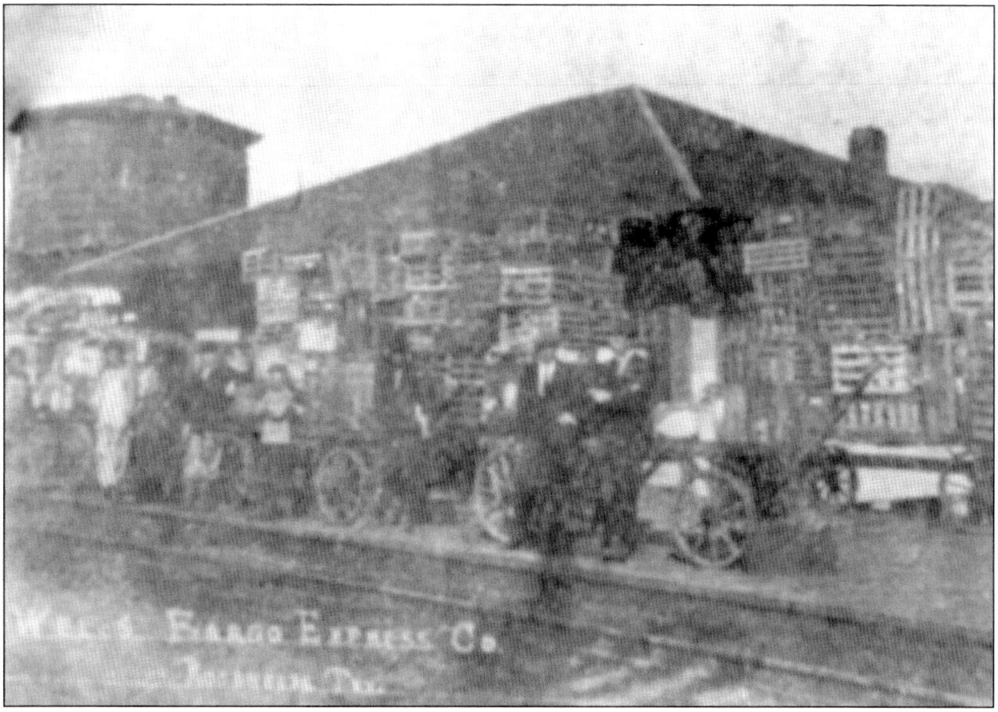

Express baggage is stacked on the platform of the Wells Fargo Express Building near the Union Station in Rosenberg.

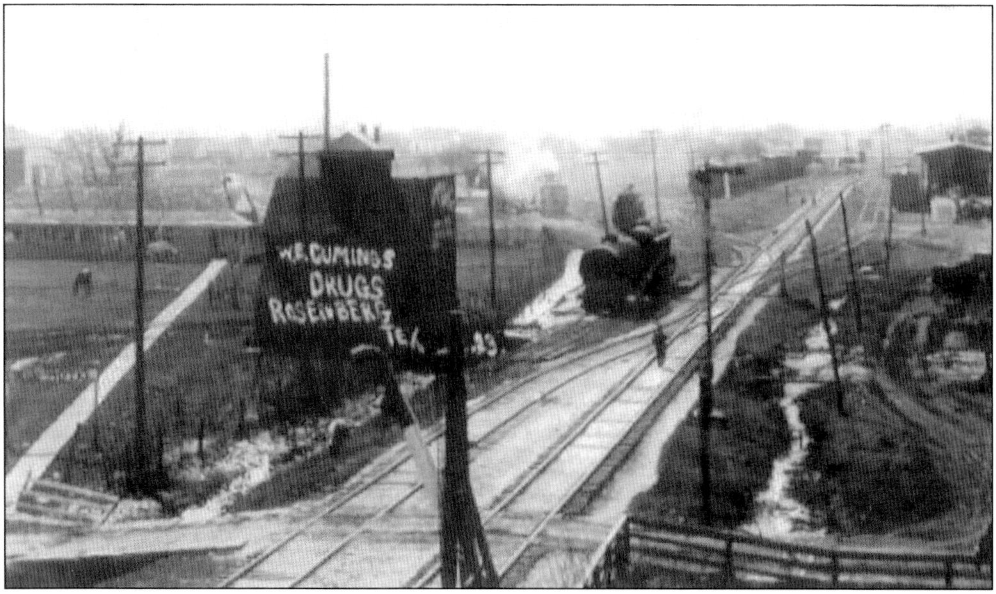

The Santa Fe rail yard is shown here as it appeared from atop the railroad's water tower looking west. The railroad's freight depot and Tower 17 are visible at the upper right-hand corner of the photograph.

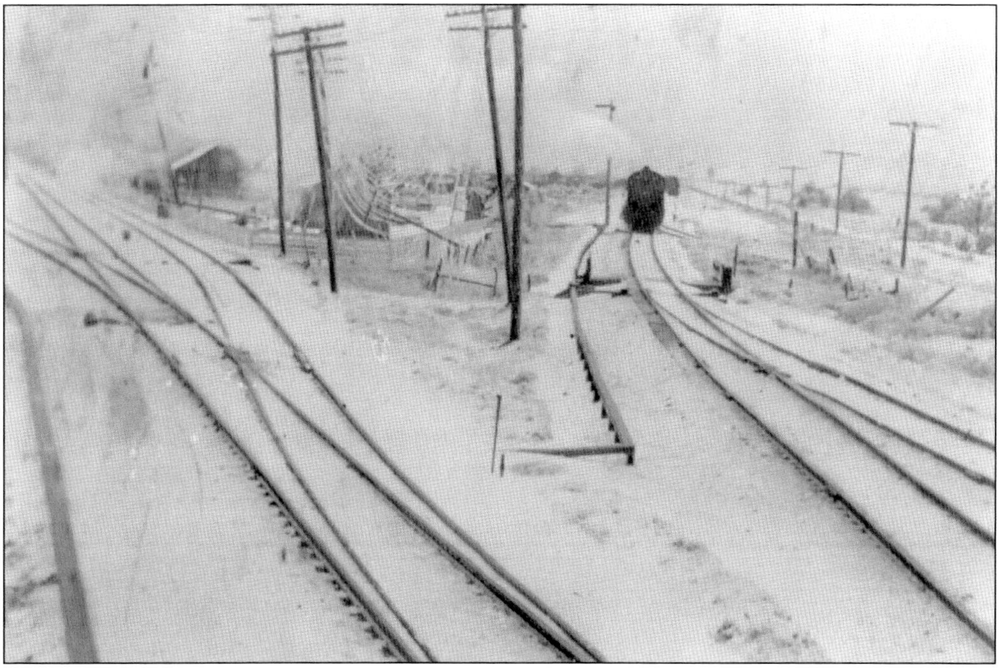

Ice and snow snap telegraph poles and freeze rail service in South Texas. This view shows a Santa Fe train stopped at Signal 4 just north of Tower 17. (Courtesy of the Rosenberg Railroad Museum Collection.)

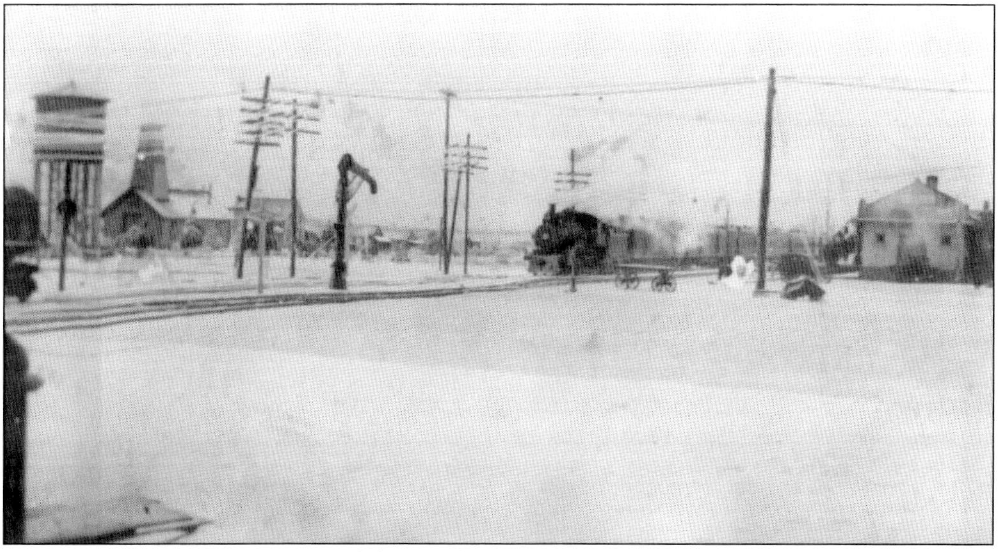

Ice and snow slow the progress of this southbound Santa Fe passenger train at the Rosenberg passenger depot. (Courtesy of the Rosenberg Railroad Museum Collection.)

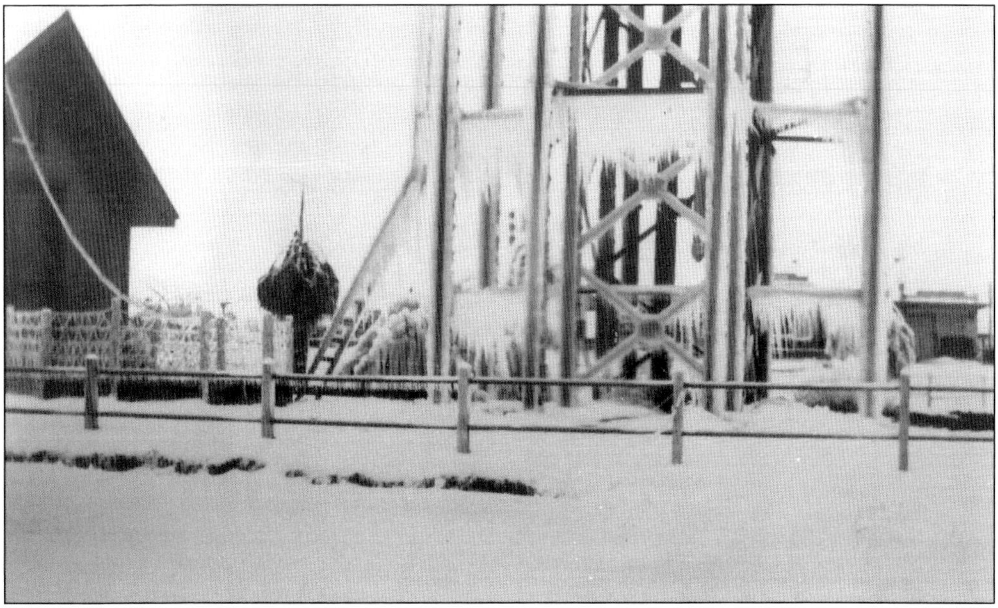

One can almost feel the chill in the air as icicles form on the water tower support structure, and palm tree branches sag under the weight. (Courtesy of the Ken E. Stavinoha Collection.)

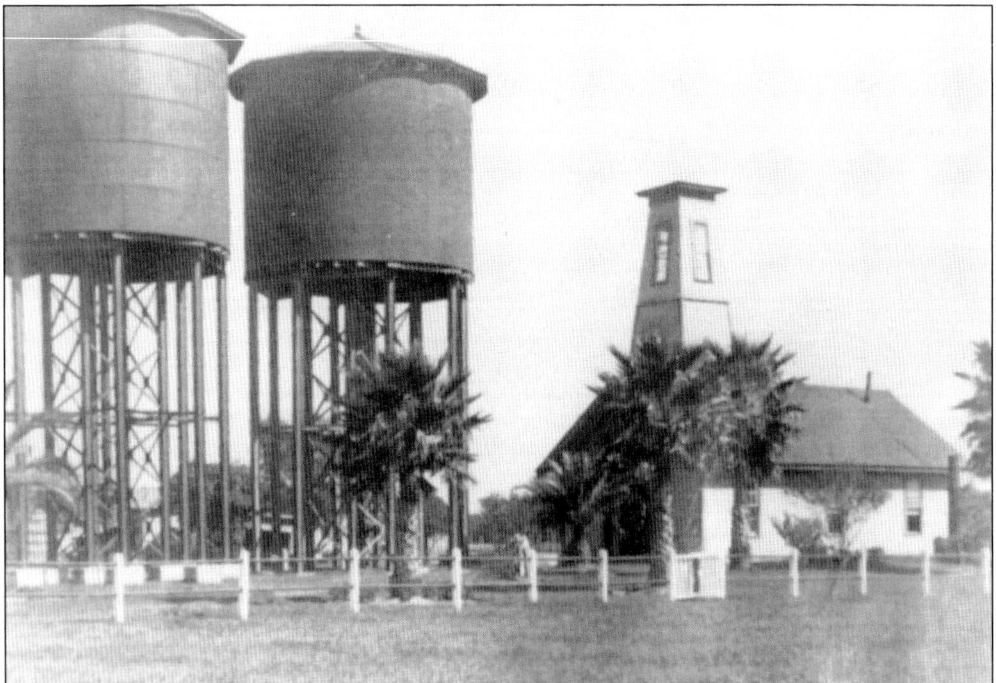

A dual water tower and pump house are telltale landmarks of the Santa Fe yards in Rosenberg, Texas.

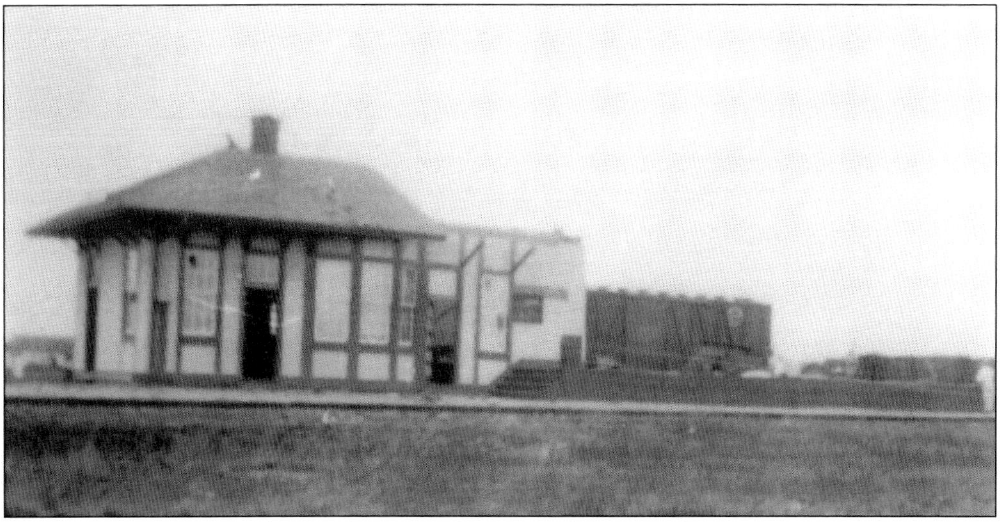

This photograph shows the Southern Pacific Railroad depot under construction in downtown Needville, Texas.

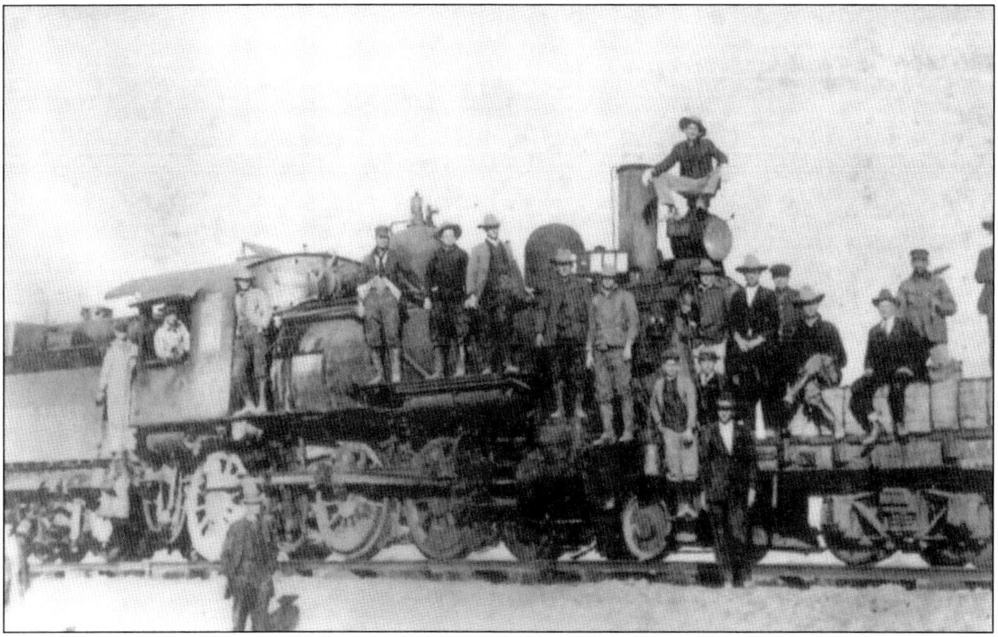

Railroad workers climb aboard the first train to arrive in Needville, Texas. (Courtesy of the Rosenberg Railroad Museum Collection.)

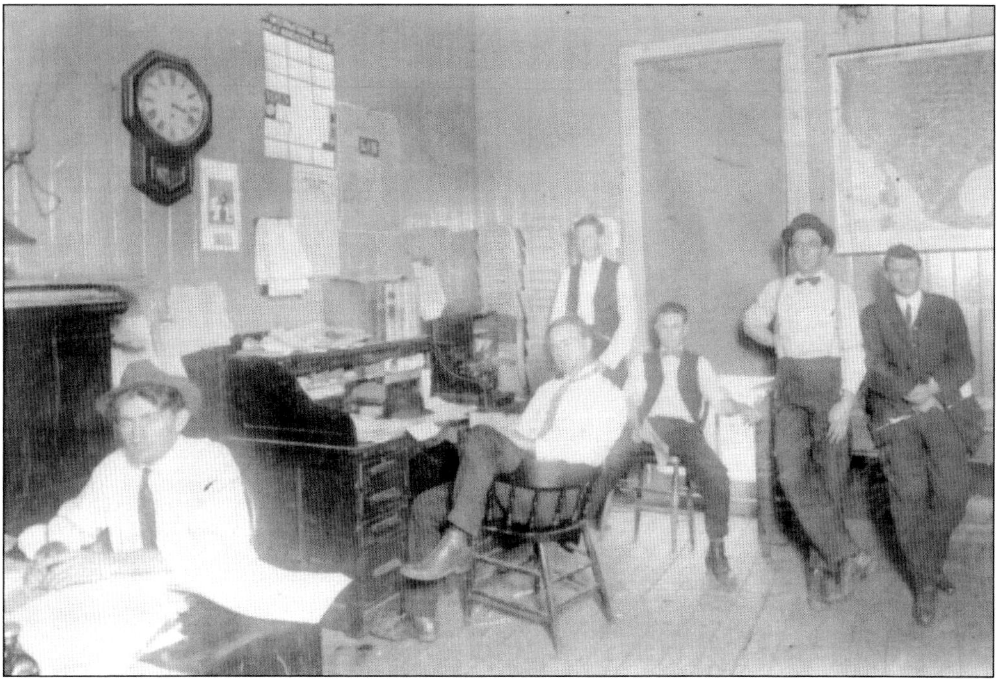

Railroad station employees take a moment to pose for this photograph inside the depot in Needville, Texas. Dave Cardwell (second from right) and Red Perrot (far left) are seen in this photograph.

(4.15) ......Time Over Subdivision...... (3.40)
16.2 ......Average Speed Per Hour...... 18.8

Eastward Trains are Superior to Trains of the Same Class in the Opposite Direction. (See Rule S-72)
EXCEPT: No. 305 is Superior to No. 306.

EASTWARD — **GUY SUBDIVISION** — WESTWARD

Timetable No. 71
December 14, 1947

Length of sidings in cars, location of bulletin, water and fuel stations, standard clocks, interlockings, turn tables, wyes and telephones.	Distance from Guy	STATIONS	Mile Post Location	Train Order Office Hours and Hours of Signal Operators at Interlocking Stations: Daily Except Sundays and Legal Holidays	Train Order Office Hours and Hours of Signal Operators at Interlocking Stations: Sundays and Legal Holidays Only
Y	0.0	GUY	15.7		
		4.7			
17 Spur East	4.7	NEEDVILLE	11.0		
		11.0			
Rosenberg Yard	15.7	GUY JUNCTION	0.0		
		0.5			
I	16.2	TO-R TOWER 17 (G.C. & S.F. Crossing)	36.3	Continuous	Continuous
SEE SAN ANTONIO DIVISION CURRENT TIME TABLE FOR TRAIN MOVEMENTS BETWEEN TOWER 17 AND ROSENBERG					
		0.4			
KWYP	16.6	ROSENBERG	35.9		

Eastward Trains are Superior to Trains of the Same Class in the Opposite Direction. (See Rule S-72)

The railroad timetable for the Guy Subdivision shows the station stops and major junctions along the route south to Guy, Texas. (Courtesy of the Ken E. Stavinoha Collection)

Two

The Houston Tap and Brazoria Railroad

The Houston Tap and Brazoria (HT&B) Railroad became the second railroad company to build through Fort Bend County. Chartered on September 1, 1856, the HT&B connected from the Buffalo Bayou, Brazos, and Colorado Railroad near Houston to the city of Columbia located on the Brazos River in Brazoria County some 50 miles away. Towns located along the line in Fort Bend County include Fresno, Arcola, and Juliff. The line was extended to Sandy Point before opening to East Columbia in 1860. The HT&B was also authorized to build from Columbia into Wharton County. The railroad completed most of the right-of-way grade and several bridges to Wharton, but the War Between the States caused great hardships and devastated the railroad. By the end of the 1860s, the line had deteriorated to a point where only infrequent service was attempted. The few remaining customers of the railroad were served by a mule-drawn cart for a time after the war ended. In 1871, the Houston Tap and Brazoria was sold under foreclosure. The HT&B was merged with the Houston and Great Northern Railroad on May 8, 1873, and became part of the International and Great Northern Railroad. The I&GN eventually had over 1,100 miles in Texas and became a major part of the Missouri Pacific Railroad when purchased on January 1, 1925. Today the remaining portion of the old Houston Tap and Brazoria line is owned and operated by the Union Pacific Railroad.

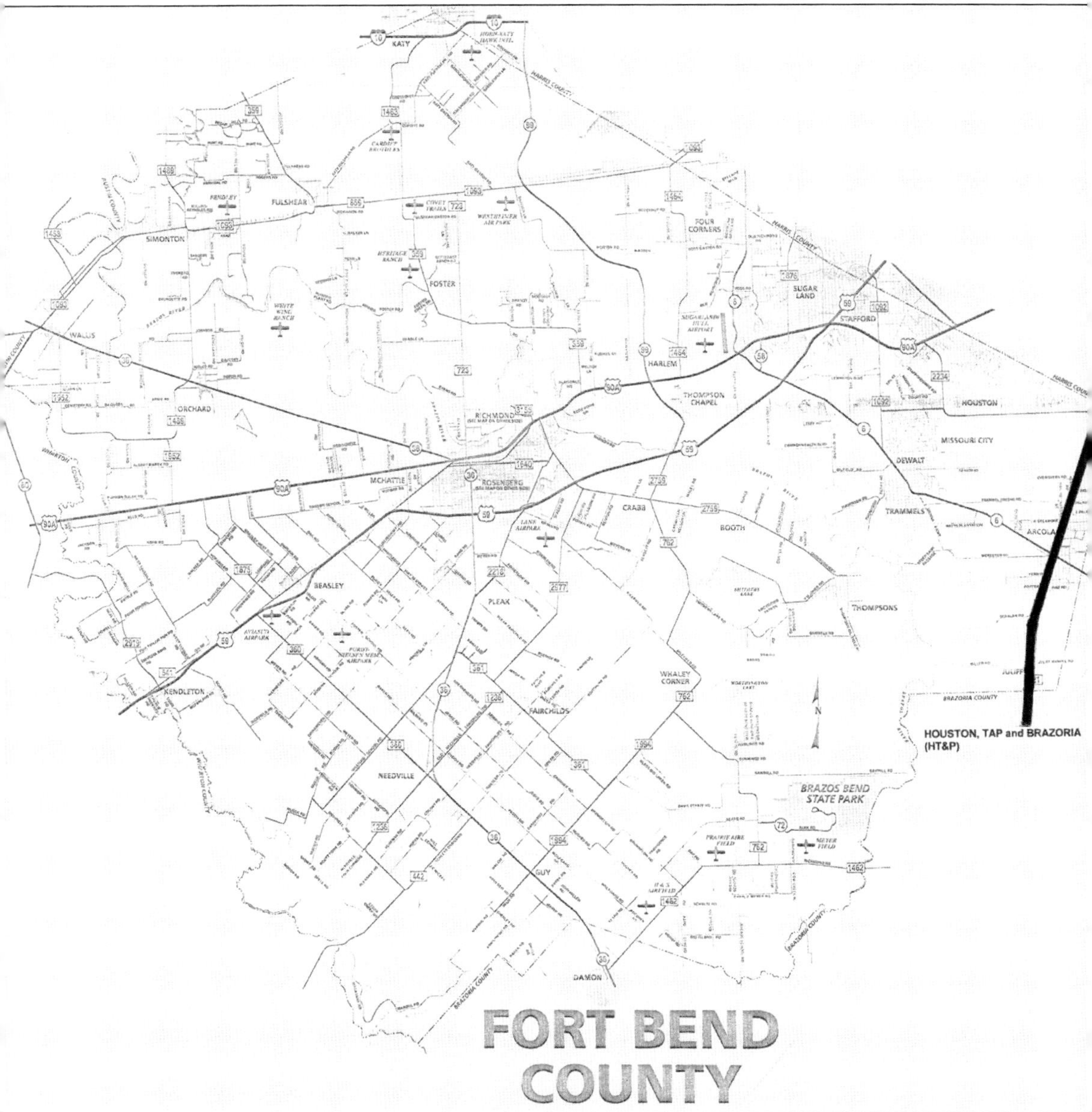

This map of Fort Bend County reflects the route of the Houston, Tap and Brazoria Railroad. "The Tap" was the second railroad to build through Fort Bend County. Starting at its connection with the Buffalo Bayou, Brazos and Colorado Railroad near Houston, the line was constructed to the city of Columbia in Brazoria County, Texas. Towns located along this line in Fort Bend County include Fresno, Arcola and Juliff, Texas.

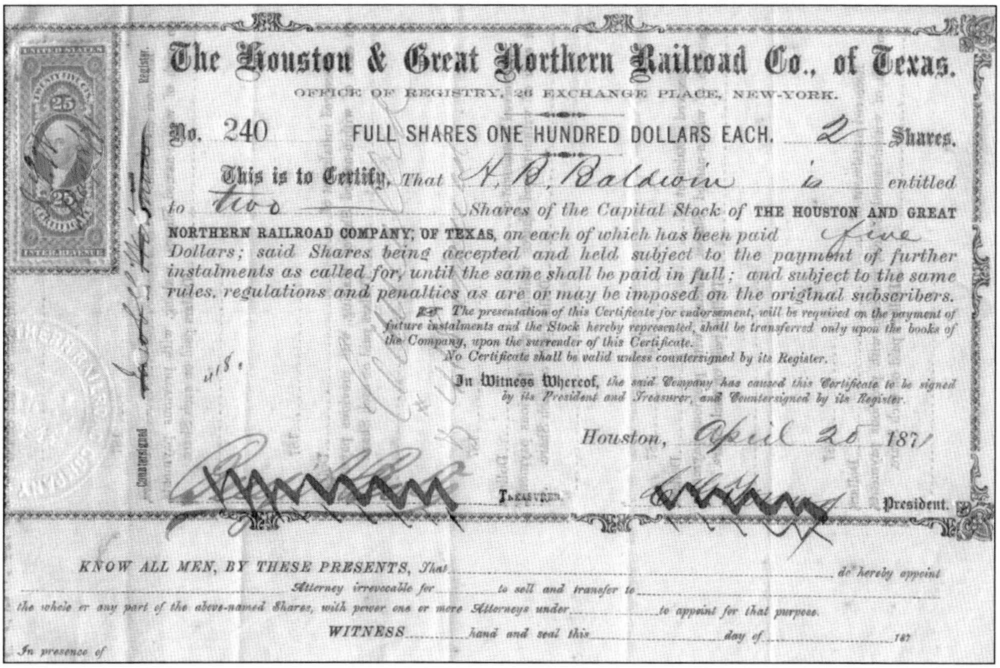

The Houston & Great Northern Railroad Co., of Texas.

OFFICE OF REGISTRY, 26 EXCHANGE PLACE, NEW-YORK.

No. 240 FULL SHARES ONE HUNDRED DOLLARS EACH. 2 Shares.

This is to Certify, That H. B. Baldwin is entitled to two Shares of the Capital Stock of THE HOUSTON AND GREAT NORTHERN RAILROAD COMPANY, OF TEXAS, on each of which has been paid five Dollars; said Shares being accepted and held subject to the payment of further instalments as called for, until the same shall be paid in full; and subject to the same rules, regulations and penalties as are or may be imposed on the original subscribers.

☞ The presentation of this Certificate for endorsement, will be required on the payment of future instalments and the Stock hereby represented, shall be transferred only upon the books of the Company, upon the surrender of this Certificate.

No Certificate shall be valid unless countersigned by its Register.

In Witness Whereof, the said Company has caused this Certificate to be signed by its President and Treasurer, and Countersigned by its Register.

Houston, April 20 1871

Register. Countersigned. Treasurer. President.

KNOW ALL MEN, BY THESE PRESENTS, That do hereby appoint Attorney irrevocable for to sell and transfer to the whole or any part of the above-named Shares, with power one or more Attorneys under to appoint for that purpose.

WITNESS hand and seal this day of 187

In presence of

This stock certificate for two shares of the Houston and Great Northern Railway Company is dated April 20, 1871, and is signed by Mr. C. G. Young, president of the company. (Courtesy of the Ken E. Stavinoha Collection.)

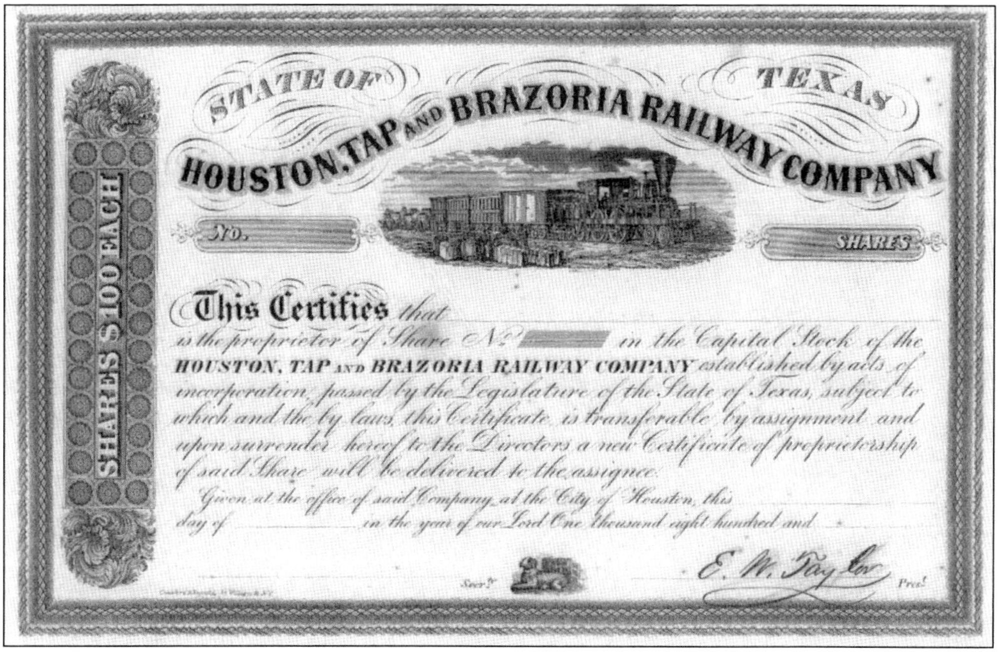

STATE OF TEXAS

HOUSTON, TAP AND BRAZORIA RAILWAY COMPANY

No. SHARES

SHARES $100 EACH

This Certifies that is the proprietor of Share No. in the Capital Stock of the HOUSTON, TAP AND BRAZORIA RAILWAY COMPANY established by acts of incorporation passed by the Legislature of the State of Texas, subject to which and the by laws, this Certificate is transferable by assignment and upon surrender hereof to the Directors a new Certificate of proprietorship of said Share will be delivered to the assignee.

Given at the office of said Company at the City of Houston, this day of in the year of our Lord One thousand eight hundred and

Secry. E. W. Taylor Presd.

This stock certificate from the late 1800s was for the Houston Tap and Brazoria Railway Company and was signed by Mr. E. W. Taylor, president of the company. (Courtesy of the Ken E. Stavinoha Collection.)

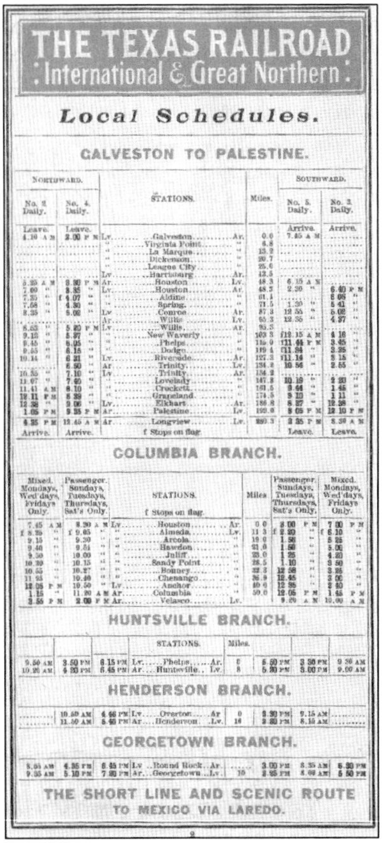

THE TEXAS RAILROAD
International & Great Northern

Local Schedules.

GALVESTON TO PALESTINE.

Northward. No. 2 Daily.	Northward. No. 4 Daily.	Stations.	Miles.	Southward. No. 5 Daily.	Southward. No. 3 Daily.
Leave.	Leave.			Arrive.	Arrive.
4.10 A M	2.00 P M	Lv. Galveston Ar.	0.0	7.45 A M	....
....	....	" Virginia Point "	6.8	....	....
....	....	" La Marque "	13.2	....	....
....	....	" Dickenson "	20.7	....	....
....	....	" League City "	25.6	....	....
....	....	Lv. Harrisburg Ar.	42.5	....	....
5.25 A M	3.30 P M	Ar. Houston Lv.	48.3	6.15 A M	....
7.00 "	3.35 "	Lv. Houston Ar.	48.3	2.30 "	6.40 P M
7.35 "	f 4.07 "	" Aldine "	61.4	....	6.06 "
7.58 "	4.30 "	" Spring "	71.5	1.30 "	5.41 "
8.35 "	5.02 "	Lv. Conroe Ar.	87.3	12.55 "	5.02 "
....		Ar. Willis Lv.	95.3	12.35 "	4.37 "
8.53 "	5.20 P M	Lv. Willis Ar.	95.3	....	....
9.12 "	5.37 "	" New Waverly "	103.3	f12.15 A M	4.16 "
9.45 "	6.05 "	" Phelps "	115.0	f11.44 P M	3.45 "
9.55 "	6.15 "	" Dodge "	119.4	f11.34 "	3.35 "
10.14 "	6.21 "	Lv. Riverside Ar.	127.3	f11.14 "	3.15 "
....	6.50 "	Ar. Trinity Lv.	134.2	10.54 "	2.55 "
10.35 "	7.10 "	Lv. Trinity Ar.	134.2	....	....
11.07 "	7.40 "	" Lovelady "	147.8	10.19 "	2.20 "
11.41 A M	8.10 "	" Crockett "	161.5	9.44 "	1.45 "
12.11 P M	8.39 "	" Grapeland "	174.5	9.10 "	1.11 "
12.38 "	9.06 "	Lv. Elkhart Ar.	186.8	8.37 "	12.38 "
1.05 P M	9.35 P M	Ar. Palestine Lv.	199.0	8.05 P M	12.10 P M
4.35 P M	12.45 A M	Ar. Longview Lv.	280.3	2.35 P M	8.30 A M
Arrive.	Arrive.	f Stops on flag.		Leave.	Leave.

COLUMBIA BRANCH.

Mixed. Mondays, Wed'days, Fridays Only.	Passenger. Sundays, Tuesdays, Thursdays, Sat's Only.	Stations. f Stops on flag.	Miles	Passenger. Sundays, Tuesdays, Thursdays, Sat's Only.	Mixed. Mondays, Wed'days, Fridays Only.
7.45 A M	8.20 A M	Lv. Houston Ar.	0.0	3.00 P M	7.00 P M
f 8.25 "	f 9.05 "	" Almeda Lv.	11.3	f 2.20 "	f 6.10 "
9.15 "	9.30 "	" Arcola "	19.0	1.58 "	5.25 "
9.40 "	9.51 "	" Hawdon "	21.0	1.50 "	5.05 "
9.50 "	10.00 "	" Juliff "	23.0	1.25 "	4.20 "
10.30 "	10.15 "	" Sandy Point "	28.5	1.10 "	3.50 "
10.55 "	10.27 "	" Bonney "	32.3	12.58 "	3.25 "
11.25 "	10.40 "	" Chenango "	36.9	12.45 "	3.00 "
12.05 P M	10.50 "	Lv. Anchor "	40.0	12.35 "	2.40 "
1.15 "	11.20 A M	Ar. Columbia "	50.0	12.05 P M	1.45 P M
3.55 P M	2.00 P M	Ar. Velasco Lv.		9.20 A M	10.00 A M

HUNTSVILLE BRANCH.

			Stations.	Miles.			
9.50 AM	3.50 PM	6.15 PM	Lv. Phelps Ar.	0	5.50 PM	3.30 PM	9.30 AM
10.25 AM	4.20 PM	6.45 PM	Ar. Huntsville Lv.	8	5.20 PM	3.00 PM	9.00 AM

HENDERSON BRANCH.

....	10.50 AM	4.46 PM	Lv. Overton Ar	0	3.30 PM	9.15 AM	....
....	11.50 AM	5.46 PM	Ar. Henderson Lv.	16	2.30 PM	8.15 AM	....

GEORGETOWN BRANCH.

8.55 AM	4.35 PM	6.45 PM	Lv. Round Rock Ar.	......	3.00 PM	8.35 AM	6.30 PM
9.35 AM	5.10 PM	7.20 PM	Ar. Georgetown Lv.	10	2.25 PM	8.00 AM	5.50 PM

THE SHORT LINE AND SCENIC ROUTE TO MEXICO VIA LAREDO.

9

A 1907 International and Great Northern Railroad timetable shows the system's Columbia branch, which includes the Fort Bend County towns of Arcola, Hawdon, Juliff, and Sandy Point on its way south to Columbia in Brazoria County. (Courtesy of the Ken E. Stavinoha Collection.)

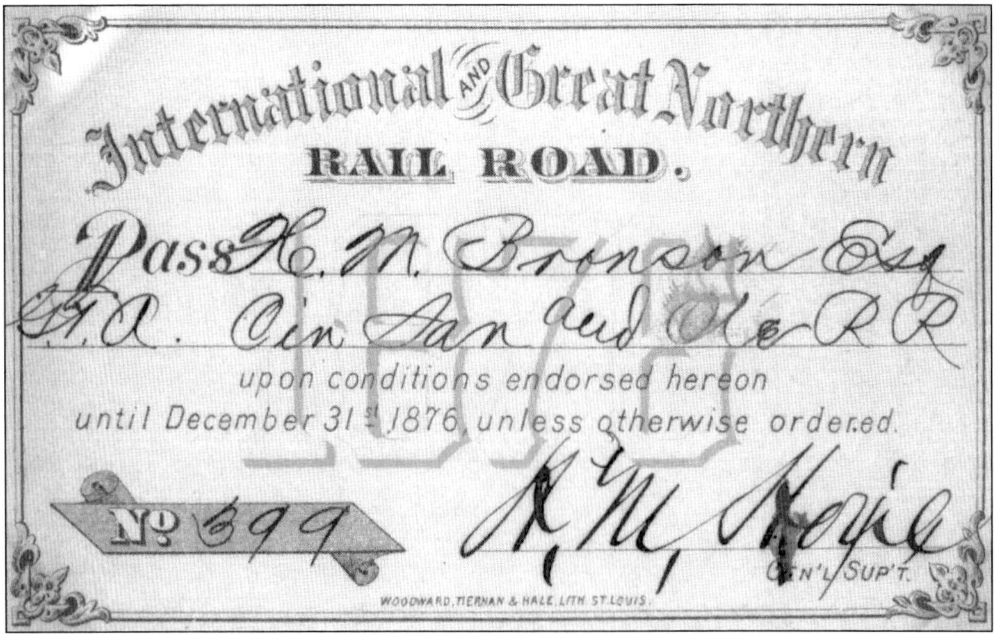

This photograph shows the International and Great Northern Railroad Company 1876 pass No. 399 issued to Mr. H. M. Bronson by H. M. Hoxie. (Courtesy of the Ken E. Stavinoha Collection.)

Three

The Gulf, Colorado, and Santa Fe Railroad

Incorporated on May 28, 1873, the Gulf, Colorado, and Santa Fe (GC&SF) Railroad was organized as a direct line from Galveston to the Canadian River in Northwest Texas. Reaching Arcola in 1877, the GC&SF became the third railroad to enter Fort Bend County. The city of Richmond is the county seat of Fort Bend County and already had the Galveston, Harrisburg, and San Antonio Railroad serving the town. Therefore, the city did not want to pay the monetary bonus and donate the right-of-way to the GC&SF Railroad. The GC&SF engineers laid tracks exactly 1 mile from the courthouse but avoided the town proper. The GC&SF continued to the future site of the city of Rosenberg, where it crossed the GH&SA Railroad at grade. This point in the railroad was named Rosenberg Junction after the second president of the GC&SF Railroad, Henry Rosenberg. The town of Rosenberg was platted and lots were sold in the early 1880s. Towns along the line in Fort Bend County include Arcola, Thompsons, Booth, Richmond, Rosenberg, and Orchard. In 1885, the GC&SF became part of the Atchison, Topeka, and Santa Fe Railroad.

On March 10, 1898, a group of Eagle Lake businessmen—including William Dunovant and William T. Eldridge—chartered the Cane Belt Railroad. As indicated by the title, sugarcane would be the primary commodity transported by the railroad, but later it included rice, gravel, and eventually sulfur. In 1903, the Santa Fe Railroad purchased the Cane Belt. In 1930 and 1931, the Cane Belt Railroad constructed a branch from Lane City (in Wharton County) to Thompsons (in Fort Bend County) that served two sulfur operations: New Gulf in Wharton County and Long Point in Fort Bend County. This branch also created a shortcut from Matagorda to Galveston for the Santa Fe and was titled the Hall District in employee timetables from the period. Passenger service was offered on a mixed train from Thompsons to Cane Junction and back but was discontinued in 1942.

Today the Burlington Northern Santa Fe Railroad remains one of the busiest rail lines along the Gulf Coast.

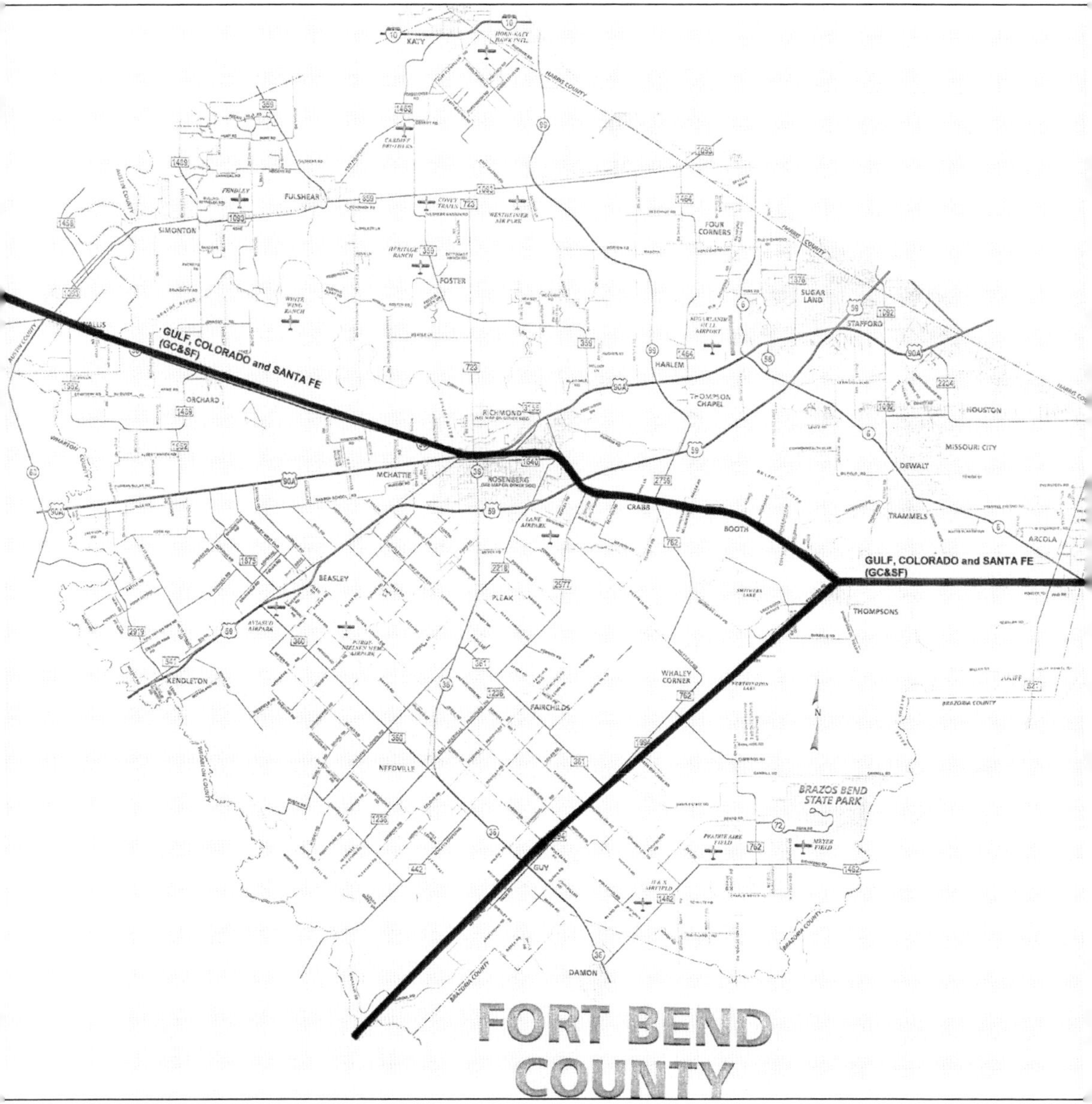

This map of Fort Bend County reflects the route of the Gulf, Colorado, and Santa Fe Railroad. Towns along this route through Fort Bend County include Arcola, Thompsons, Booth, Crabb, Richmond, Rosenberg, Dyer, and Orchard, Texas.

A Gulf, Colorado, and Santa Fe Railroad employee timetable is pictured here. Fort Bend County towns along this route include Arcola, Thompsons, Booth, Crabb, Richmond, Rosenberg, Dryer, and Orchard, Texas. (Courtesy of the Ken E. Stavinoha Collection.)

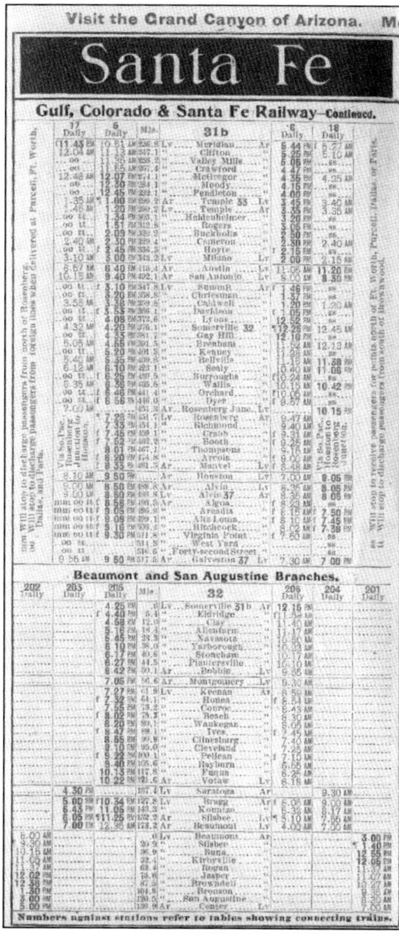

Visit the Grand Canyon of Arizona. Mo

Santa Fe

Gulf, Colorado & Santa Fe Railway—Continued.

17 Daily	5 Daily	Mls.	31b	6 Daily	18 Daily
11.43 PM	10.51 AM	236.8	Lv ..... Meridian ..... Ar	5.44 PM	f 5.27 AM
12.04 AM	11.13 AM	247.1	" ..... Clifton ..... "	5.25 PM	5.10 AM
oo	11.35 AM	258.2	" ..... Valley Mills ..... "	5.05 PM	ss
oo	11.55 AM	267.4	" ..... Crawford ..... "	4.47 PM	ss
12.48 AM	12.07 PM	274.1	" ..... McGregor ..... "	4.35 PM	4.25 AM
oo	12.30 PM	284.1	" ..... Moody ..... "	4.15 PM	ss
oo	12.45 PM	292.1	" ..... Pendleton ..... "	4.00 PM	ss
1.35 AM	1.00 PM	299.2	Ar ..... Temple 33 Lv	3.45 PM	3.40 AM
1.45 AM	1.20 PM	299.2	Lv ..... Temple ..... Ar	3.35 PM	3.35 AM
oo tt	1.34 PM	303.1	" ..... Heidenheimer ..... "	3.20 PM	ss
oo tt	1.51 PM	312.8	" ..... Rogers ..... "	3.05 PM	ss
oo tt	2.09 PM	320.2	" ..... Buckholts ..... "	2.50 PM	ss
2.40 AM	2.30 PM	329.4	" ..... Cameron ..... "	2.30 PM	2.40 AM
oo tt	f 2.45 PM	334.3	" ..... Hoyte ..... "	f 2.15 PM	ss
3.10 AM	3.00 PM	343.2	Lv ..... Milano Lv	2.00 PM	2.15 AM
6.57 AM	6.40 PM	418.4	Ar ..... Austin Lv	11.05 AM	11.20 PM
10.15 AM	9.40 PM	492.1	Ar ..... San Antonio Lv	8.00 AM	8.30 PM
oo tt	f 3.10 PM	347.8	Lv ..... Summit ..... Ar	f 1.46 PM	ss
oo tt	3.20 PM	358.8	" ..... Chriesman ..... "	1.37 PM	ss
3.58 AM	3.38 PM	359.8	" ..... Caldwell ..... "	1.20 PM	1.20 AM
oo tt	f 3.53 PM	366.1	" ..... Davidson ..... "	f 1.05 PM	ss
oo tt	4.08 PM	372.6	" ..... Lyons ..... "	12.52 PM	ss
4.32 AM	4.20 PM	376.1	" ..... Somerville 32 ..... "	12.25 PM	12.45 AM
oo tt	4.33 PM	381.7	" ..... Gay Hill ..... "	12.10 PM	ss
5.05 AM	4.55 PM	391.5	" ..... Brenham ..... "	11.52 AM	12.13 AM
oo tt	5.20 PM	401.5	" ..... Kenney ..... "	11.28 AM	ss
5.40 AM	5.35 PM	409.8	" ..... Bellville ..... "	11.15 AM	11.38 PM
6.12 AM	6.10 PM	423.1	" ..... Sealy ..... "	10.40 AM	11.08 PM
oo tt	f 6.25 PM	427.5	" ..... Burroughs ..... "	f 10.24 AM	ss
6.35 AM	6.36 PM	435.5	" ..... Wallis ..... "	10.15 AM	10.42 PM
oo tt	f 6.46 PM	441.4	" ..... Orchard ..... "	f 10.05 AM	ss
oo tt	f 6.56 PM	446.0	" ..... Dyer ..... "	f 9.57 AM	ss
7.00 AM		451.3	Ar .. Rosenberg Junc. .. Lv		10.15 PM
Via So. Pac. Rosenberg Junction to Houston.	7.28 PM	451.7	Lv ..... Rosenberg ..... Ar	9.47 AM	Via So. Pac. Houston to Rosenberg Junction.
	7.33 PM	454.1	" ..... Richmond ..... "	9.40 AM	
	f 7.45 PM	459.1	" ..... Crabb ..... "	f 9.31 AM	
	f 7.52 PM	462.2	" ..... Booth ..... "	f 9.25 AM	
	8.01 PM	467.1	" ..... Thompsons ..... "	9.15 AM	
	f 8.20 PM	474.8	" ..... Arcola ..... "	f 9.00 AM	
	f 8.35 PM	481.5	Ar ..... Manvel Lv	f 8.48 AM	
8.10 AM	9.50 PM		Ar ..... Houston Lv	7.00 AM	9.05 PM
9.00 AM	8.50 PM	488.8	Ar ..... Alvin Lv	8.35 AM	8.05 PM
9.00 AM	8.50 PM	488.8	Lv ..... Alvin 37 ..... Ar	8.35 AM	8.05 PM
mm oo tt	f 8.58 PM	496.3	Ar ..... Algoa ..... "	f 8.23 AM	ss
mm oo tt	f 9.05 PM	496.9	" ..... Arcadia ..... "	f 8.15 AM	f 7.50 PM
mm oo tt	f 9.09 PM	499.1	" ..... Alta Loma ..... "	f 8.10 AM	f 7.45 PM
mm oo tt	f 9.16 PM	503.4	" ..... Hitchcock ..... "	8.02 AM	f 7.38 PM
mm oo tt	f 9.30 PM	511.8	" ..... Virginia Point ..... "	f 7.50 AM	ss
oo tt		514.8	" ..... West Yard ..... "		ss
oo tt		516.6	" . Forty-second Street . "		ss
9.55 AM	9.50 PM	517.3	Ar ..... Galveston 37 Lv	7.30 AM	7.00 PM

mm Will stop to discharge passengers from north of Rosenberg.
oo Will stop to discharge passengers from foreign lines when delivered at Purcell, Ft. Worth, Dallas, and Paris.

ss Will stop to receive passengers for points north of Ft. Worth, Purcell, Dallas, or Paris.
tt Will stop to discharge passengers from south of Brownwood.

Beaumont and San Augustine Branches.

202 Daily	203 Daily	205 Daily	Mls.	32	206 Daily	204 Daily	201 Daily
		4.25 PM	.0	Lv ... Somerville 31b ... Ar	12.15 PM		
		f 4.40 PM	6.4	" ..... Eldridge ..... "	f 11.59 AM		
		4.58 PM	12.0	" ..... Clay ..... "	11.40 AM		
		5.16 PM	18.4	" ..... Allenfarm ..... "	11.17 AM		
		5.45 PM	28.3	" ..... Navasota ..... "	10.50 AM		
		6.10 PM	38.0	" ..... Yarborough ..... "	10.23 AM		
		6.17 PM	40.6	" ..... Stoneham ..... "	10.17 AM		
		6.27 PM	44.5	" ..... Plantersville ..... "	10.10 AM		
		6.42 PM	50.1	Ar ..... Bobbin Lv	9.55 AM		
		7.05 PM	56.6	Ar ..... Montgomery Lv	9.30 AM		
		7.27 PM	61.9	Lv ..... Keenan ..... Ar	8.59 AM		
		f 7.32 PM	64.1	" ..... Honea ..... "	f 8.54 AM		
		7.55 PM	73.2	" ..... Conroe ..... "	8.43 AM		
		f 8.02 PM	75.3	" ..... Beach ..... "	8.30 AM		
		8.20 PM	80.1	" ..... Waukegan ..... "	8.05 AM		
		f 8.47 PM	88.1	" ..... Ives ..... "	f 7.45 AM		
		8.55 PM	90.8	" ..... Clinesburg ..... "	7.40 AM		
		9.10 PM	95.0	" ..... Cleveland ..... "	7.25 AM		
		f 9.22 PM	100.1	" ..... Pelican ..... "	f 7.10 AM		
		9.40 PM	105.6	" ..... Rayburn ..... "	6.55 AM		
		10.13 PM	117.8	" ..... Fuqua ..... "	6.25 AM		
		10.22 PM	121.6	Ar ..... Votaw Lv	6.18 AM		
	4.30 PM		137.4	Lv ..... Saratoga ..... Ar		9.30 AM	
	5.00 PM	f 10.34 PM	127.8	Lv ..... Bragg ..... Ar	f 6.08 AM	9.00 AM	
	5.43 PM	11.05 PM	143.3	" ..... Kountze ..... "	5.32 AM	8.17 AM	
	6.05 PM	11.25 PM	152.2	Ar ..... Silsbee Lv	5.10 AM	7.55 AM	
	7.00 PM	12.35 AM	173.2	Ar ..... Beaumont Lv	4.00 AM	7.00 AM	
8.00 AM			.0	Lv ..... Beaumont ..... Ar			3.00 PM
9.30 AM			20.9	" ..... Silsbee ..... "			1.40 PM
10.15 AM			26.9	" ..... Buna ..... "			12.55 PM
11.05 AM			32.4	" ..... Kirbyville ..... "			12.05 PM
11.37 AM			62.4	" ..... Rogan ..... "			11.37 AM
12.02 PM			73.8	" ..... Jasper ..... "			11.07 AM
12.38 PM			87.5	" ..... Browndell ..... "			10.27 AM
1.30 PM			104.8	" ..... Bronson ..... "			9.35 AM
3.00 PM			120.5	" ..... San Augustine ..... "			8.30 AM
5.00 PM			130.9	Ar ..... Center Lv			7.00 AM

Numbers against stations refer to tables showing connecting trains.

This is an 1881 Gulf, Colorado, and Santa Fe Railway pass, no. 87, that was issued to James Converse, general superintendent of the GH&SA railway, by John Sealy, general superintendent of the GC&SF railroad. (Courtesy of the Ken E. Stavinoha Collection.)

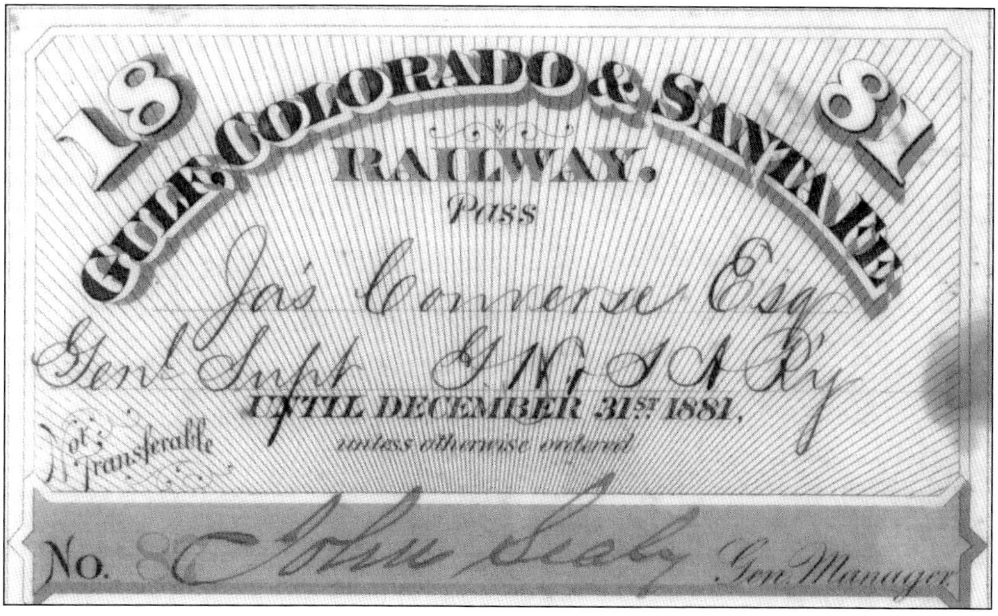

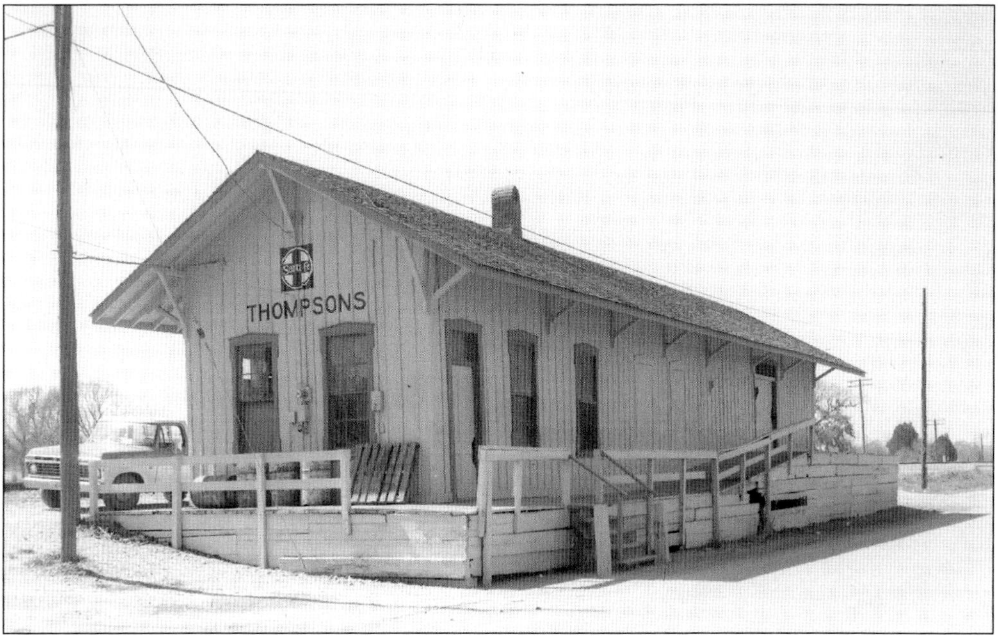

An early-1970s view looks southeast past the Gulf, Colorado, and Santa Fe depot in Thompsons, Texas. This depot remained in service until the early 1980s. The depot building was relocated to Richmond and is a private residence along State Road 359.

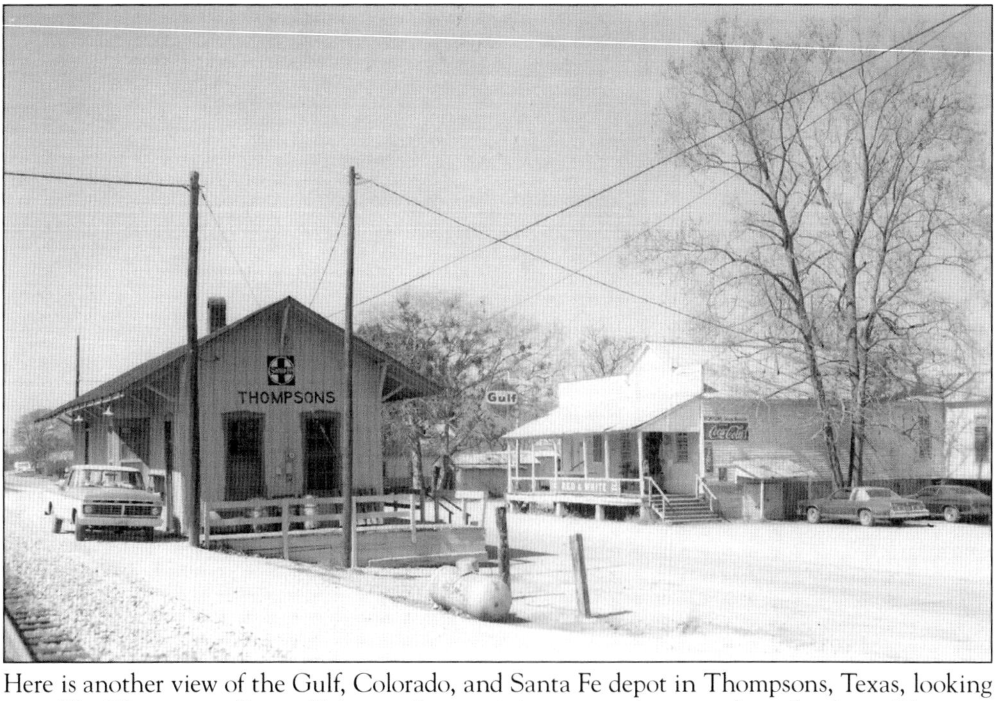

Here is another view of the Gulf, Colorado, and Santa Fe depot in Thompsons, Texas, looking west. The Thompsons General Mercantile store is just across the street from the depot. The store has closed but the building remains.

This is a 1938 copy of the Gulf, Colorado, and Santa Fe Hall District timetable. Originally part of the Cane Belt Railroad, the Santa Fe acquired the Cane Belt in 1903. Towns along the Hall District in Fort Bend County include Thompsons, Long Point, and Guy, Texas. (Courtesy of the Ken E. Stavinoha Collection.)

GULF DIVISION

HALL DISTRICT

SOUTHWARD Second Class 117 Mixed	113 Mixed	Capacity of Sidings	Distance from Thompsons	Ruling Grade Ascending	TIME TABLE No. 141 February 20, 1938	Ruling Grade Ascending	Fuel, Water, Turn Tables and Wyes	Office of Communication	NORTHWARD Second Class 114 Mixed	118 Mixed
Leave Wed. Only	Leave Daily Ex. Sunday	Cars	Miles	Ft. Per Mile	STATIONS	Ft. Per Mile			Arrive Daily Ex. Sunday	Arrive Wed. Only
	PM 12.01	126			THOMPSONS			O	PM 6.30	
				7.9	11.0	5.3				
	f12.55	112	11.0		LONG POINT				f 5.45	
				5.3	4.9	11.6				
			15.9		T. & N. O. CROSSING					
					0.2					
	f 1.25	113	16.1		GUY				f 5.20	
				6.3	11.2	10.6				
PM 2.10	2.10 PM	113	27.3		NEWGULF JCT. T. & N. O. CROSSING		W Y		4.35 PM	PM 3.50
					2.4					
			29.7		AREY					
				4.8	4.2	4.2				
2.45 PM		113	33.9		CANE JCT.		Y			3.15 PM
Arrive Wed. Only	Arrive Daily Ex. Sunday				(33.9)				Leave Daily Ex. Sunday	Leave Wed. Only
(11.3)	(12.0)				Average speed per hour				(13.7)	(11.8)

All trains must obtain Clearance Card at Thompsons.

Hall District trains and engines will use Matagorda District main track at Cane Jct., at restricted speed, keeping out of the way of Matagorda District trains and engines. Matagorda District trains and engines must operate within above limits at restricted speed, looking out for Hall District trains and engines.

Hall District trains and engines will use First District main track at Thompsons at restricted speed, keeping out of the way of First District trains and engines.

First District trains and engines must operate within above limits at restricted speed, looking out for Hall District trains and engines. No switch lights on Hall District.

NO. 113 IS SUPERIOR TO NO. 114.
NO. 117 IS SUPERIOR TO NO. 118

LOCATION AND CAPACITY OF TRACKS NOT SHOWN ON FACE OF TIME TABLE

Name	Mile Post	Car Capacity
Mooredale	19.4	5

GALVESTON TERMINAL DISTRICT

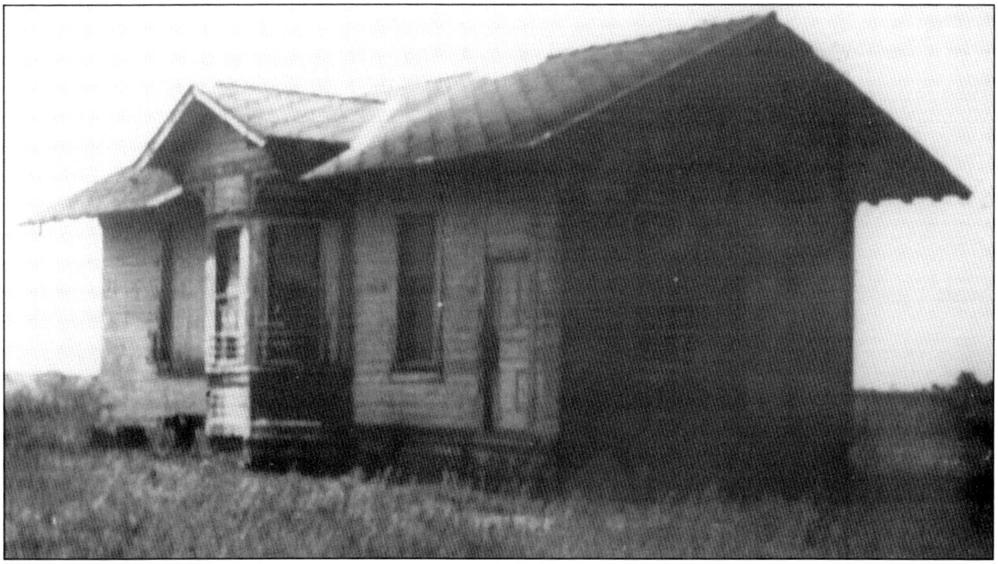

The elements have been taking their toll on the Long Point depot as it sits all alone in a field in Fort Bend County. The depot had been out of service for a while at the time of this photograph (Courtesy of the Ken E. Stavinoha Collection.)

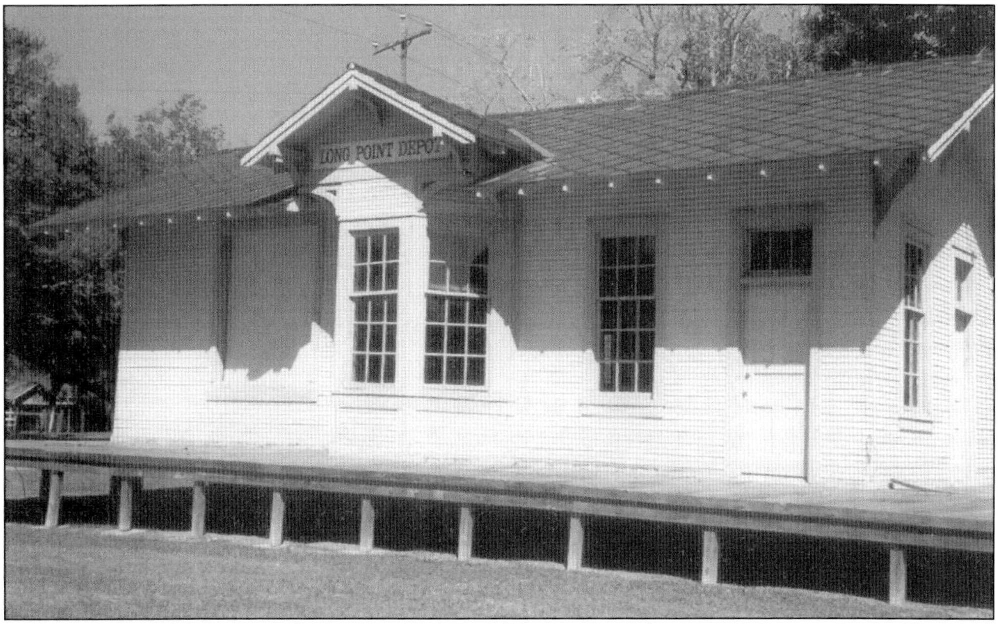

This is a view of the restored Long Point depot. (Courtesy of the Ken E. Stavinoha Collection.)

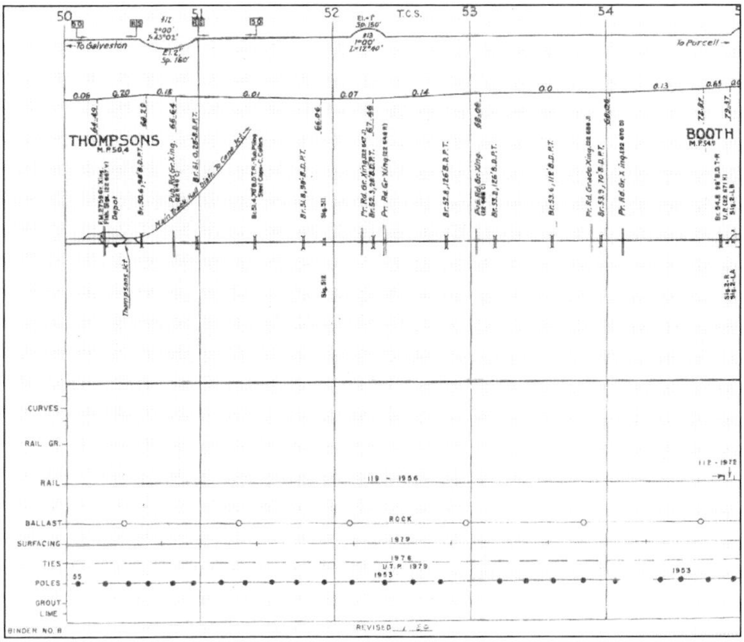

A Gulf, Colorado, and Santa Fe track chart documents the history of the line, showing the last maintenance dates for items such as poles, ties, rail, ballast, etc. (Courtesy of the Rosenberg Railroad Museum Collection.)

In this early photograph of the Gulf, Colorado, and Santa Fe railroad depot in Booth, Texas, a soldier passes the time talking with a young lady as they wait for their train.

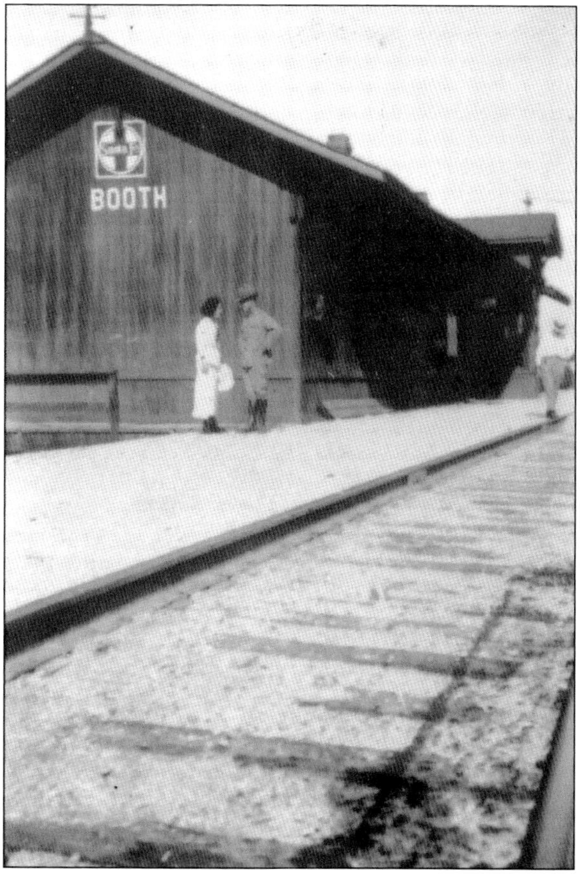

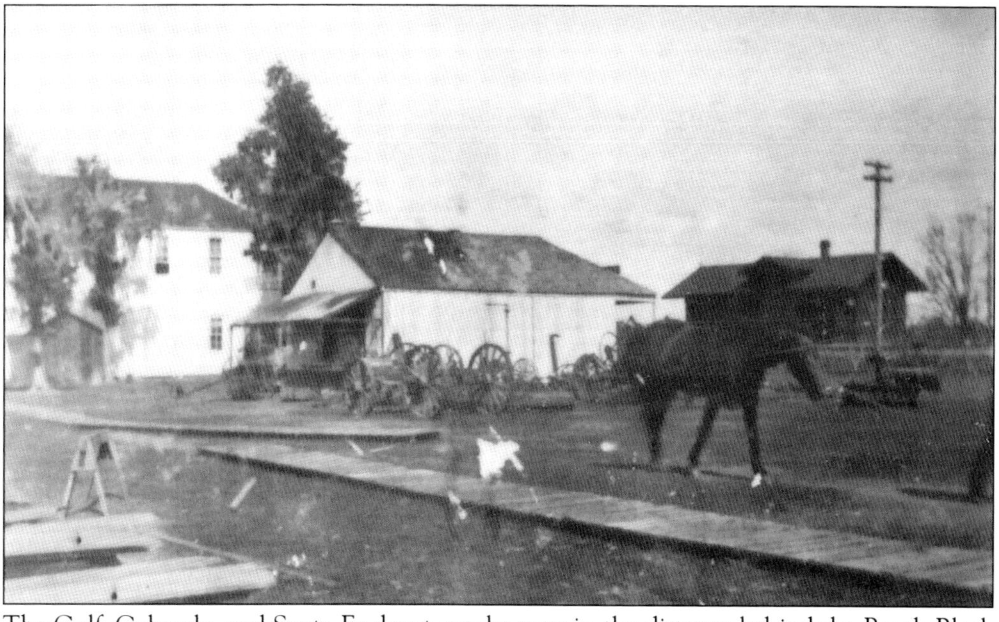

The Gulf, Colorado, and Santa Fe depot can be seen in the distance behind the Booth Black Smith shop.

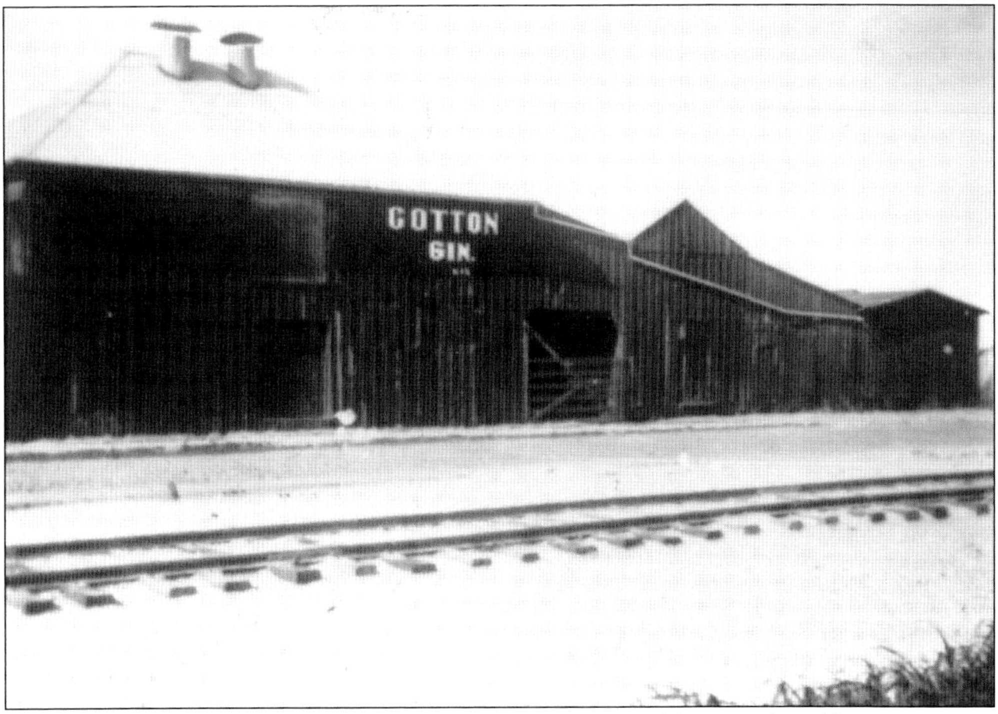

Cotton was a common commodity shipped by rail. Pictured here is the old cotton gin in downtown Booth.

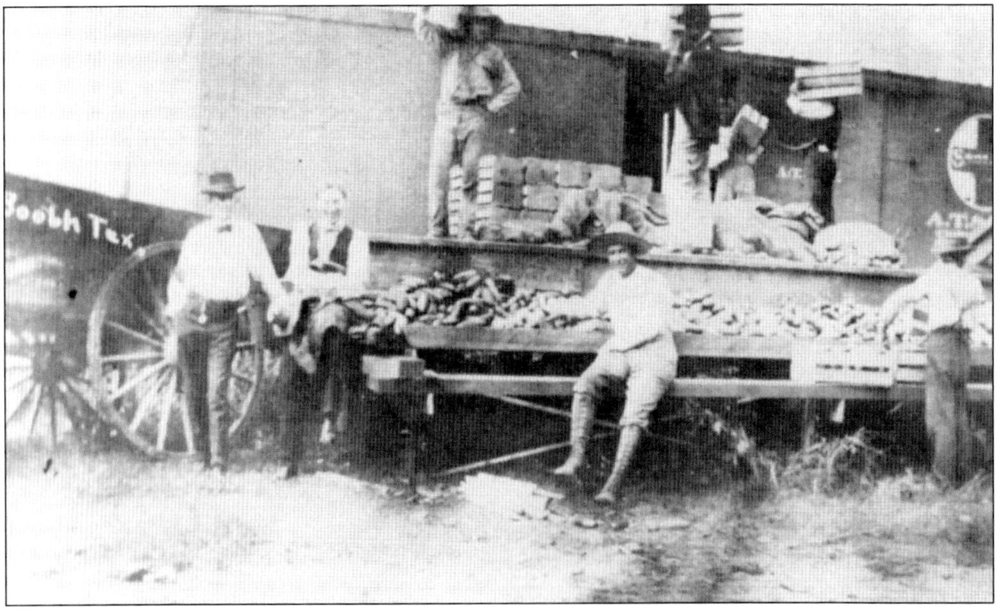

Cucumbers are packaged for shipping and being loaded into CG&SF refrigerated boxcars in Booth, Texas, in this photograph.

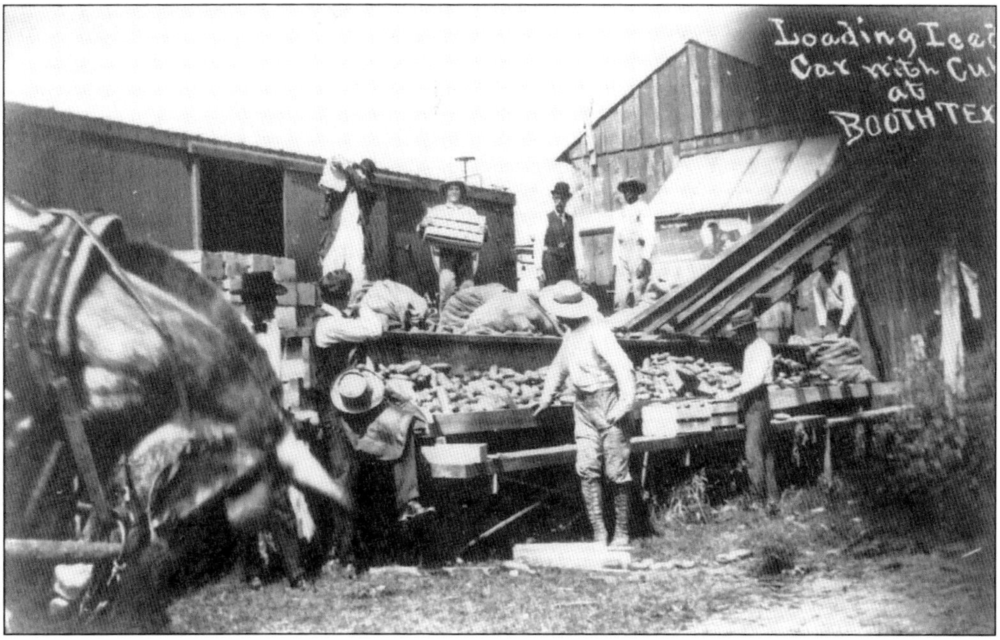

Pictured here are people loading crates of cucumbers into iced boxcars on the GC&SF in Booth, Texas.

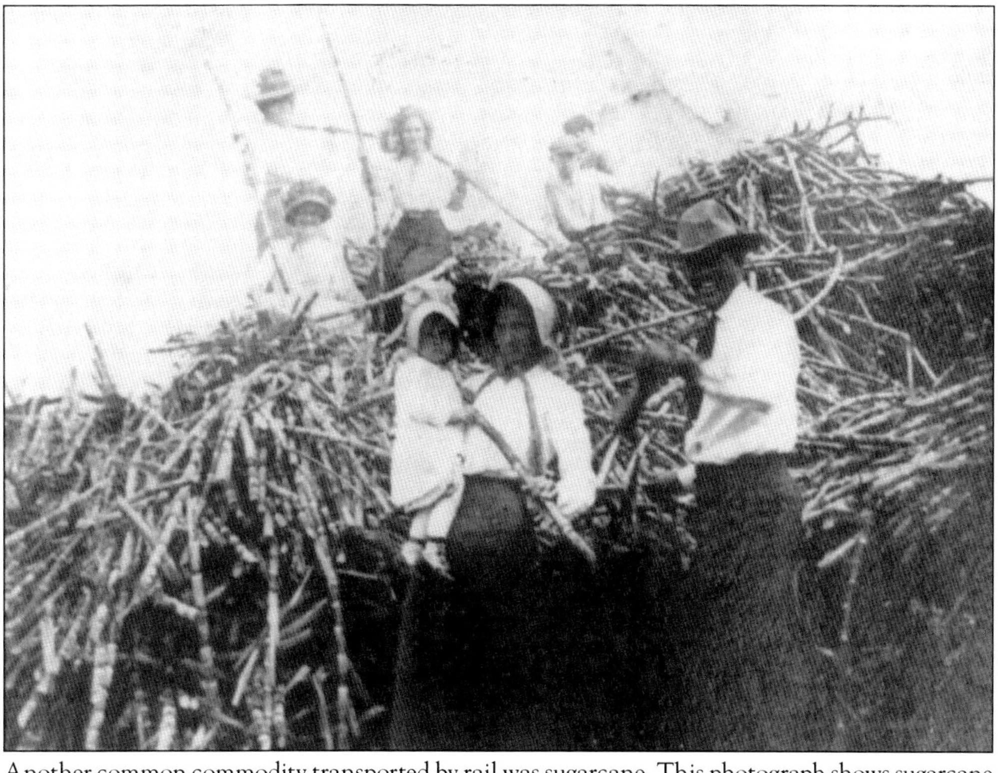

Another common commodity transported by rail was sugarcane. This photograph shows sugarcane being loaded for its trip to the syrup refinery located in Booth, Texas.

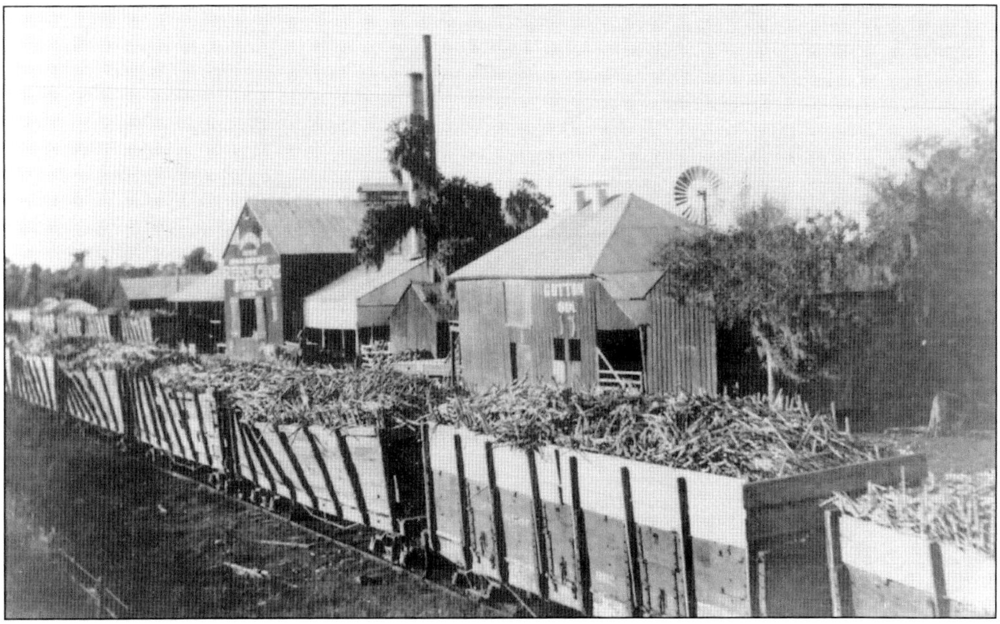

Railcars bulging with sugarcane arrive at the Booth Pure Open Kettle Ribbon Cane Syrup refinery in Booth, Texas. Cotton and sugarcane were common commodities shipped by rail.

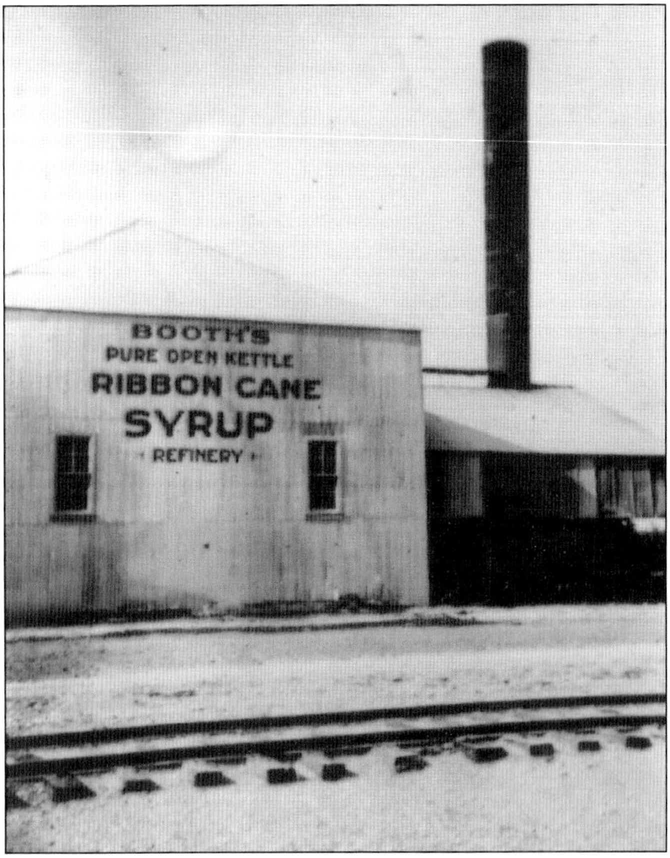

In this photograph is the Booth Pure Open Kettle Ribbon Cane Syrup refinery located along the Gulf, Colorado, and Santa Fe Railroad.

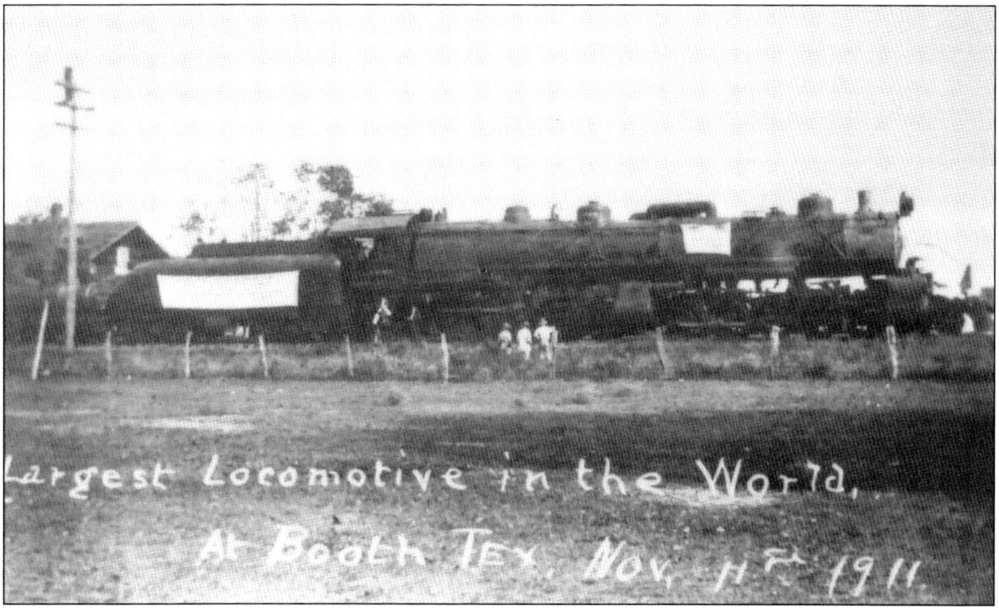

On November 11, 1911, the Gulf, Colorado, and Santa Fe, the world's largest locomotive, visits Booth, Texas, drawing residents from the area trackside to have a look.

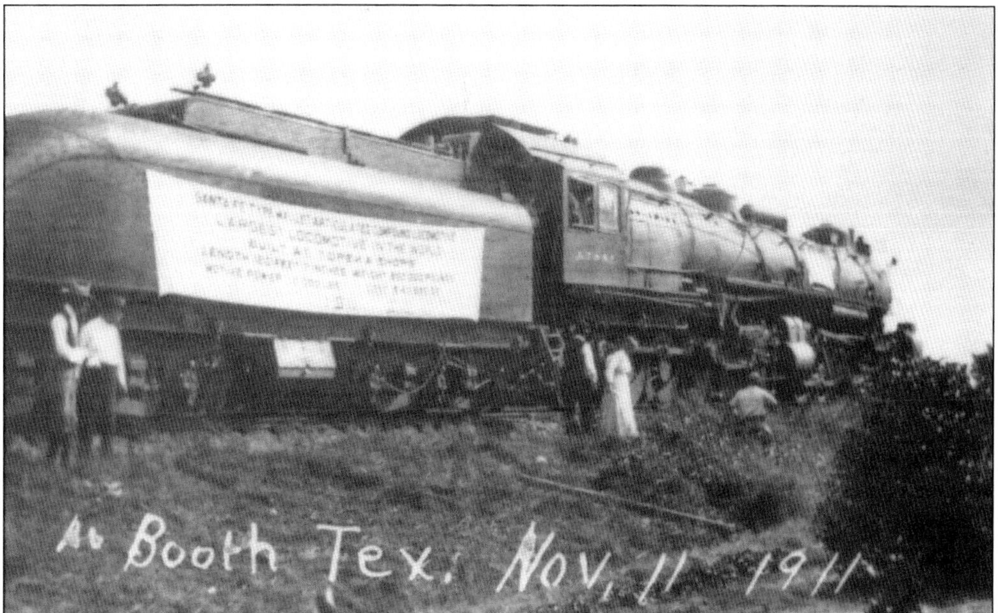

Built at the AT&SF locomotive shops in Topeka, Kansas, the world's largest locomotive weighs in at 850,000 pounds, is 120 feet and 7 inches long, and cost $43,680 to build. This Mallet-type locomotive is constructed as an articulated locomotive to allow it to maneuver around curves along the Santa Fe route.

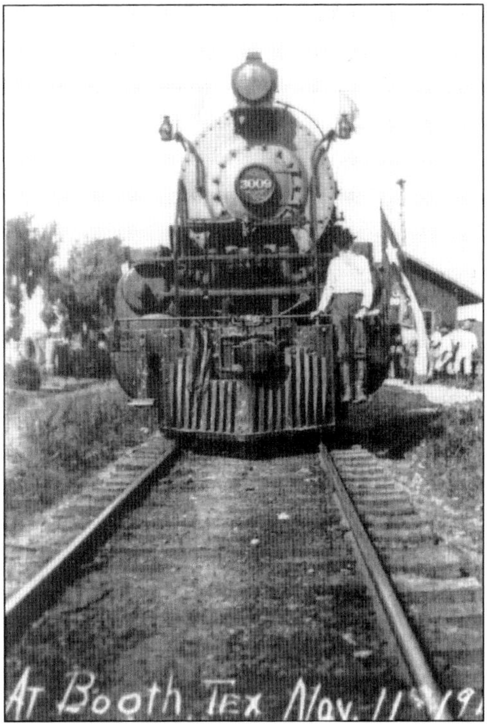

Posing at the front of locomotive No. 3009, a local resident has his picture taken with the Santa Fe Railway's largest locomotive in the world at the depot in Booth, Texas.

This track chart of the Santa Fe through Richmond, Texas, provides the location of road crossings and bridges as well as a maintenance history of the line, including such things as pole, rail, and ballast installation dates. (Courtesy of the Rosenberg Railroad Museum Collection.)

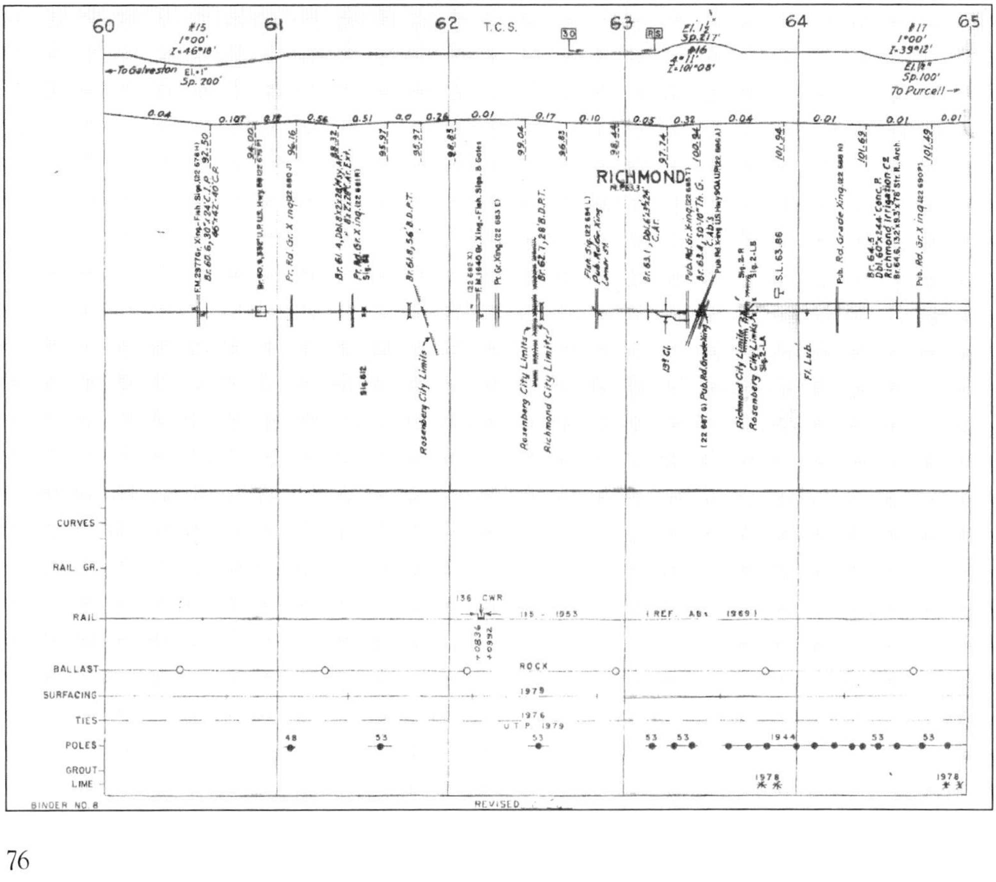

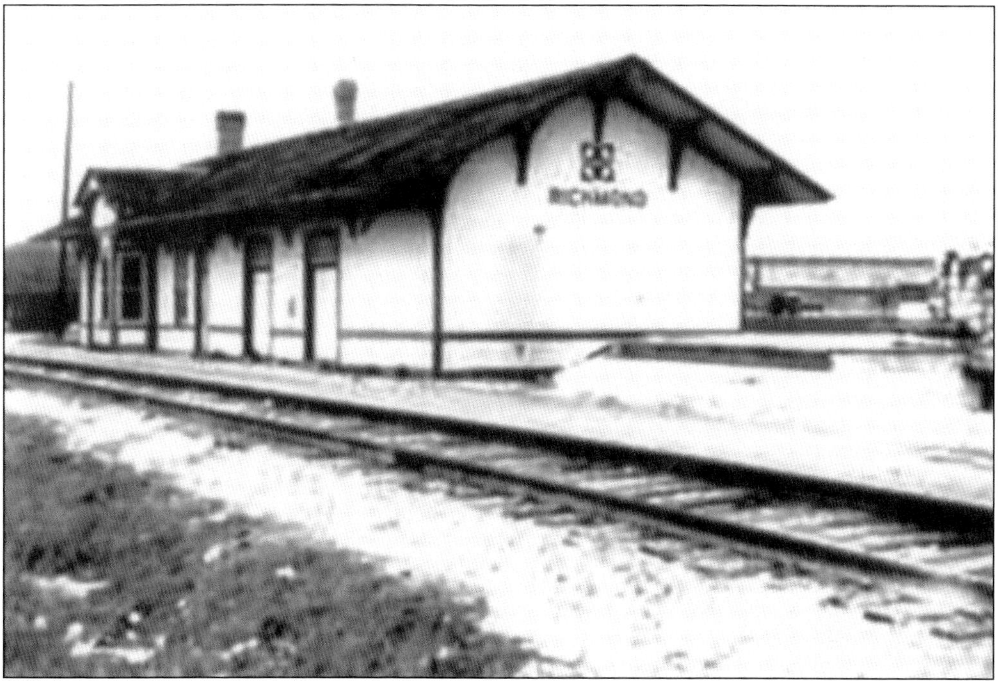

Pictured here is the Santa Fe depot in Richmond, Texas. The wooden-style depot is a typical design used along the Santa Fe route.

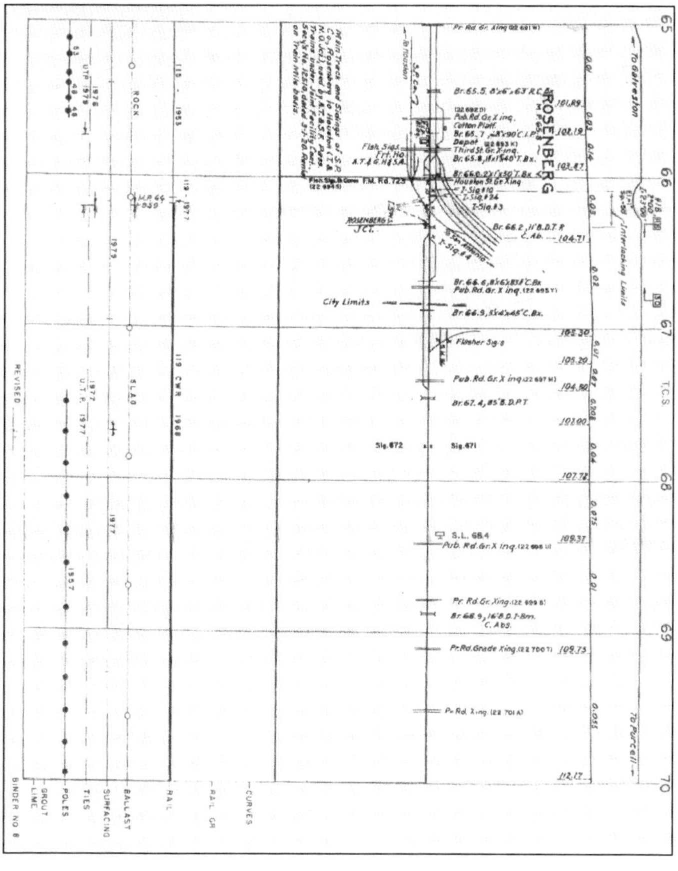

This track chart of the Santa Fe through Rosenberg, Texas, provides the location of road crossings and maintenance information. An interesting point about Rosenberg is that it is the location of Interlocking Tower 17. This is the location where the Santa Fe Railway and the Southern Pacific rail lines cross each other at grade. The interlocking limits are identified on this chart just past mile marker 66. (Courtesy of the Rosenberg Railroad Museum Collection.)

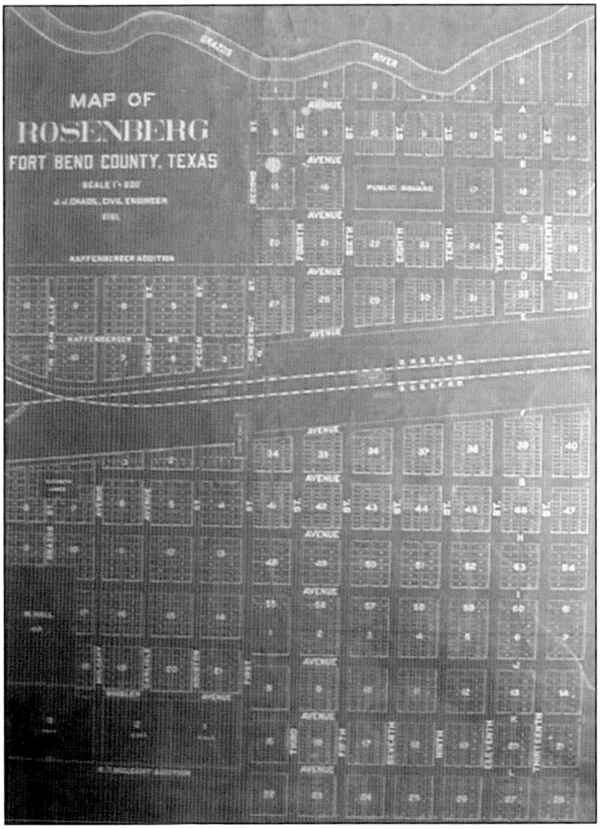

An early map of Rosenberg, Texas, shows the platted lots, public square, the GC&SF, and GH&SA rail lines through town and the Brazos River running to the north of town.

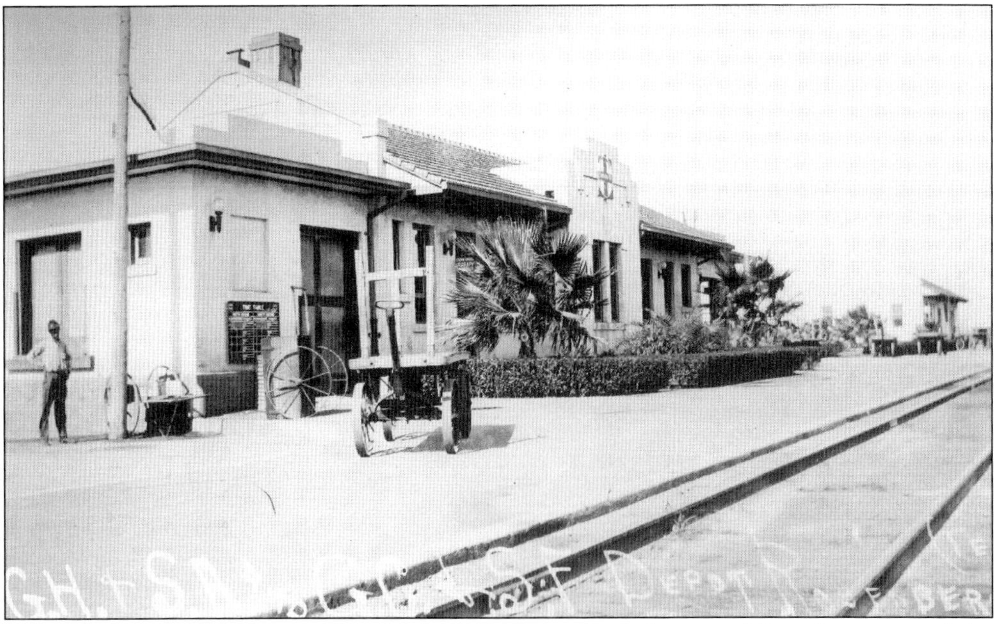

The depot in Rosenberg served both the Galveston, Harrisburg, and San Antonio and the Gulf, Colorado, and Santa Fe Railroads. This depot, like many others, had a beautiful park that welcomed visitors to town. (Courtesy of the Ken E. Stavinoha Collection.)

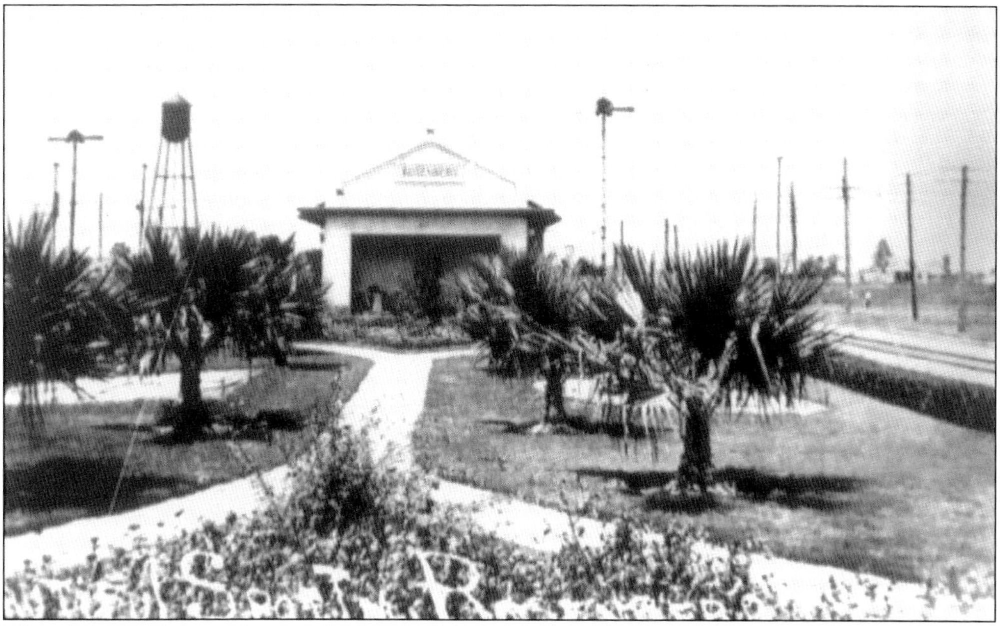

This photograph provides another view of the Rosenberg depot and park. Located on either side of the sidewalk are the symbols of the Santa Fe and the Southern Pacific Railroads built into the landscape. (Courtesy of the Ken E. Stavinoha Collection.)

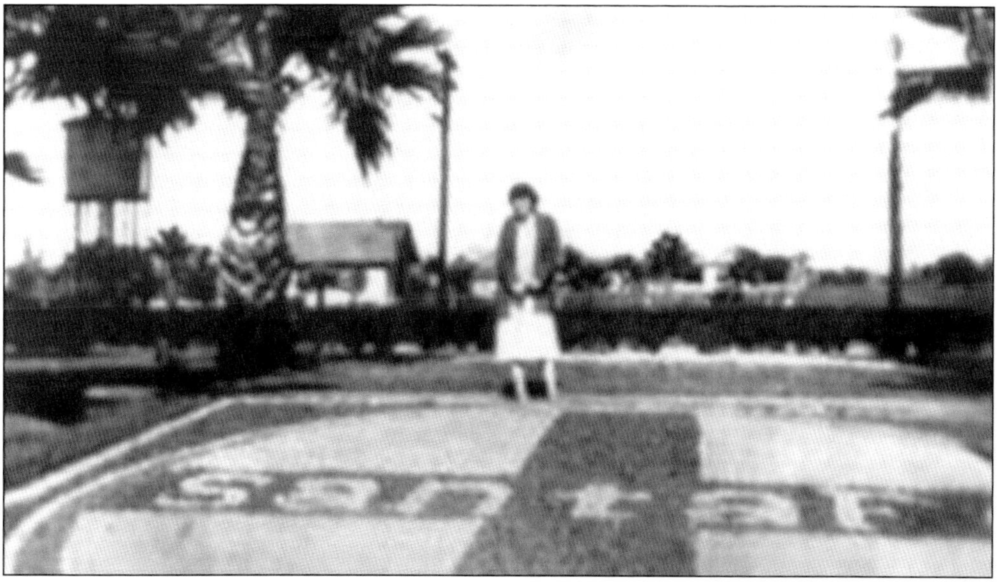

A young girl has her picture taken at the Santa Fe emblem in the park of the Rosenberg depot. The Wells Fargo Express Building and a railroad water tower are seen in the background.

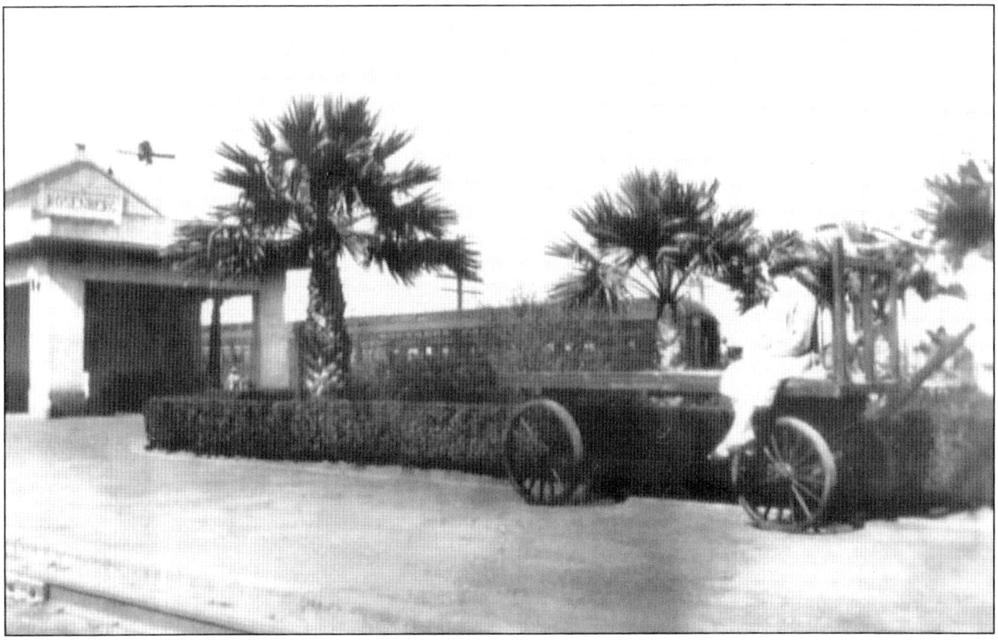

The Sunset Limited Train No. 1 has arrived at the Rosenberg depot. A young lady sits on a baggage cart along the Santa Fe tracks.

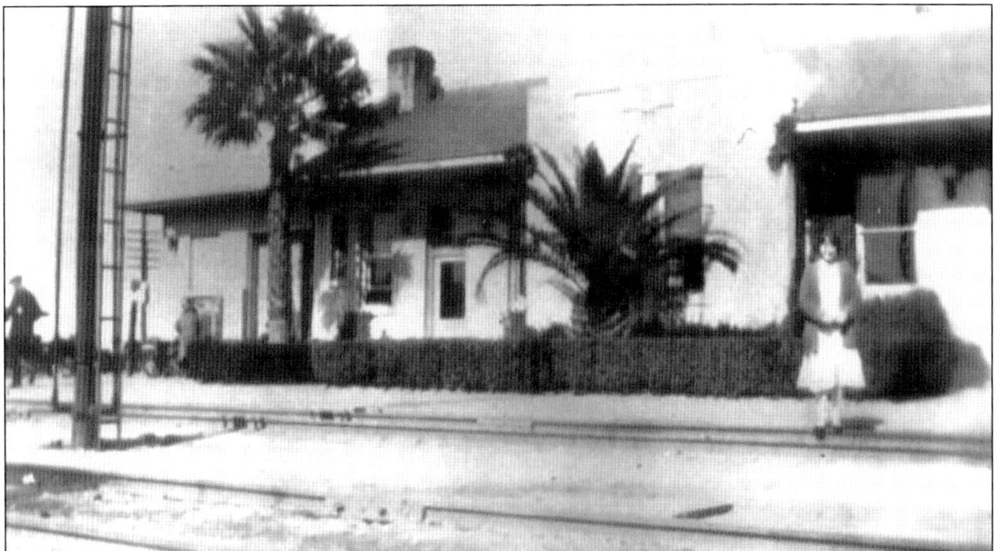

The same young girl has another picture taken outside the Rosenberg depot along the Santa Fe tracks as a traveler checks the station bulletin board for his train schedule in the background.

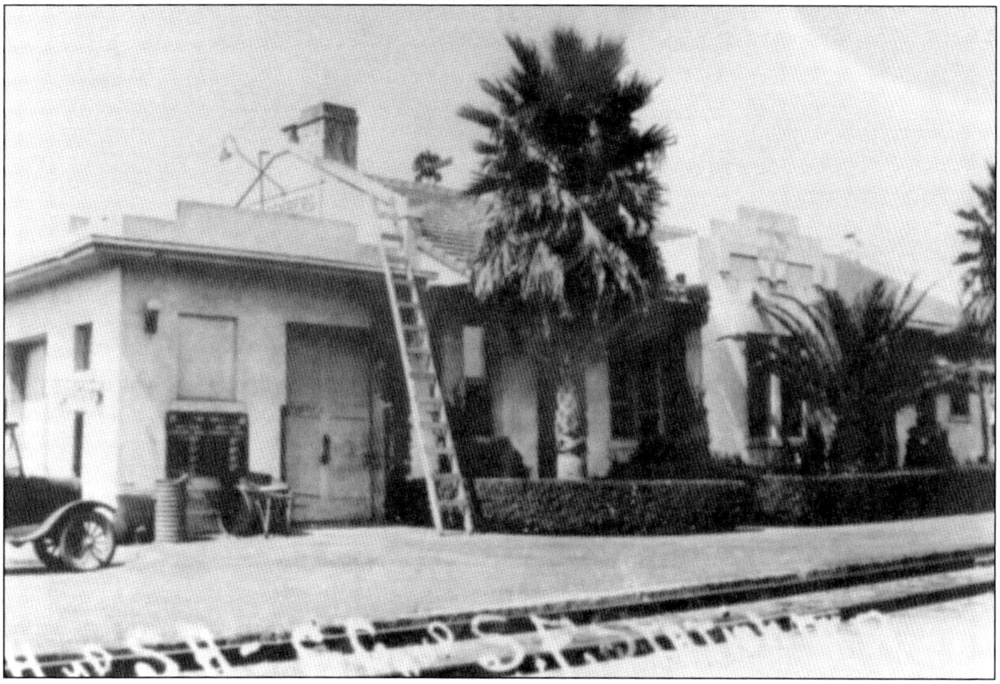

Here is a view of the joint GH&SA and GC&SF passenger depot in the early 1920s.

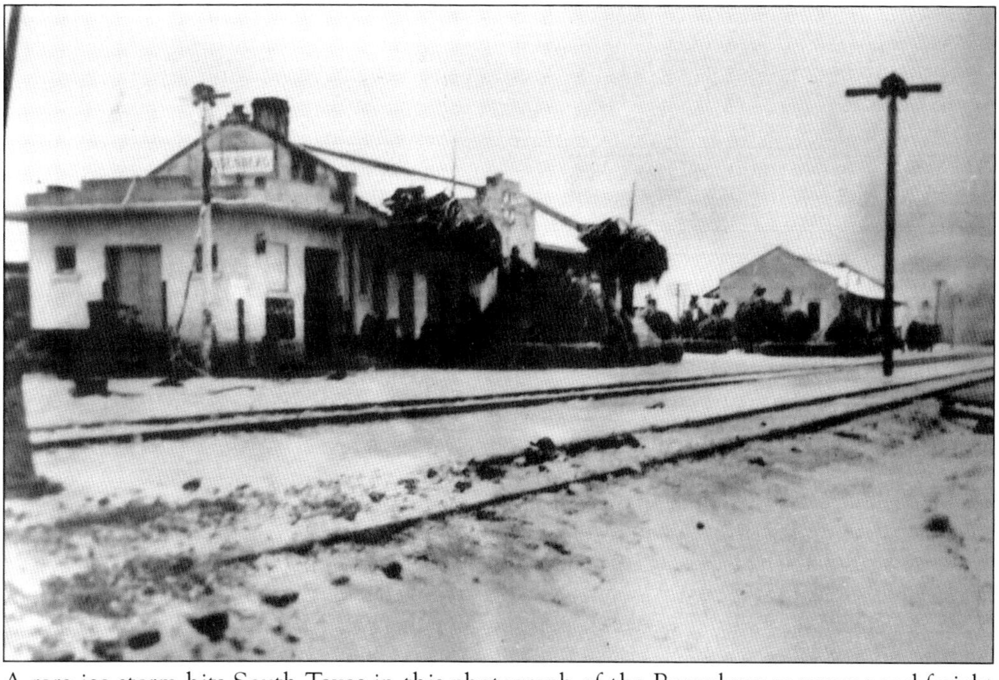

A rare ice storm hits South Texas in this photograph of the Rosenberg passenger and freight depots. The branches of the palm trees outside the depot sag from the weight of the ice that has formed on their branches.

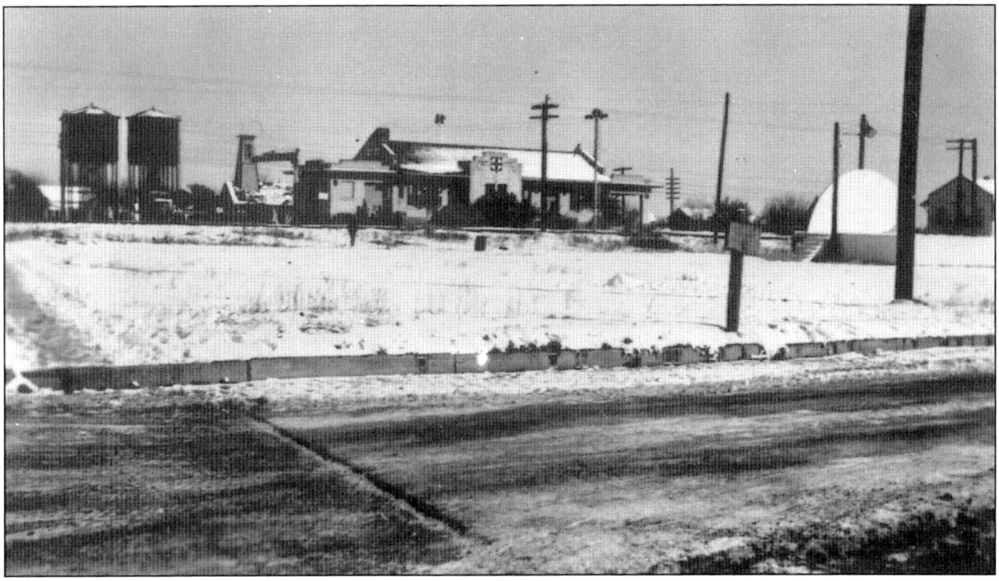

One can feel the chill in the air in this view of the ice and snow at the Rosenberg passenger and freight depots. Also seen are the dual railroad water towers and pump house.

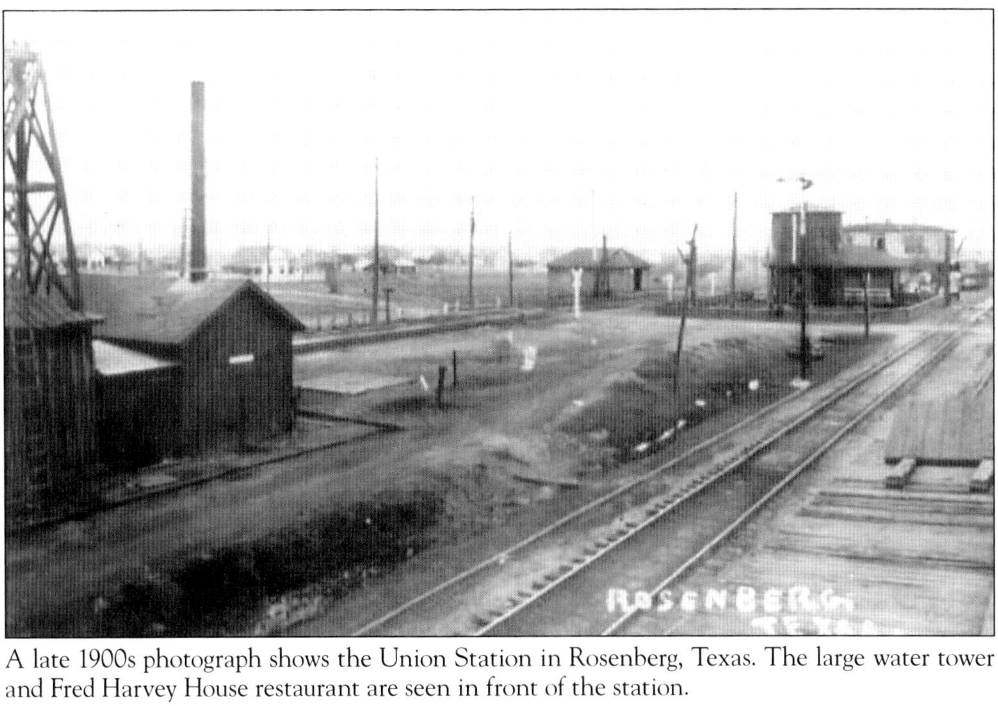

A late 1900s photograph shows the Union Station in Rosenberg, Texas. The large water tower and Fred Harvey House restaurant are seen in front of the station.

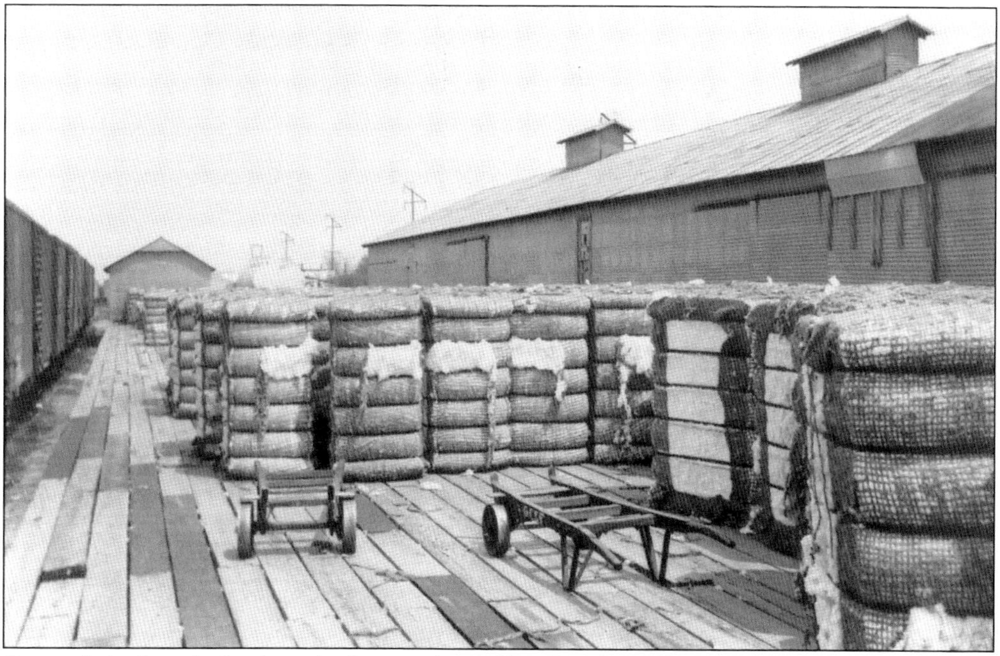

Cotton bales line the loading platform in the Gulf, Colorado, and Santa Fe rail yard in Rosenberg. Cotton was a chief commodity shipped on the railroads of Fort Bend County.

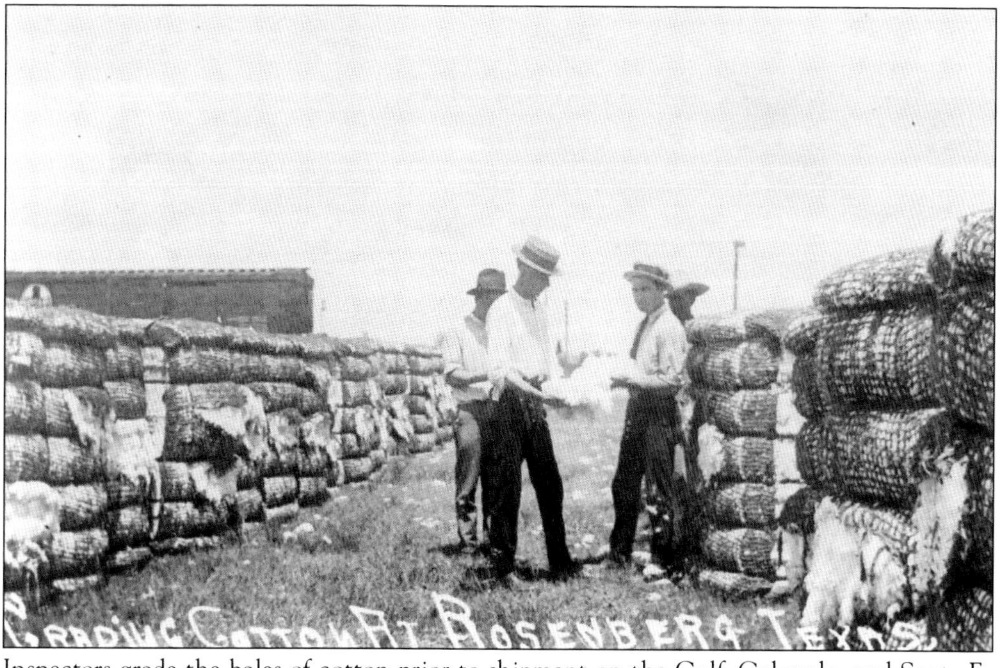

Inspectors grade the bales of cotton prior to shipment on the Gulf, Colorado, and Santa Fe Railroad in Rosenberg, Texas.

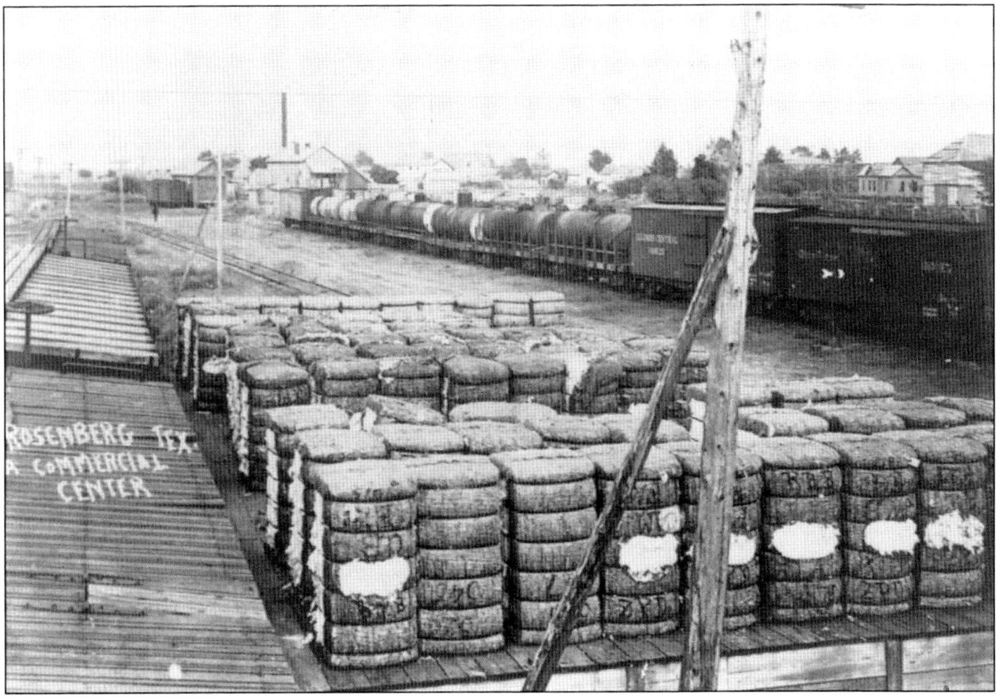

This photograph of the GC&SA rail yard in Rosenberg, taken from atop a railcar in the yard, shows a very busy facility with bales of cotton ready to be loaded and shipped.

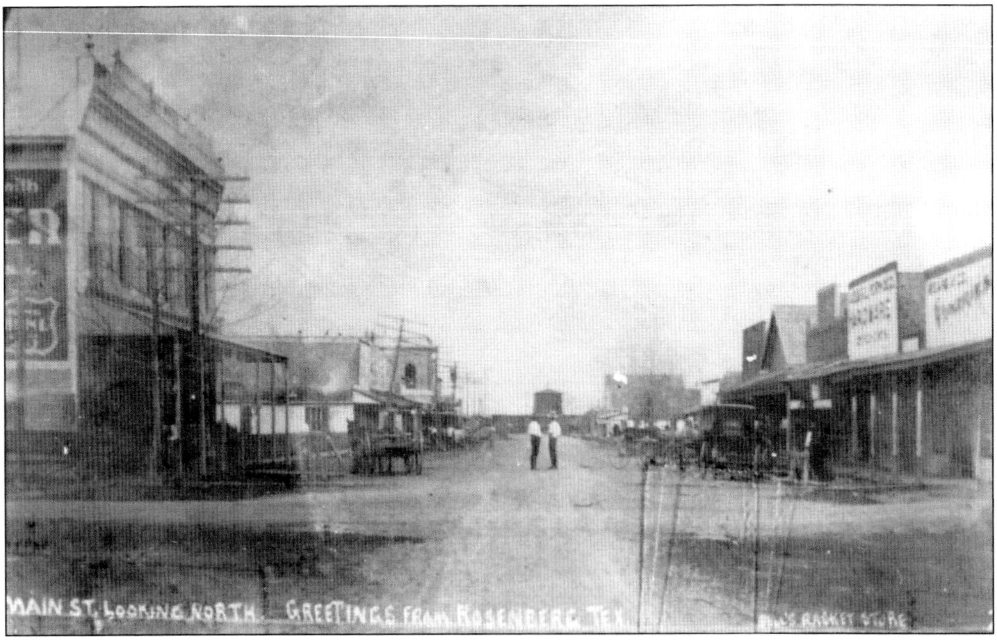

An early-1900s view down Third Street looks from Main Street (U.S. Highway 90A) in Rosenberg and includes a Santa Fe freight train stopped at the depot. On the left is the J. J. Neuman General Merchandise store. A saloon is on the right and was the location of a 1916 shoot-out that left a man dead.

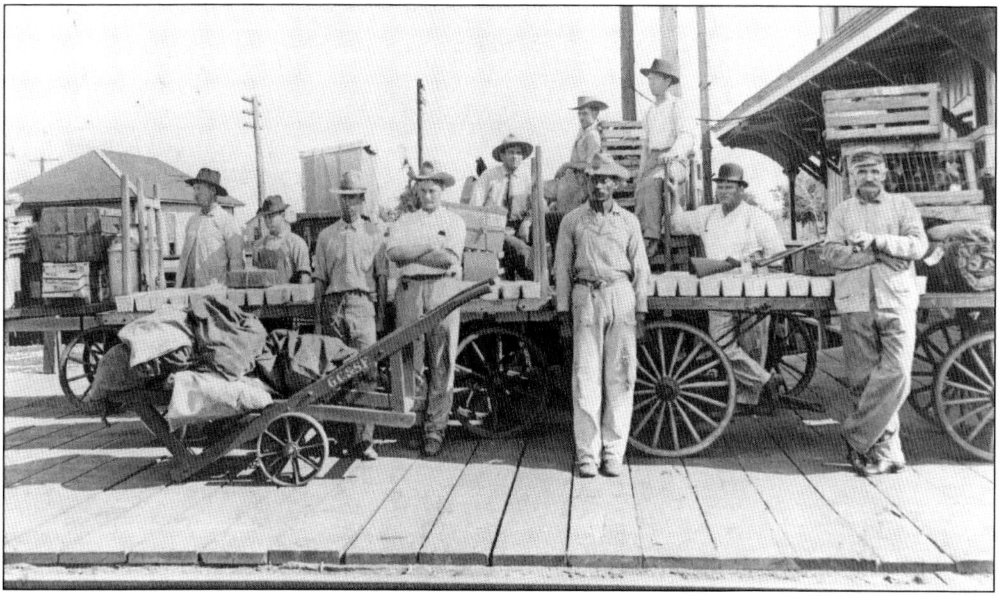

Cotton was not the only commodity shipped by the railroads. A heavily guarded silver shipment is seen here along with other freight waiting to be loaded onto a GC&SF train in Rosenberg. Seen second from the right is Taylor Ray, a Wells Fargo agent and later mayor of Rosenberg.

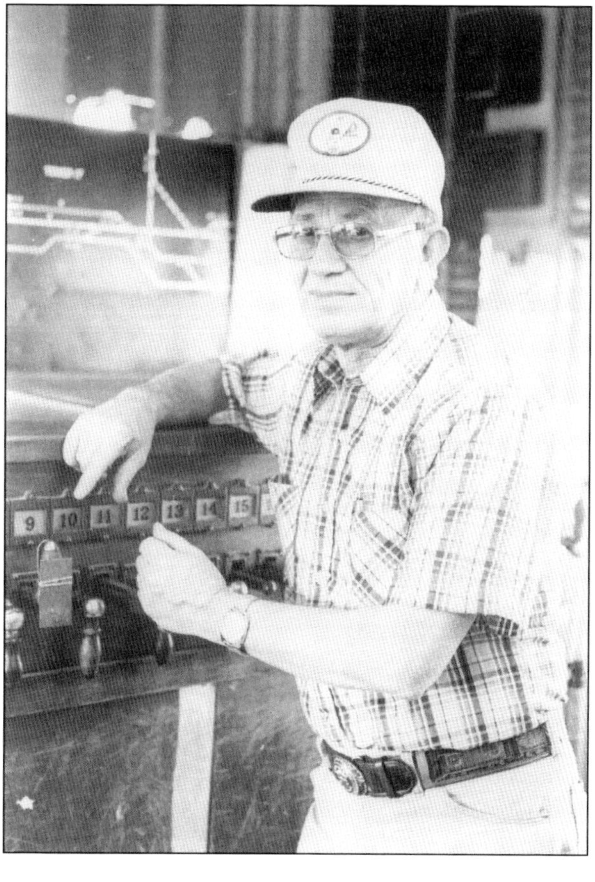

Longtime Tower 17 operator Marvin Slough poses at the control handles of the interlocker machine located on the second floor of the tower on the day of his retirement from the Southern Pacific Railroad Company in the mid-1980s. (Courtesy of the Ken E. Stavinoha Collection.)

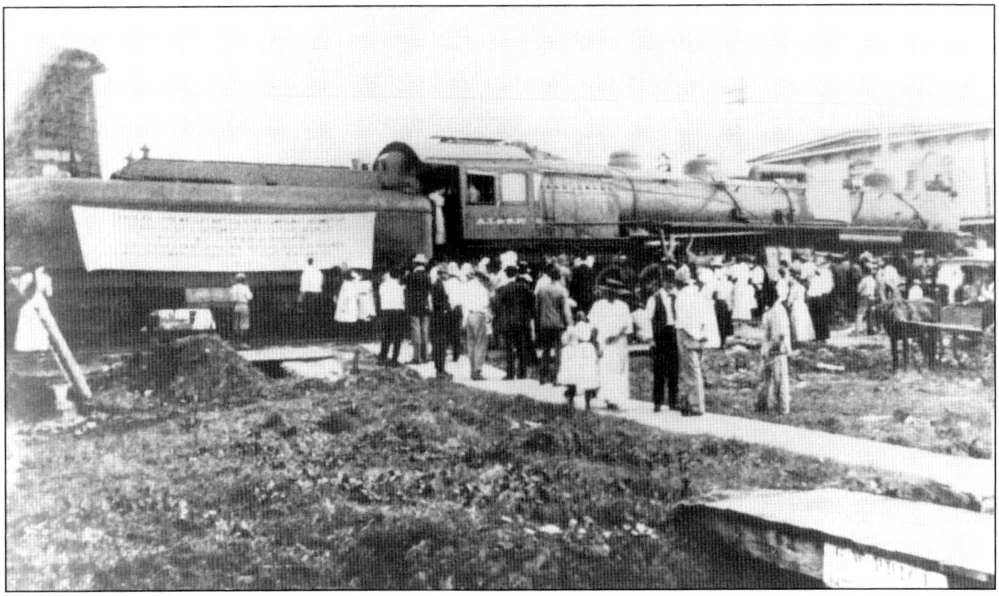

A crowd of townspeople gathers to have a look at the world's largest steam locomotive at the Rosenberg Union Station.

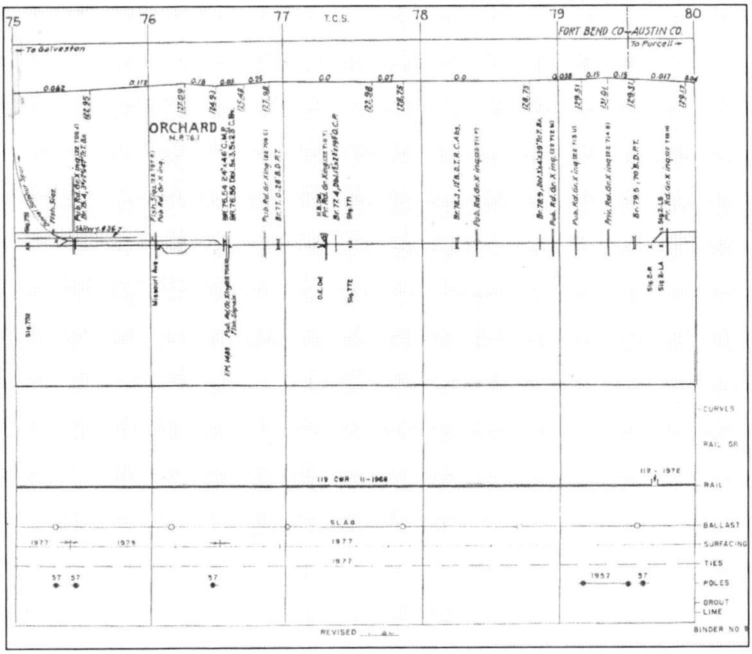

This track chart of the Santa Fe through Orchard, Texas, provides the location of road crossings and bridges as well as a maintenance history of the line, including such things as pole, rail, and ballast installation dates. This chart also shows the spur track that cuts off to the Duval Sulfur Mines at mile marker 75. (Courtesy of the Rosenberg Railroad Museum Collection.)

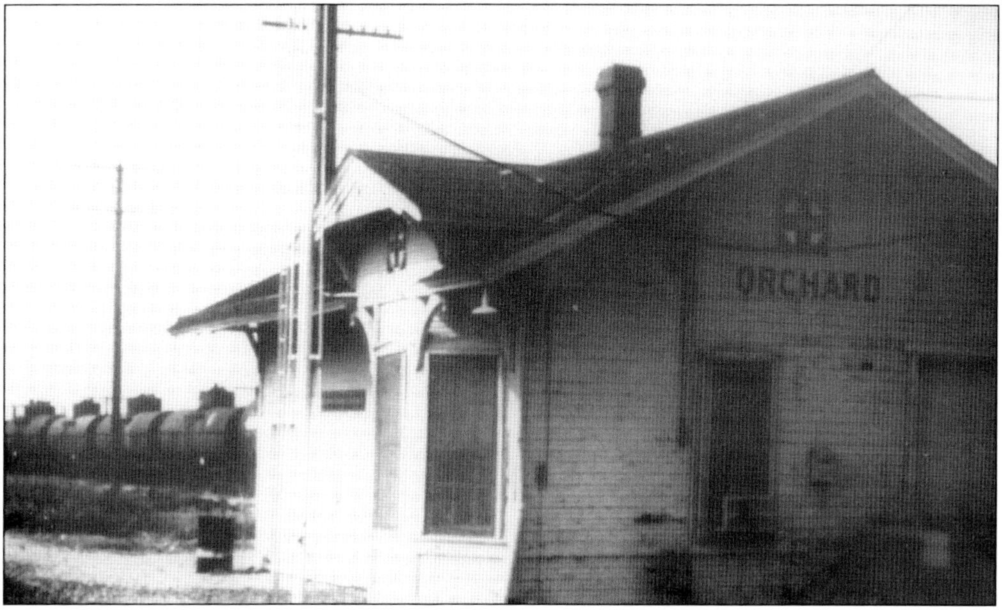

A string of sulfur tank cars sit in a siding at the Orchard depot. Molten sulfur is shipped by rail using specially insulated tank cars. (Courtesy of the Ken E. Stavinoha Collection.)

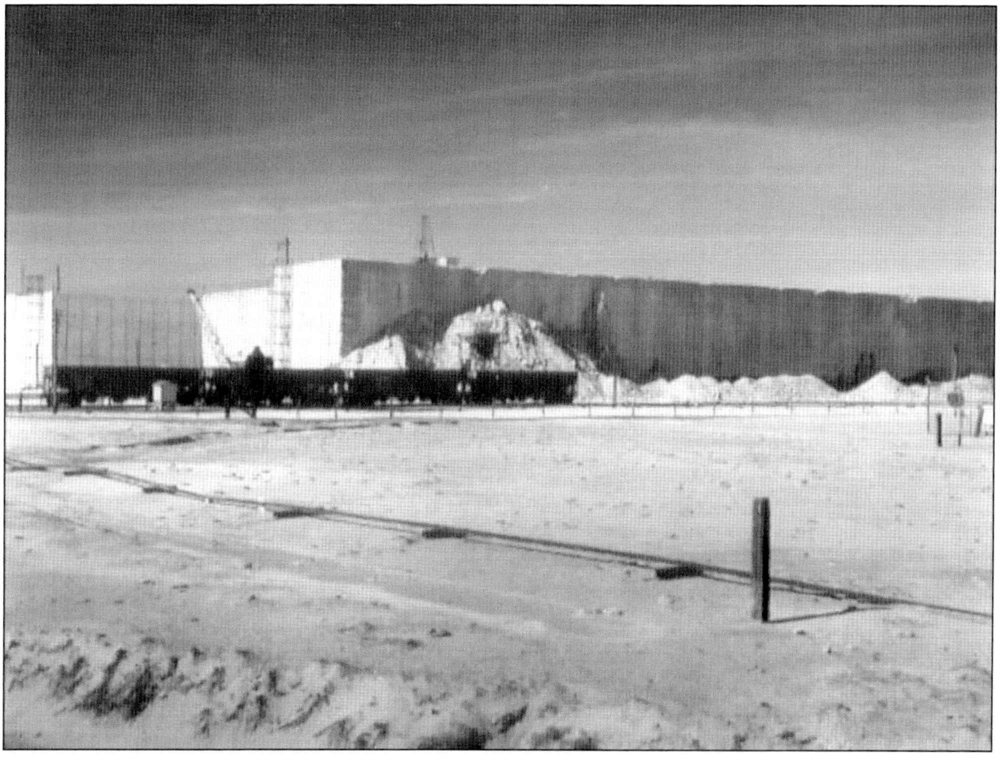

Large stockpiles of sulfur are seen in this photograph at the sulfur mines in Orchard, Texas.

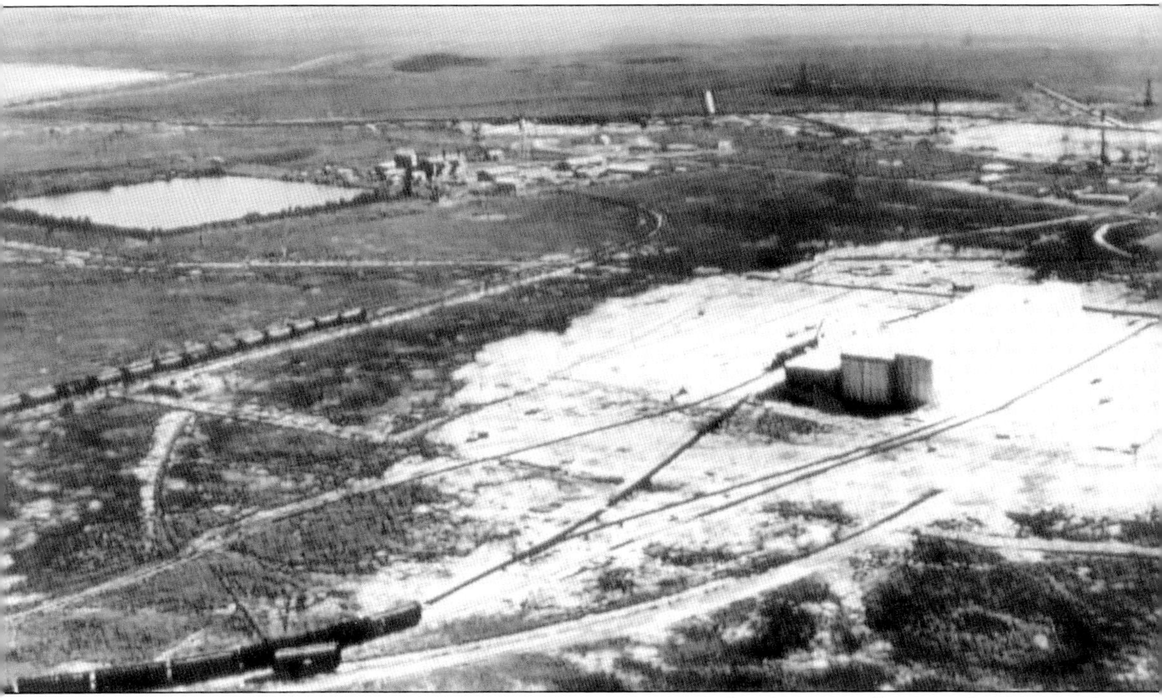

An aerial view shows the Duval Sulfur Mine complex in Orchard, Texas. This complex remained in operation into the 1970s.

Four

The Texas Western Narrow-Gauge Railroad

Created by a February 6, 1875, amendment to the charter of the former Western Narrow Gauge Railway Company, the Texas Western Narrow Gauge Railroad was the fourth railroad company to build through Fort Bend County. Passing through the northernmost part of the county, the Texas Western was originally conceived to be built between Houston and San Antonio and further west into Mexico to Guaymas, on the Gulf of California. Ground was broken in 1872, but actual construction did not start until 1875. The initial 10 miles opened in July 1875 and took another year for the next 10-mile portion to be constructed. It was not until April 1877 that the railroad opened 42 miles between Houston and Pattison, Texas. Within the first two years, the railroad was in financial trouble and was reorganized as the Texas Western Railway Company. At this time, former U.S. president Ulysses S. Grant became interested in the railroad project and became a member of the board of directors while his son Frederick D. Grant was named president. In 1882, the railroad was able to bridge the Brazos River and completed another 10-mile extension into Sealy, Texas, where a connection was made with the Gulf, Colorado, and Santa Fe Railroad. However, due to the difference in track gauge between the two railroads, the Texas Western was unable to interchange cars with the GC&SF. The railroad went back into the hands of the courts in July 1884 when a receiver was appointed for the company. A receiver sale was held on May 5, 1885, and was approved on November 25. In 1887, the receiver made an unsuccessful attempt to extend the Texas Western west from Sealy to Cat Springs. The fate of the railroad was sealed in 1893 when the Missouri-Kansas-Texas Railway Company of Texas built into Sealy along the projected route of the Texas Western Railroad. The Texas Western was sold in 1895 and was no longer in operation after June 30, 1896. The line was abandoned in 1899, and the rails were removed by the end of June 1900.

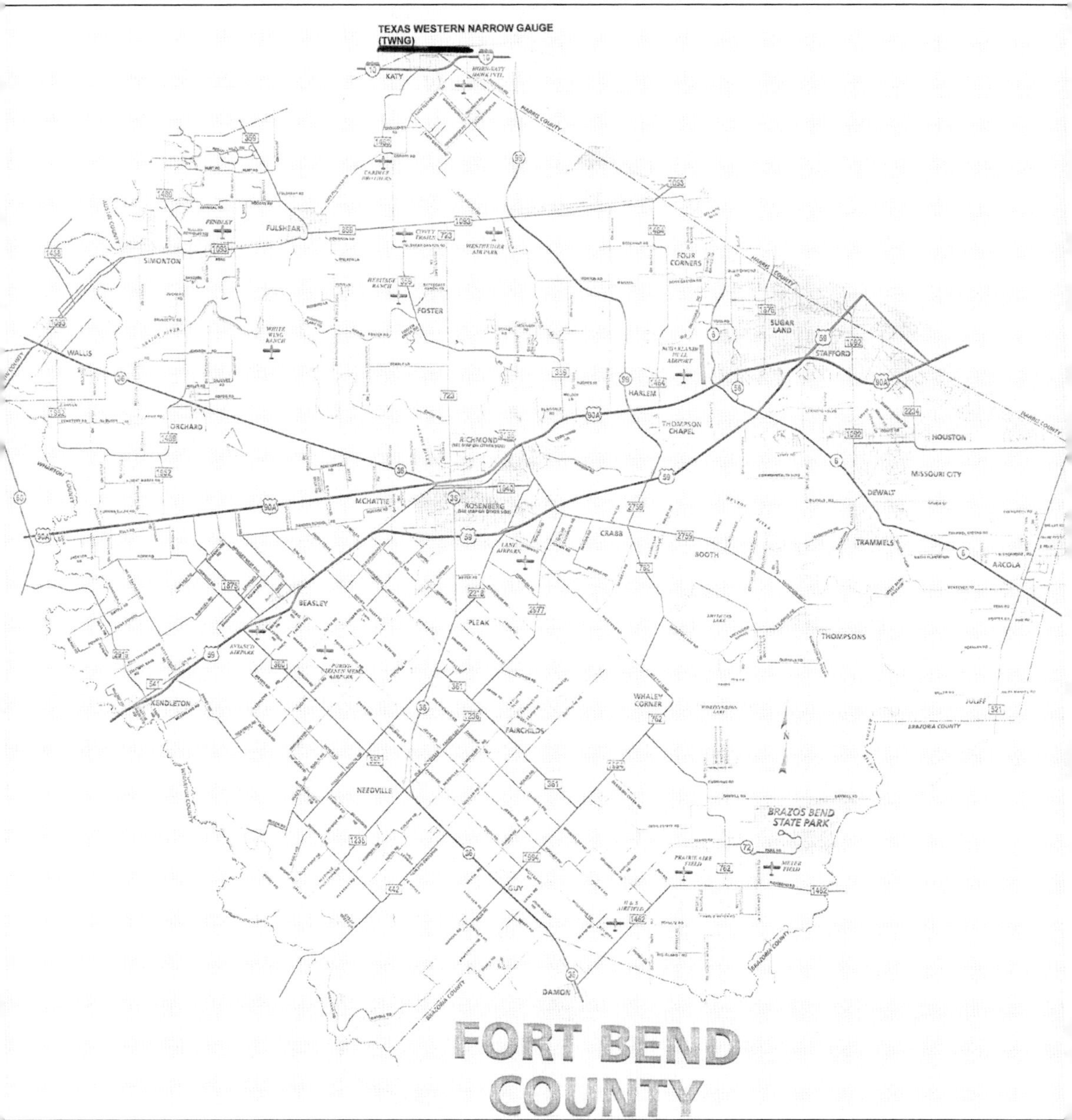

This map of Fort Bend County reflects the route of the Texas Western Narrow Gauge Railroad. Pattison, Texas, is the only Fort Bend County town in which this rail line passed through.

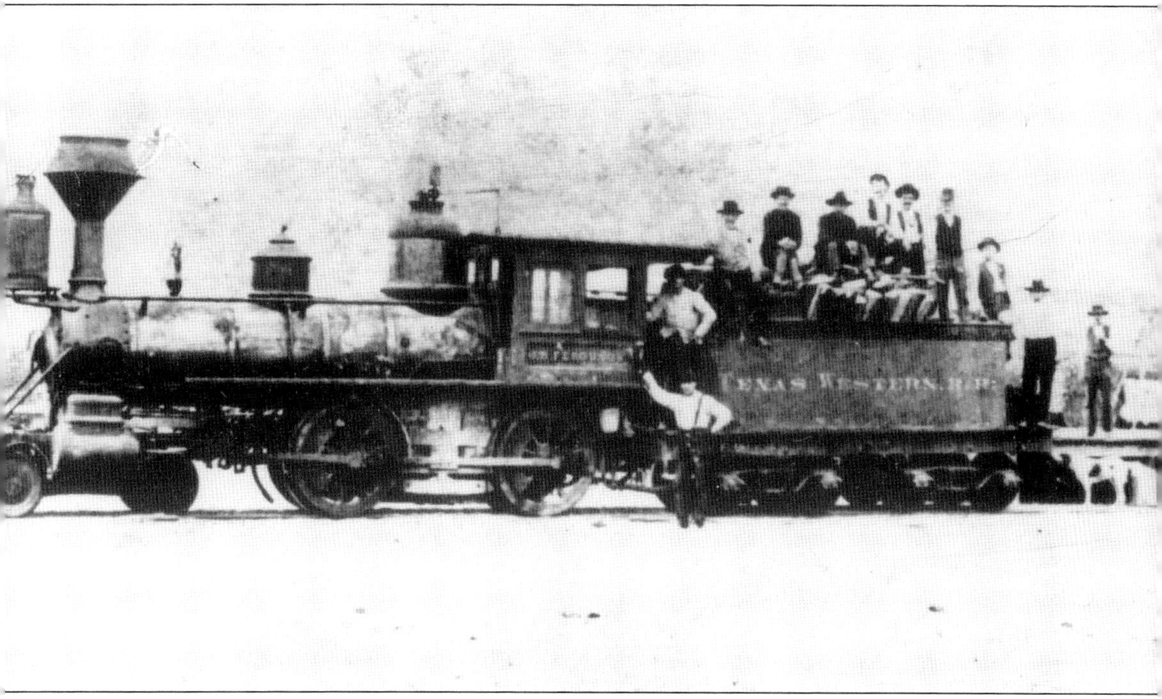

A Texas Western Railroad locomotive, the *J. H. Ferguson*, and its crew pose for this 1890s photograph. (Courtesy of the Rosenberg Railroad Museum Collection.)

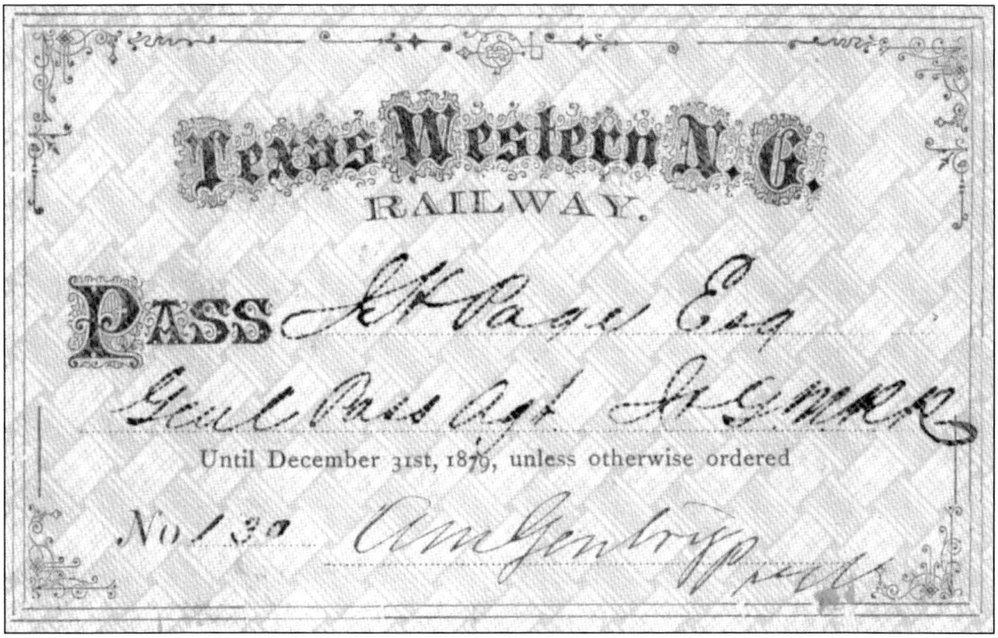
Texas Western N. G.
RAILWAY.
PASS J H Page Esq
Genl Pass Agt I & G N R R
Until December 31st, 1879, unless otherwise ordered
No 130 A M Gentry Prest

This photograph shows a Texas Western Narrow Gauge Railway 1879 pass issued to J. H. Page. (Courtesy of the Ken E. Stavinoha Collection.)

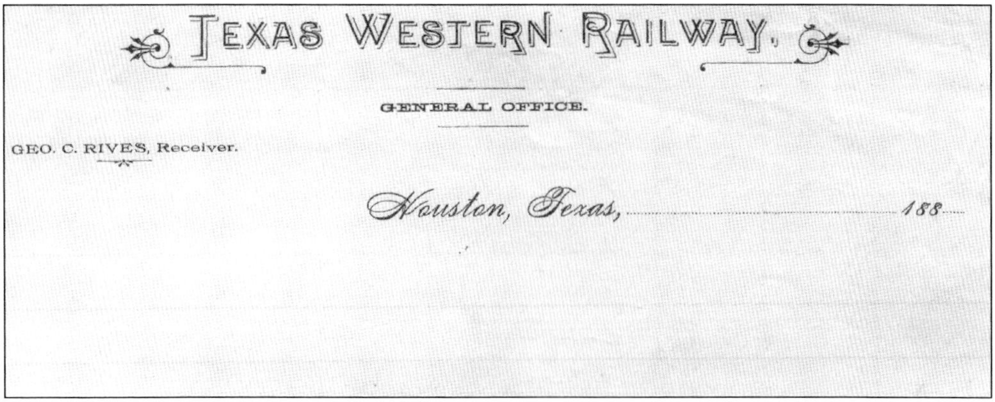
TEXAS WESTERN RAILWAY.
GENERAL OFFICE.
GEO. C. RIVES, Receiver.
Houston, Texas, ... 188....

This 1880s Texas Western Railway document is from the general office located in Houston and reflects George C. Rives as the receiver. (Courtesy of the Ken E. Stavinoha Collection.)

Five

The New York, Texas, and Mexican Railroad

In a charter signed on October 18, 1880, in Paris, France, Count Joseph Telfener and a group of associates formed a Texas corporation to construct a railroad from Richmond, Texas, in Fort Bend County, south to Brownsville, Texas. This charter was filed in Austin, Texas, on November 17, 1880. The New York, Texas, and Mexican Railroad (NYT&M) was to begin in Texas, from the Galveston, Harrisburg, and San Antonio Railroad at Richmond, and extend through Fort Bend, Wharton, Jackson, Victoria, Goliad, Bee, Refugio, San Patricio, Nueces, Hidalgo, and Cameron Counties and was to terminate in Brownsville, Texas. Count Telfener brought over 1,200 laborers from Italy to perform the heavy construction on this line, and his hope was that they would settle, become citizens, and purchase land along the line. As an added incentive, Count Telfener paid for the Italians' passage to Texas as well as supplied them with food, clothing, and shelter until they could begin work. The pasta diet of the Italian laborers lent itself to the railroad's nickname as the "Macaroni Line." The NYT&M had hoped to use proceeds from the sale of land grants awarded by the State of Texas to finance further construction, but Texas repealed the land grants in 1882, when it was discovered that the number of those issued exceeded the amount of available land. The railroad completed 91 miles of track installation from Rosenberg Junction to Victoria, Texas, in 1882 and became the fifth railroad company to operate in Fort Bend County. Six stations established along the line, Inez, Louise, Edna, Hungerford, Telfener, and Mackay, were named after family members. The line proved not to be as successful as originally envisioned and was sold to the Southern Pacific Railroad in 1885. It remained in operation until the late 1980s when the line was abandoned and portions of the track were later removed. In 2009, the Kansas City Southern (KCS) Railroad completed a total rebuilding of the line between Rosenberg and Victoria, and once again trains are running on the Macaroni Line, and it is contributing toward the economic development of the county.

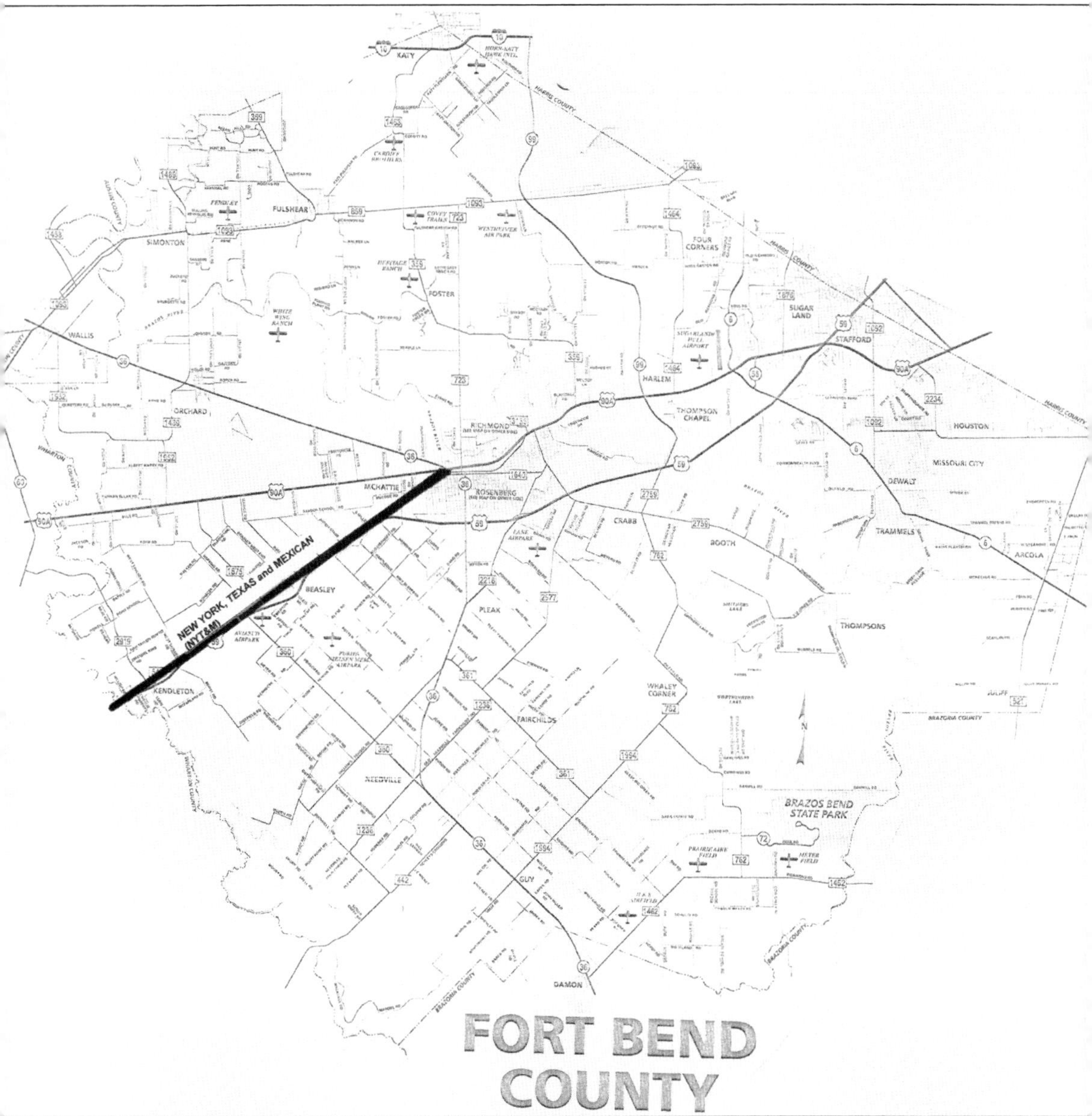

This map of Fort Bend County reflects the route of the New York, Texas, and Mexican Railroad. Towns along this route through Fort Bend County include Rosenberg, Beasley, and Kendleton, Texas.

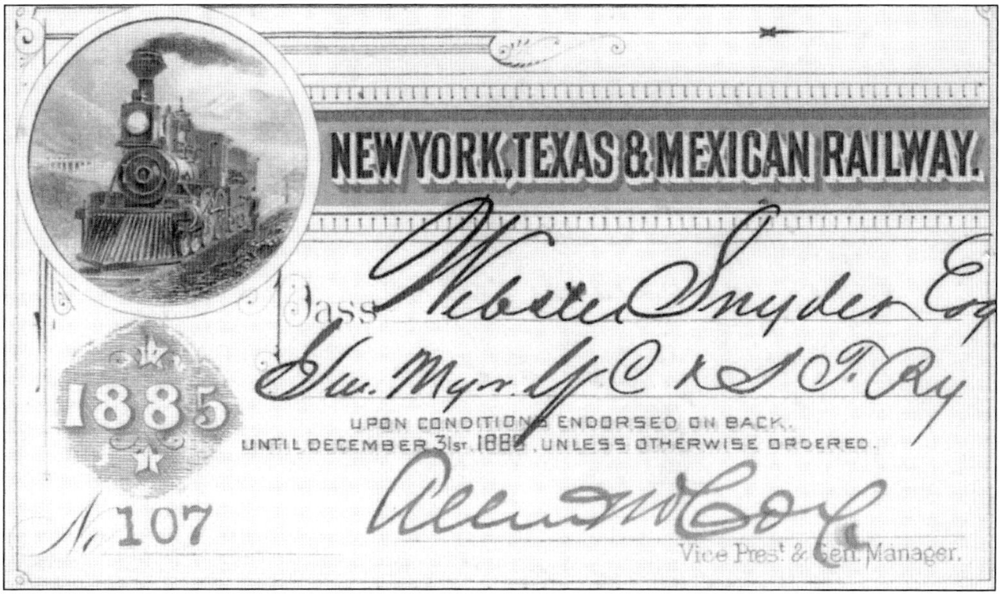

An 1885 New York, Texas, and Mexican Railroad pass No. 107 issued to Mr. Webster Snyder by vice president and general manager Allen W. Cox. (Courtesy of the Ken E. Stavinoha Collection.)

2 VICTORIA DIVISION--Rosenberg to Cuero.

WEST. 3d Class. No. 153 Daily Except Sunday FREIGHT	2d Class. No. 167 Daily Except Sunday MIXED	1st Class. No. 151 DAILY PASSENGER	Distance from Rosenberg.	STATIONS.	Distance from Cuero.	Length of Side Tracks in Feet	EAST. 1st Class. No. 152 DAILY PASSENGER	2d Class. No. 168 Daily Except Sunday MIXED	3d Class. No. 154 Daily Except Sunday FREIGHT
5 45 am	....	8 35 am	36.25	Leave........HOUSTON, 5th Ward. ....Arrive	156.51	....	3 55 pm	....	8 00 pm
....	....	8 40 am / 9 25 am	36.46	........HOUSTON, H. & T. C. Depot........	156.30	....	3 45 pm / 3 35 pm	....	....
8 30 am	....	11 00 am	....	........† ROSENBERG........w	120.05	6,647	2 00 pm	....	4 35 pm
				8.21					
8 50	....	f 11 18	8.21	........BEASLEY........	111.84	3,900	f 1 42	....	4 00
				5.67					
9 10	....	s 11 32	13.88	........†KENDLETON........	106.17	1,395	s 1 28	....	3 30
				6.14					
9 30	....	s 11 46	20.02	........† HUNGERFORD........	100.03	1,646	s 1 14	....	3 00
				5.17					
9 53	....	11 59 am	25.19	........WHARTON JUNCTION........	94.86	....	1 01	....	2 32
				0.42					
....	....	....	25.61	........C. B. CROSSING........	94.44	....	....	....	....
				0.37					
9 55 / 10 35	....	s 12 00 pm	25.98	........† WHARTON........w	94.07	5,314	s 1 00	....	2 30 / 2 00
				1.69					
10 48	....	12•03	27.67	........SHANGHAI........	92.38	1,850	12 55	....	1 50
				3.04					
11 10	....	f 12 10	30.71	........MACKAY........	89.34	1,713	f 12 49	....	1 40
				3.45					
11 35 am	....	s 12 18	34.16	........†PIERCE........	85.89	1,443	s 12 42	....	1 25
				5.02					
12 05 pm / 1 00	....	s 12 30	39.18	........† EL CAMPO........w	80.87	3,819	s 12 30	....	1 00
				5.82					
1 20	....	f 12 42	45.00	........HILLJE........	75.05	1,774	f 12 19	....	12 42
				4.75					
1 40	....	s 12 52	49.75	........†LOUISE........	70.30	2,013	s 12 09 pm	....	12 09 pm
				7.71					
2 15	....	s 1 07	57.46	........†GANADO........w	62.59	1,978	s 11 54 am	....	11 28 am
				7.23					
2 40	....	f 1 22	64.69	........EDNA STOCK PENS........	55.36	1,484	f 11 39	....	11 05
				1.96					
3 00	....	s 1 26	66.65	........† EDNA........	53.40	3,275	s 11 36	....	10 55
				4.03					
3 45	....	f 1 35	70.68	........EL TORO........	49.37	1,284	f 11 28	....	10 41
				6.01					
4 05	....	s 1 48	76.69	........INEZ........w	43.36	1,964	s 11 15	....	10 25
				7.16					
4 30	....	f 2 03	83.85	........KEERAN........	36.20	1,723	f 11 01	....	10 00
				7.67					
5 00 pm	9 20 am	s 2 20 / 2 30	91.52	........†VICTORIA........w	28.53	19,868	s 10 45 / 10 30	4 50 pm	9 40 am
				3.89					
....	f 9 35	f 2 40	95.41	........WOMACK SPUR........	24.64	479	f 10 18	f 4 36	....
				4.92					
....	f 9 53	f 2 49	100.33	........CRAIG........	19.72	1,809	f 10 11	f 4 26	....
				2.33					
....	s 10 05	s 2 55	102.66	........NURSERY........	17.39	1,998	s 10 05	s 4 20	....
				6.27					
....	s 10 23	s 3 07	108.93	........†THOMASTON........	11.12	1,742	s 9 52	s 4 03	....
				3.92					
....	f 10 35	f 3 15	112.85	........BURNS........	7.20	1,303	f 9 44	s 3 51	....
				7.20					
....	10 55 am	3 30 pm	120.05	Arrive........†CUERO........w Leave	....	23,396	9 30 am	3 30 pm	....

Trains between Rosenberg and 5th Ward, Houston, will run subject to Time Tables and Rules of the G. H. & S. A. R'y; and between H. & T. C. crossing and H. & T. C. depot, will be subject to Rules and Time Table of the H. & T. C. R'y.

This is the Victoria Division employee timetable for the New York, Texas, and Mexican Railroad route between Rosenberg and Cuero, Texas. Fort Bend County towns along this route include Rosenberg, Beasley, and Kendleton, Texas. (Courtesy of the Ken E. Stavinoha Collection.)

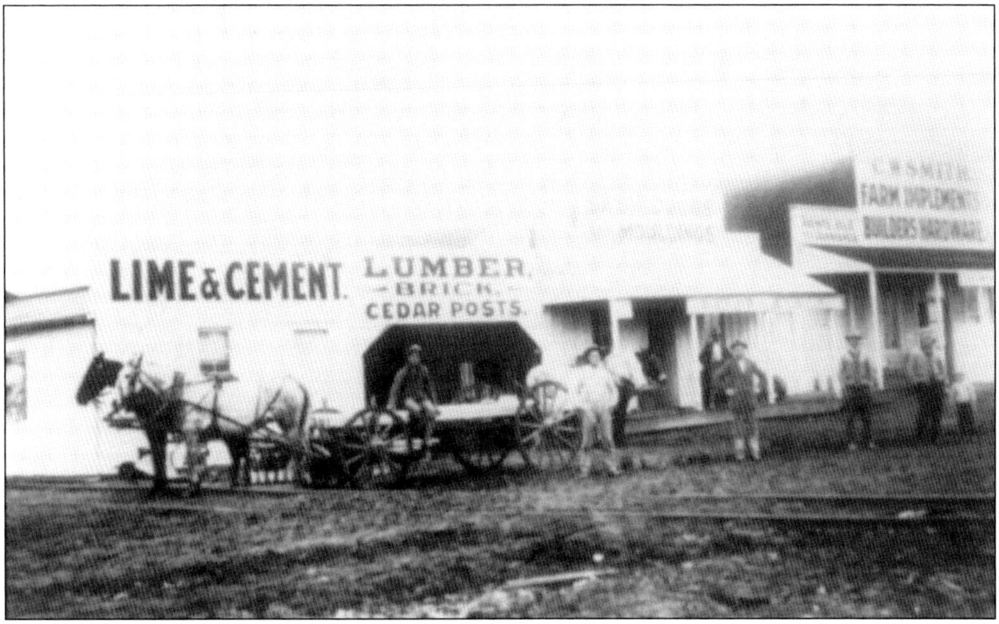

To the far right in the photograph with the same style of sweaters, Beasley Lumber owner Glen Hamlink (left) and C. W. Smith (right) pose for the camera; Leonard Hamlink is just to the right of the back wagon wheel. Fort Bendy Lumber Company was an early business serviced by the NYT&M Railroad.

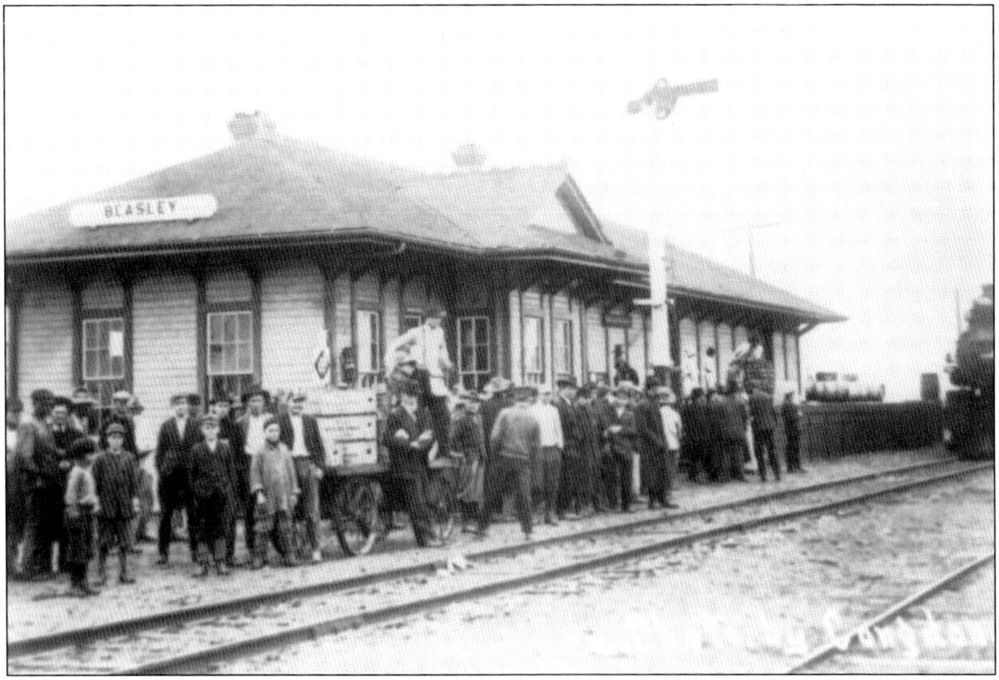

Beasley depot's train order signal indicates a "stop" for the locomotive engineer. Crowds await the arrival of the next train from out of town.

Six

The San Antonio and Aransas Pass Railroad

The sixth railroad company to operate in Fort Bend County was the San Antonio and Aransas Pass Railroad (SA&AP). It was chartered in August 1884 and connected San Antonio with Aransas Pass, Texas. This line, better known as "the Sap," completed a 176-mile rail line between Kennedy and Houston. Construction through Fort Bend County began in 1888 as part of the railroad's route into Houston. Principal towns in Fort Bend County along this route were Simonton, Fulshear, and Clodine. As a result of lawsuits filed against the company because of a wreck in 1890, the San Antonio and Aransas Pass entered receivership. The Southern Pacific Railroad began acquiring a majority of the SA&AP stock in 1892. It was being operated as a separate company of the Southern Pacific until the Texas Railroad Commission decided, in March 1903, that acquisition of the SAP was illegal. The Southern Pacific divested itself of the SAP until March 25, 1925, when the Texas Railroad Commission granted the Southern Pacific permission to reacquire the San Antonio and Aransas Pass Railroad. The part of the Sap through Fort Bend County was included in the Southern Pacific's Bellaire branch, portions of which remained in operation until 1998. The rails were removed in 2001, and part of the right-of-way is now in use as the West Park Toll Road into Houston.

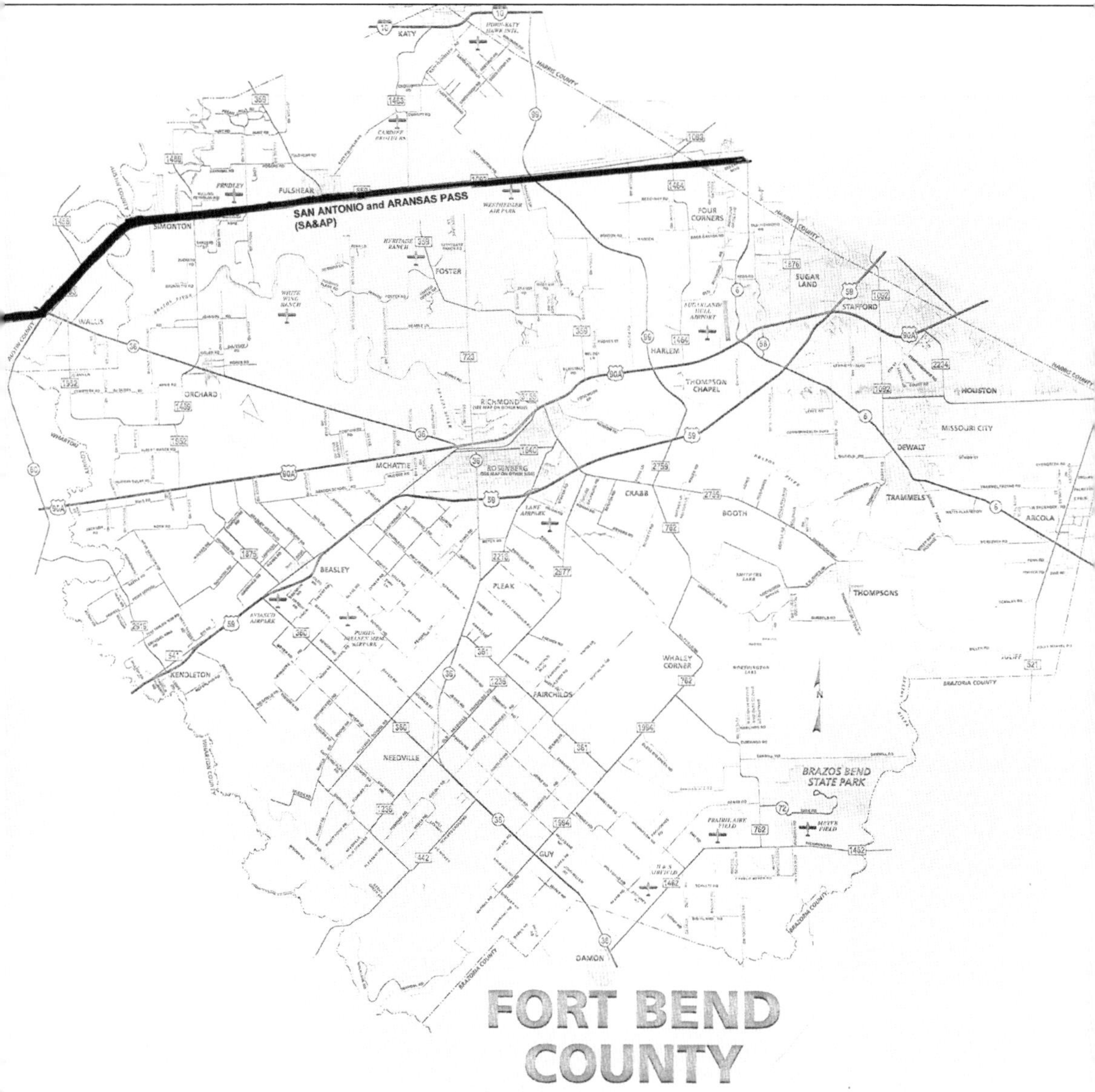

This map of Fort Bend County reflects the route of the San Antonio and Aransas Pass Railroad. Towns along this route through Fort Bend County include Clodine, Fulshear, and Simonton.

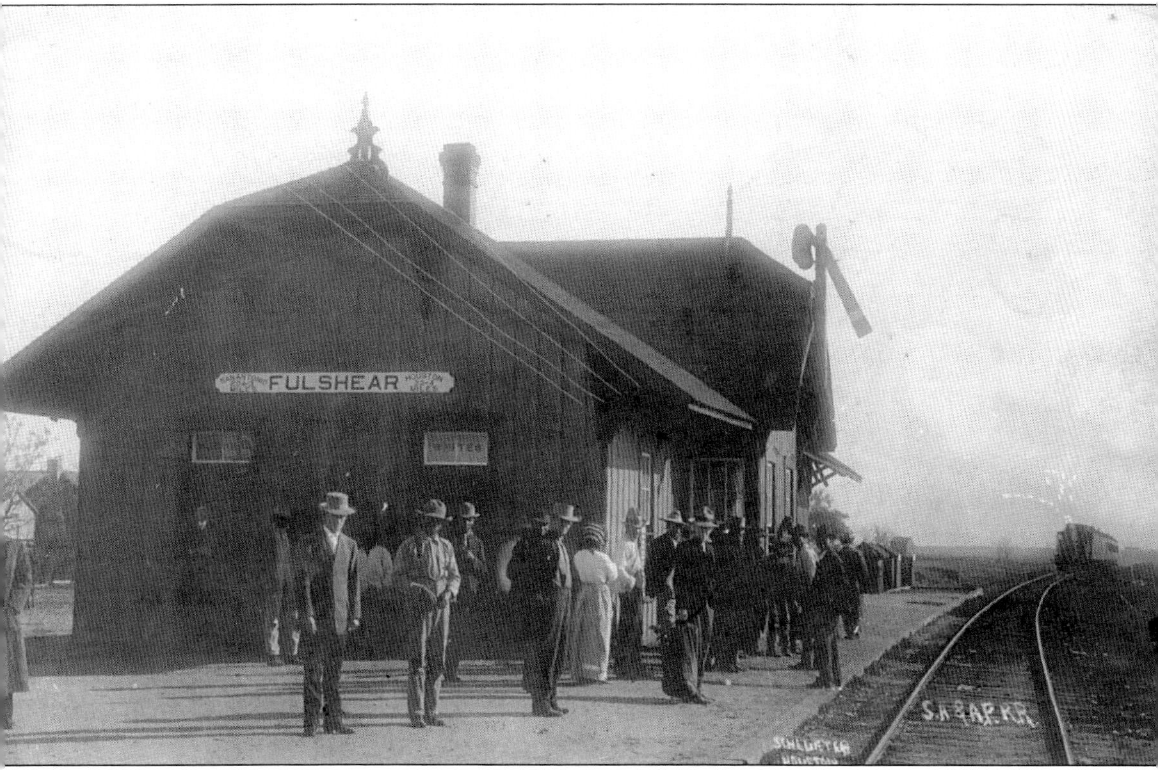

This photograph of the Fulshear depot serving the San Antonio and Aransas Pass Railroad shows passengers awaiting the arrival of a short SA&AP passenger train. This short train consists of a baggage car and a passenger coach. (Courtesy of the Ken E. Stavinoha Collection.)

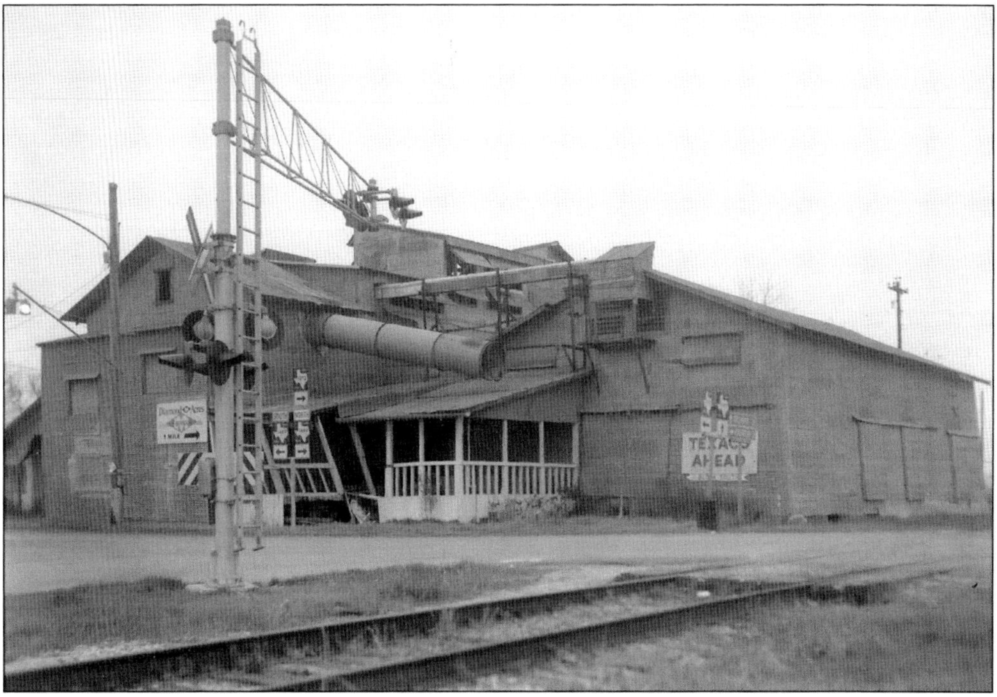

HOUSTON AND SAN ANTONIO

READ DOWN			Miles	STATIONS (Grand Central Station)	Population	READ UP		
	No. 3 Daily	No. 1 Daily				No. 2 Daily	No. 4 Daily	
	6 30PM	9 05AM	0	Lv. ¶Houston... Ar.	78,800	7 10PM	9 05AM	
	* 6 59 "	* 9 37 "	7	" Bellaire...... "	10	* 6 37 "	* 8 35 "	
	* 7 04 "	* 9 44 "	11	" Jeanetta...... "	10	* 6 31 "	* 8 30 "	
	* 7 13 "	* 9 53 "	15	" Alief........ "	15	* 6 22 "	* 8 21 "	
	7 28 "	10 06 "	21	" Clodine..... "	20	6 10 "	8 10 "	
	* 7 37 "	*10 17 "	27	" Gaston...... "	50	* 5 57 "	* 7 57 "	
	* 7 44 "	*10 25 "	30	" Flewellen... "	15	* 5 49 "	* 7 50 "	
	7 51 "	10 33 "	34	" Fulshear..... "	200	5 43 "	7 44 "	
	* 8 02 "	10 46 "	38	" Simonton.... "	150	5 33 "	* 7 33 "	
	8 23 "	11 03 "	45	" ¶Wallis....... "	1,200	5 18 "	7 16 "	
	* 8 41 "	11 20 "	54	" Chesterville. "	400	4 56 "	* 6 56 "	
	9 02 "	11 41AM	62	" ¶Eagle Lake.. "	1,717	4 38 "	6 38 "	
	9 22 "	12 02PM	70	" Altair....... "	150	4 20 "	6 20 "	
	9 38 "	12 18 "	77	" ¶Rock Island. "	700	4 02 "	6 00 "	
		*12 29 "	83	" Cheetham... "	75	* 3 49 "	* 5 47 "	
	9 52 "	12 33 "	84	" Sheridan ... "	200	3 47 "	5 45 "	
	*10 08 "	12 50 "	92	" Sublime...... "	228	3 31 "	5 29 "	
	10 33 "	1 13 "	101	" ¶Hallettsville "	1,379	3 10 "	5 06 "	
		* 1 26 "	107	" Mont....... "	50	* 2 58 "		
	*10 57 "	1 37 "	112	" Sweet Home Ar	250	2 47 "	* 4 40 "	
	11 10PM	1 50PM	119	Ar ¶Yoakum... Lv	4,657	2 35PM	4 25AM	
	11 25PM	2 15PM	118	Lv ¶Yoakum... Ar	4,657	2 15PM	4 20AM	
		2 32 "	127	Ar Edgar...... "	300	1 55 "		
	12 04AM	2 52 "	135	" ¶Cuero...... "	3,109	1 37 "	3 45 "	
		* 3 08 "	143	" Buschel..... "	10	* 1 17 "		
	12 41 "	3 27 "	152	" ¶Yorktown.. "	1,180	1 00 "	3 08 "	
	1 02 "	3 47 "	160	" Nordheim... "	300	12 38 "	2 47 "	
	1 18 "	4 03 "	167	" Runge....... "	2,000	12 22 "	2 31 "	
	1 40AM	4 25PM	177	Ar ¶Kenedy....Lv	1,200	12 01PM	2 10AM	
	6 15AM		...	Ar Corpus Christi Lv	20,000	7 50AM	10 25PM	
No. 12	No. 14	No. 16				No. 11	No. 13	No. 15
11 45AM	2 55AM	4 45PM	177	Lv ¶Kenedy....Ar	1,200	11 45AM	1 20AM	3 45PM
11 59AM	3 15 "	4 58 "	183	Ar Karnes City "	1,000	11 32 "	1 05 "	3 33 "
*12 14PM	* 3 33 "	* 5 12 "	191	" Hobson...... "	100	*11 17 "		* 3 17 "
12 24 "	3 44 "	5 22 "	194	" Falls City... "	400	11 07 "	12 31 "	3 10 "
12 39 "	* 3 59 "	5 37 "	201	" Poth........ "	250	10 52 "	*12 14AM	* 2 55 "
12 55 "	4 19 "	5 53 "	208	" ¶Floresville "	1,398	10 36 "	11 57PM	2 40 "
1 27 "	4 59 "	6 24 "	222	" Elmendorf.. "	500	10 03 "	*11 17 "	2 05 "
2 05PM	5 55AM	7 05PM	238	Ar ¶San Antonio Lv	96,614	9 25AM	10 30PM	1 25PM

Tourist Pullman Sleepers between San Antonio and Yoakum on trains 13-4 and 3-14.

SAN ANTONIO AND KERRVILLE

No. 156 Freight Daily Ex. Sunday See Note	READ DOWN No. 42 Pass. Daily	No. 44 Pass. Sunday Only	Miles	STATIONS	Population	READ UP No. 41 Pass. Daily	No. 43 Pass. Sunday Only	No. 155 Freight Daily Ex Sunday See Note
7 30AM	4 50PM	8 05AM	0	Lv ¶San Antonio. Ar	96,614	9 15AM	6 40PM	6 40PM
* 8 02 "	* 5 15 "	* 8 40 "	10	Ar Robards.... "	5	* 8 45 "	* 6 10 "	* 5 55 "
* 8 25 "	* 5 30 "	* 8 55 "	15	" Olga........ "	25	* 8 25 "	* 5 55 "	5 30 "
8 30 "	* 5 34 "	* 8 58 "	16	" Beckman ... "	25	* 8 19 "	* 5 52 "	* 5 02 "
8 42 "	5 42 "	9 05 "	19	" Viva........ "	5	8 11 "	5 42 "	* 4 50 "
8 55 "	5 50 "	9 08 "	21	" Leon Springs. "	75	8 08 "	5 36 "	4 45 "
* 9 00 "	* 5 52 "	* 9 11 "	22	" Remount.... "	0	* 8 03 "	* 5 28 "	* 4 41 "
9 15 "	6 03 "	9 22 "	25	" Van Raub... "	75	7 55 "	5 20 "	4 30 "
9 45 "	6 22 "	9 41 "	32	" ¶Boerne .... "	886	7 40 "	5 03 "	4 10 "
*10 05 "	* 6 37 "	* 9 56 "	...	" Spanish Pass "	0	* 7 28 "	* 4 50 "	* 3 35 "
*	*	*	40	" Kenilworth. "	10	*	*	*
10 20 "	6 46 "	10 06 "	41	" Welfare.... "	100	7 18 "	4 40 "	3 15 "
10 35 "	6 55 "	10 16 "	45	" Waring..... "	325	7 08 "	4 30 "	3 00 "
*	*	*	48	" Guad'pe River "	10	*	*	*
10 59 "	7 08 "	10 30 "	...	" Fred'berg Jc.. "	...	6 56 "	4 18 "	2 40 "
11 20 "	7 17 "	10 39 "	52	" Comfort.... "	1,000	6 48 "	4 08 "	2 20 "
*	*	*	56	" Moores..... "	5	*	*	*
11 50AM	7 35 "	10 57 "	60	" Center Point "	550	6 30 "	3 50 "	1 45 "
*	*	*	66	" Split Rock.. "	10	*	*	*
*	*	*	69	" Parson...... "	0	*	*	*
12 20PM	8 00PM	11 25AM	71	Ar ¶Kerrville.... Lv	1,843	6 05AM	3 25PM	1 10PM

(Note:—Trains 145 and 146 have Passenger and Baggage Car Attached

SAN ANTONIO & LEON SPRINGS

(GOV'T. TRAINING CAMP)

No. 50 Daily	No. 48 Daily	No. 45 Daily	Miles		No. 45 Daily	No. 47 Daily	No. 49 Daily
4 40PM	1 00PM	8 15AM	0	Lv San Antonio....... Ar	11 19AM	4 10PM	7 50PM
5 36 "	1 59 "	9 18 "	20	Ar Leon Springs..... Ar	10 19 "	3 08 "	6 48 "
5 41 "	2 04 "	9 21 "	21	Ar Remount........ Ar	10 17 "	3 06 "	6 46 "
6 00PM	2 20PM	9 35AM		Ar Camp Funston.. Lv	10 01AM	2 50PM	6 30PM

¶Stop on Signal. ‖Meal Station. *Stations where through tickets are sold.

12M, 9-12-17.

This image reflects a typical feed and grain facility located along the route of the San Antonio and Aransas Pass Railroad through Fort Bend County.

In 1917, the San Antonio and Aransas Pass Railroad had several routes across Texas as noted by this timetable. One of the routes reflected the railroad's Houston Division. (Courtesy of the Ken E. Stavinoha Collection.)

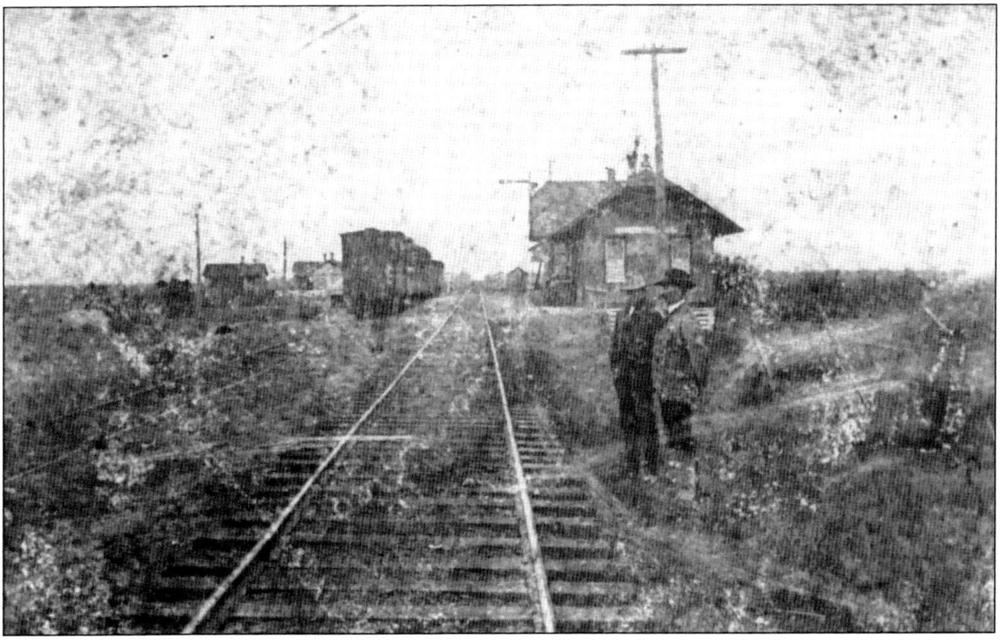

This photograph features the San Antonio and Aransas Pass Railroad depot located in Clodine, Texas. (Courtesy of the Rosenberg Railroad Museum Collection.)

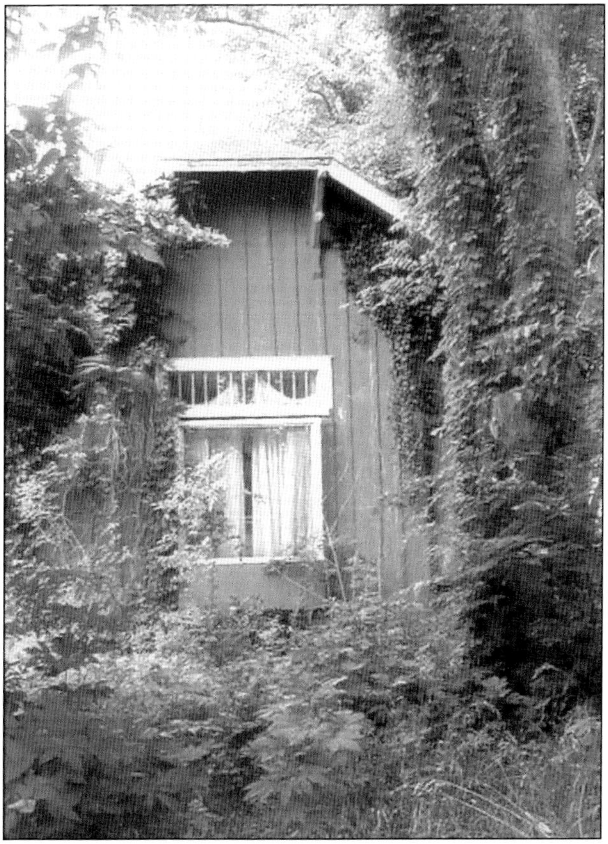

This is an end view of the Simonton depot of the San Antonio and Aransas Pass Railroad as it looks today as a private residence. (Author's collection.)

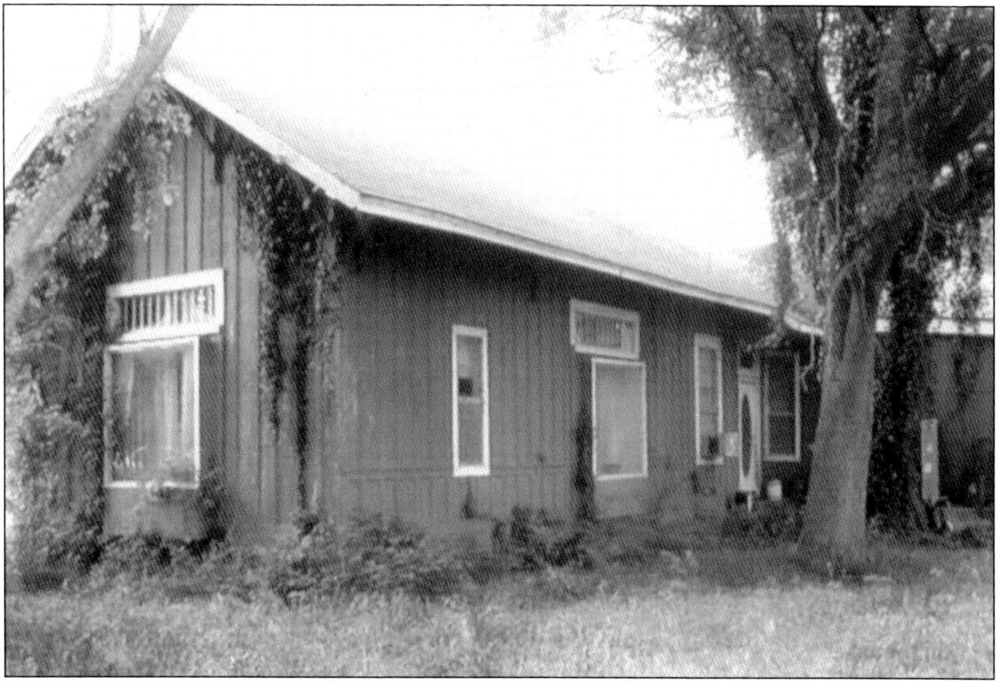

A side view of the Simonton depot of the San Antonio and Aransas Pass Railroad shows how it looks today as a private residence. (Author's collection.)

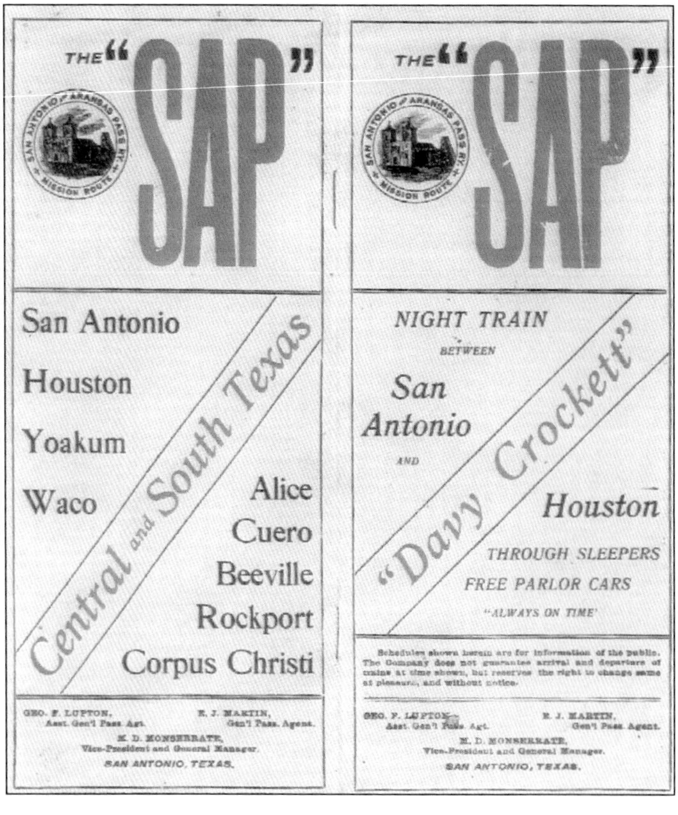

A San Antonio and Aransas Pass timetable for the Davy Crocket night train advertises sleeper cars and a free parlor car. (Courtesy of the Ken E. Stavinoha Collection.)

A February 1904 timetable shows the station stops along the route between San Antonio and Houston on the Sap line.

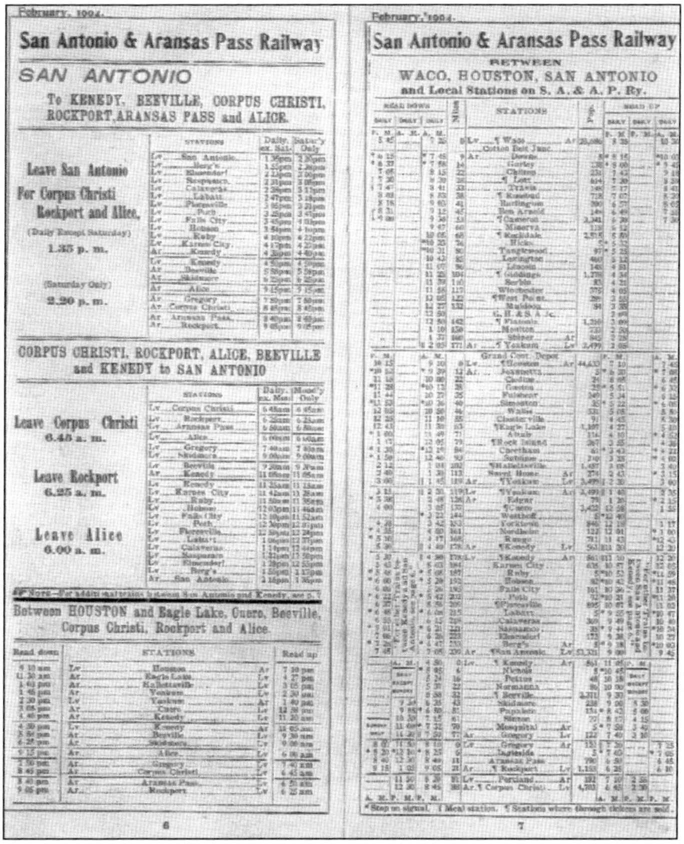
February, 1904.

San Antonio & Aransas Pass Railway

SAN ANTONIO

To KENEDY, BEEVILLE, CORPUS CHRISTI, ROCKPORT, ARANSAS PASS and ALICE.

Leave San Antonio For Corpus Christi Rockport and Alice,

(Daily Except Saturday)

1.35 p. m.

(Saturday Only)

2.20 p. m.

CORPUS CHRISTI, ROCKPORT, ALICE, BEEVILLE and KENEDY to SAN ANTONIO

Leave Corpus Christi 6.45 a. m.

Leave Rockport 6.25 a. m.

Leave Alice 6.00 a. m.

Between HOUSTON and Eagle Lake, Cuero, Beeville, Corpus Christi, Rockport and Alice.

February, 1904.

San Antonio & Aransas Pass Railway

BETWEEN

WACO, HOUSTON, SAN ANTONIO

and Local Stations on S. A. & A. P. Ry.

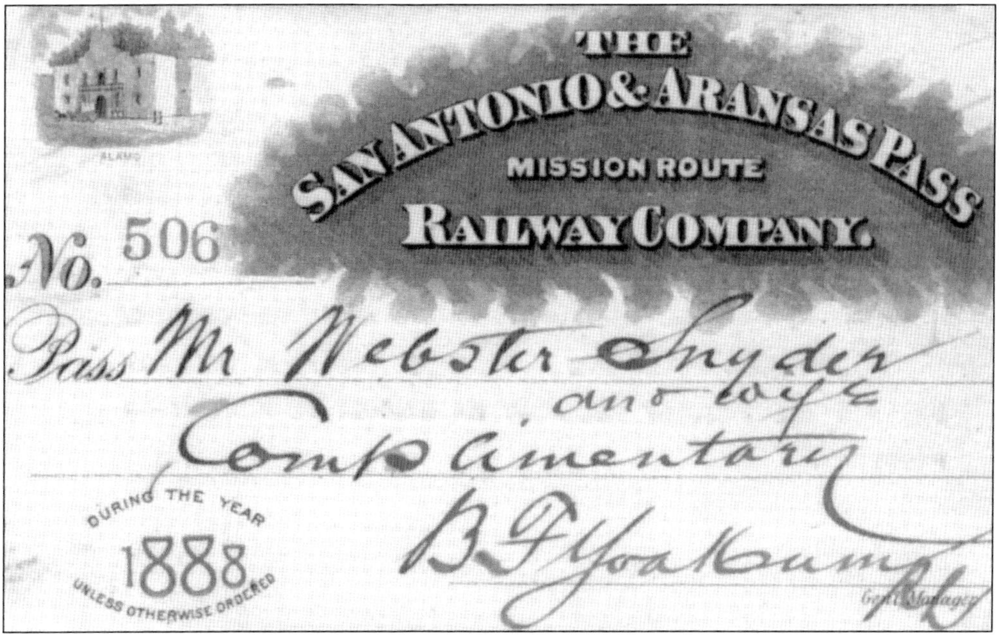

Pass No. 506 was issued in 1888 to Mr. Webster Snyder and his wife with B. F. Yoakum's signature. (Courtesy of the Ken E. Stavinoha Collection.)

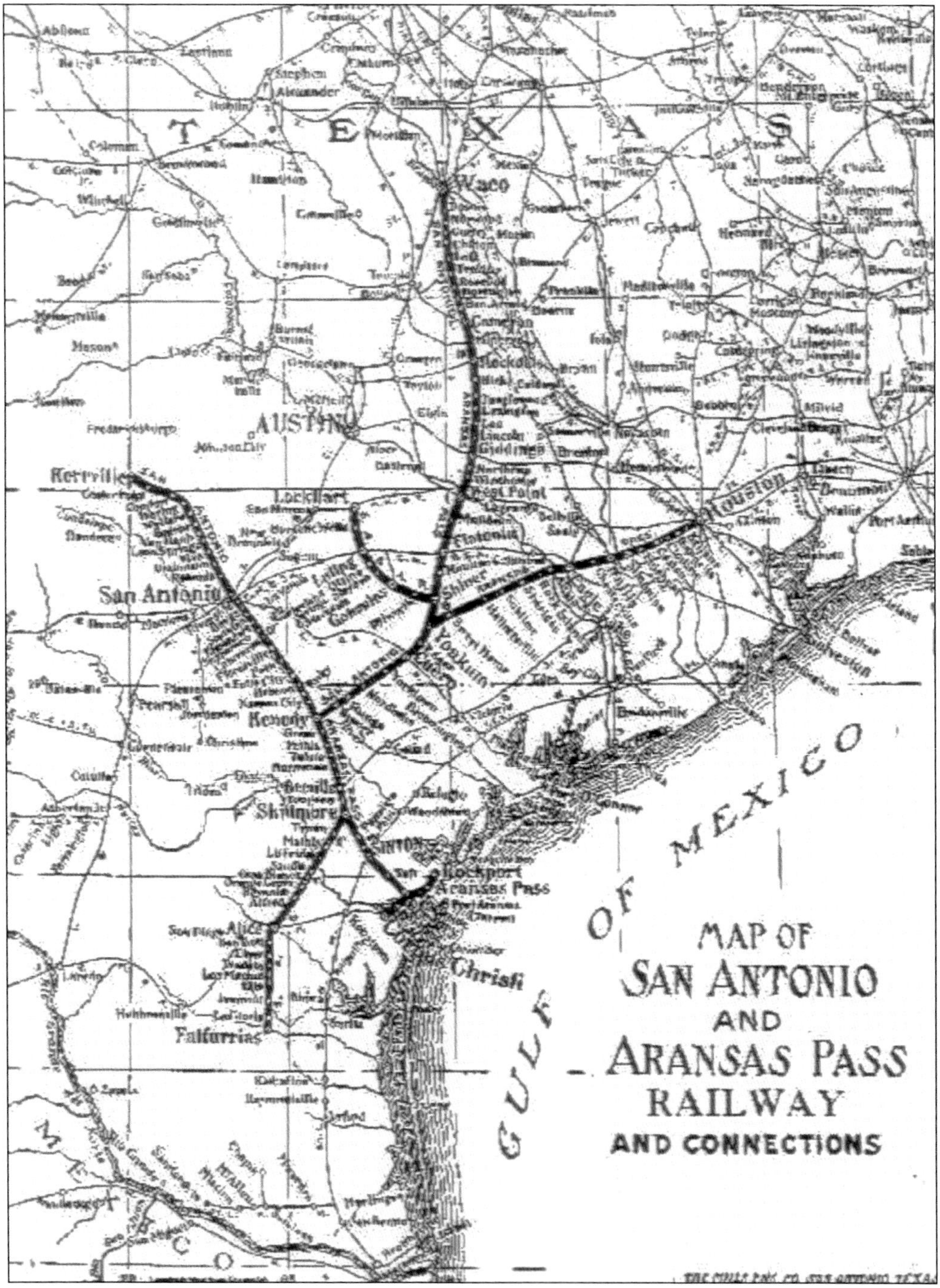

A system map of the San Antonio and Aransas Pass Railroad shows the lines and connections. (Courtesy of the Ken E. Stavinoha Collection.)

Seven

The Sugar Land Railroad

The Sugar Land Railroad became the seventh railroad company to operate in Fort Bend County in the 1880s as a private rail line. The railroad was used primarily as the means of transporting sugarcane from the fields located in Brazoria County to the refinery without having to travel through Houston. It was chartered by E. H. Cunningham in 1893 and later built through the town of Dewalt to Arcola, Texas, where it crossed the Gulf, Colorado, and Santa Fe Railroad. This crossing became known as Sugar Land Junction and was the location of Interlocking Tower 162. The line continued south and curved sharply to the east to a location known as House Junction to reach a connection with the International and Great Northern Railroad near Arcola, Texas. In 1912, the Sugar Land Railroad purchased 17 miles of private track from the Cunningham Sugar Company that ran south from House Junction. In the 1920s, the president of the sugar company, William T. Eldridge, took great pride in the Sugar Land Railroad and traveled extensively in a business car owned by the railroad. Eldridge had purchased several other Texas short lines and later sold most of them, including the Sugar Land Railroad, to the Missouri Pacific Railroad in 1925. In the 1970s, the Missouri Pacific received trackage rights on the Southern Pacific into Houston and eventually abandoned all of the remaining line to Arcola.

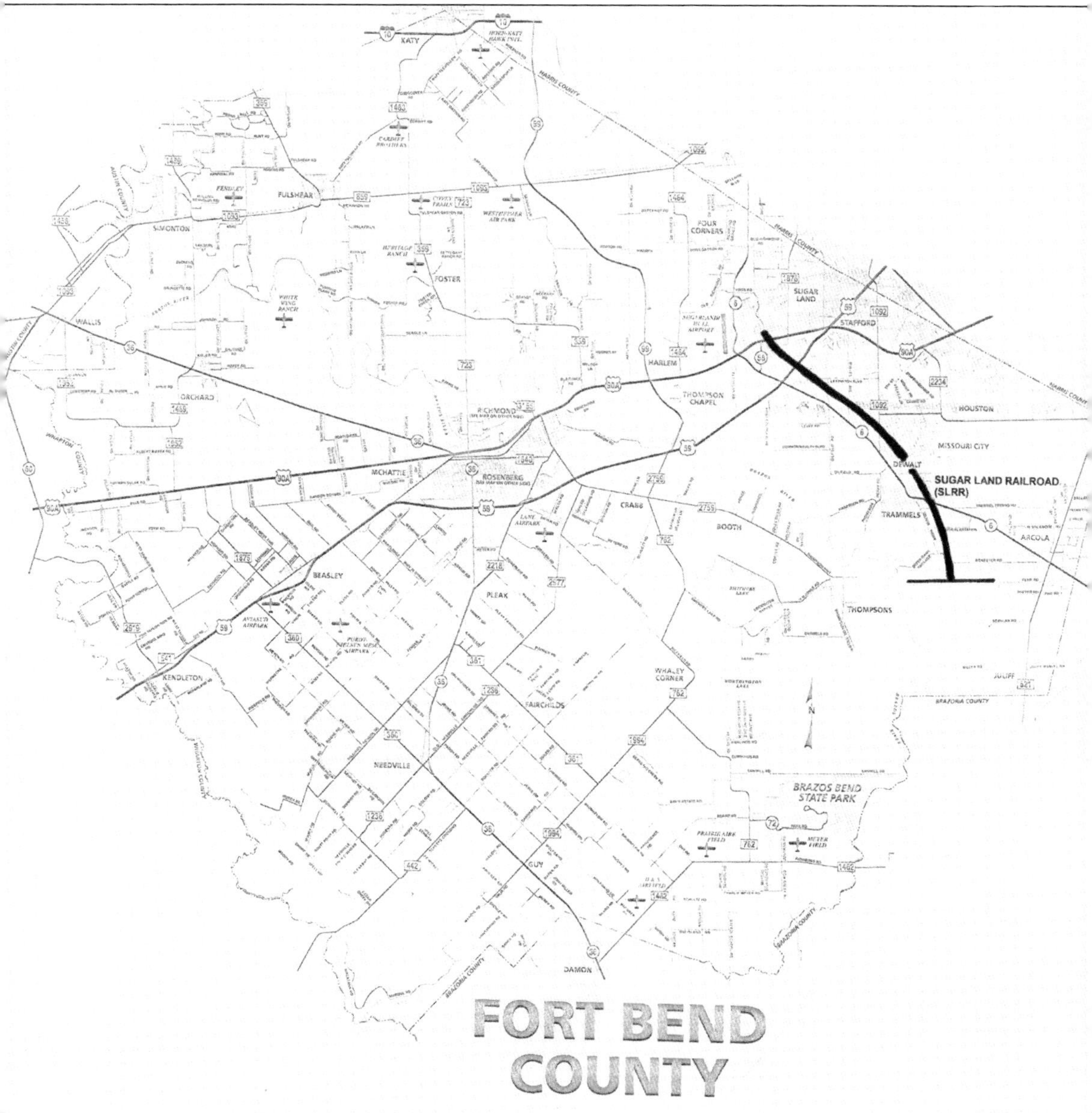

This map of Fort Bend County reflects the route of the Sugar Land Railroad. Towns along this route through Fort Bend County include Arcola, Dewalt, and Sugar Land.

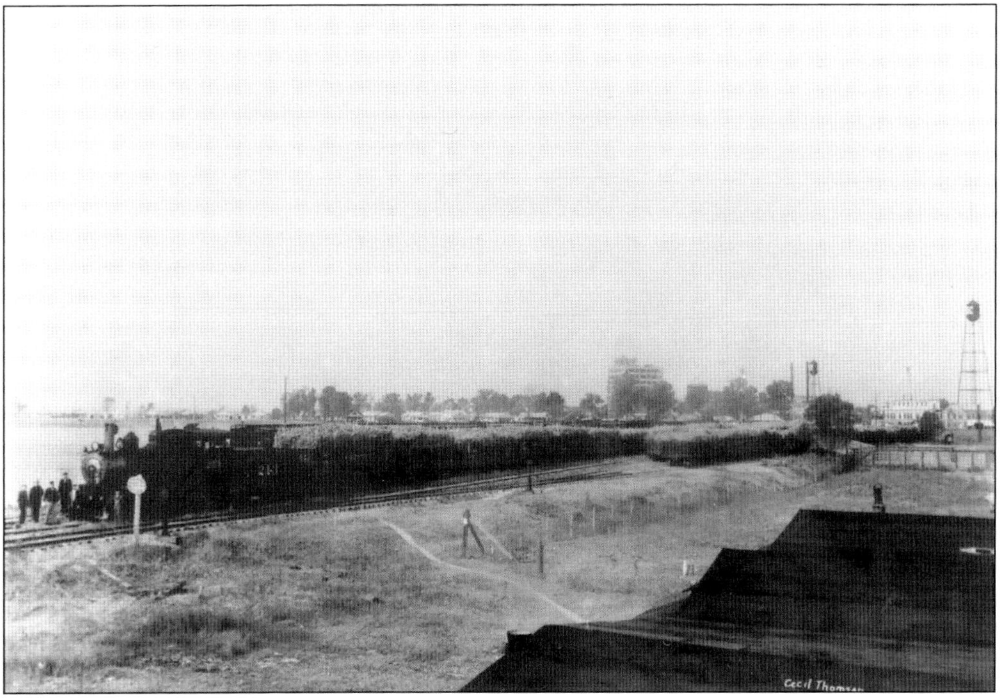

Locomotive No. 213 works in the rail yard located south of the sugar refinery with yet another load of sugarcane.

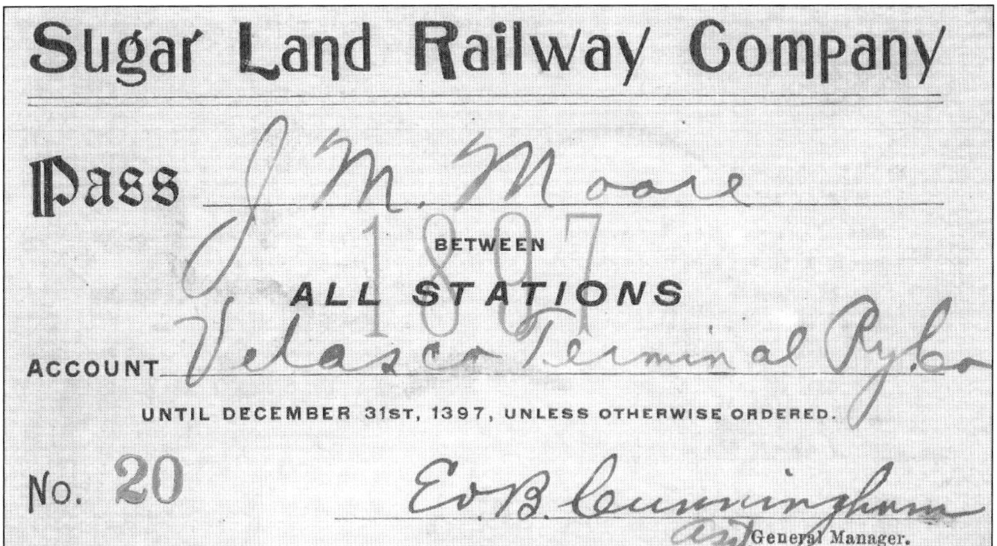

Sugar Land Railway Company

Pass J. M. Moore

1897

BETWEEN

ALL STATIONS

ACCOUNT Velasco Terminal Ry. Co

UNTIL DECEMBER 31ST, 1397, UNLESS OTHERWISE ORDERED.

No. 20

E. B. Cunningham

Asst. General Manager.

This photograph shows pass No. 20 of the Sugar Land Railroad issued to Mr. J. M. Moore by E. B. Cunningham, assistant manager of the Cunningham Sugar Refinery. (Courtesy of the Ken E. Stavinoha Collection.)

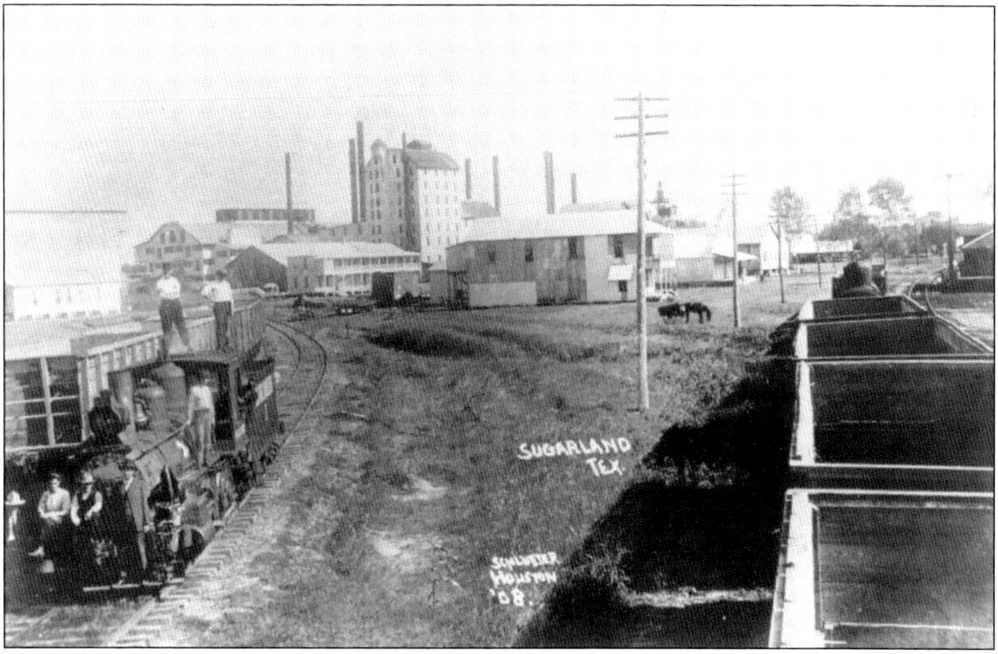

Sugar Land Railroad Locomotive No. 1 takes a moment from its switching duties so the crew can pose for this early-1900 photograph.

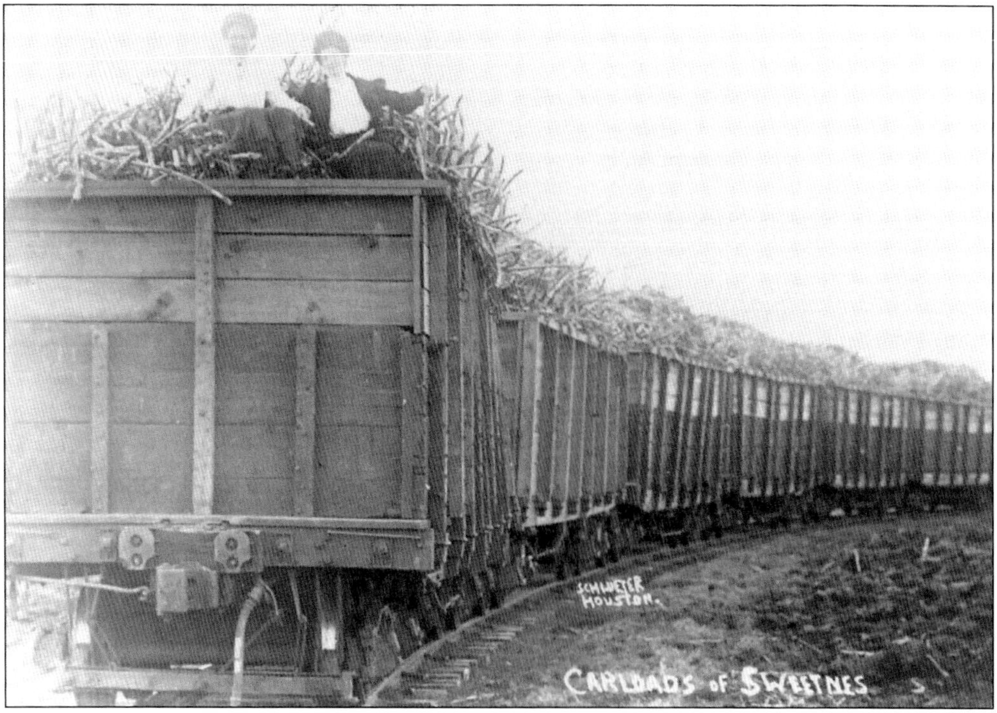

This photograph is titled "Car Loads of Sweetness," which is a reference to the carloads of sugarcane and not to the young ladies who decided to climb aboard.

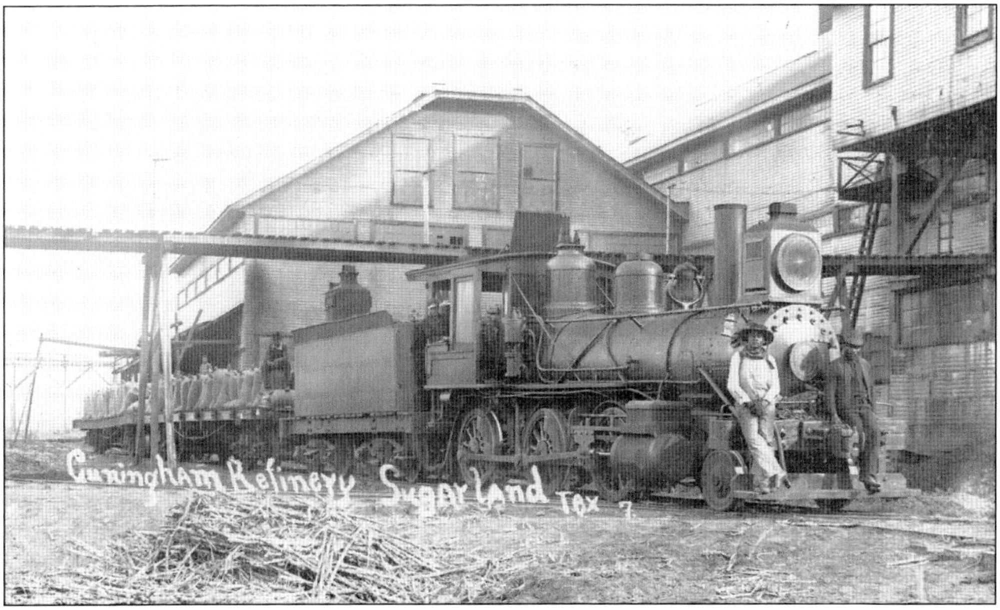

A train crew positions flat cars loaded with sacked sugar at the loading dock of the Cunningham Sugar Refinery in Sugar Land, Texas. These crew members take a moment from their work to pose for the camera. (Courtesy of the Ken E. Stavinoha Collection.)

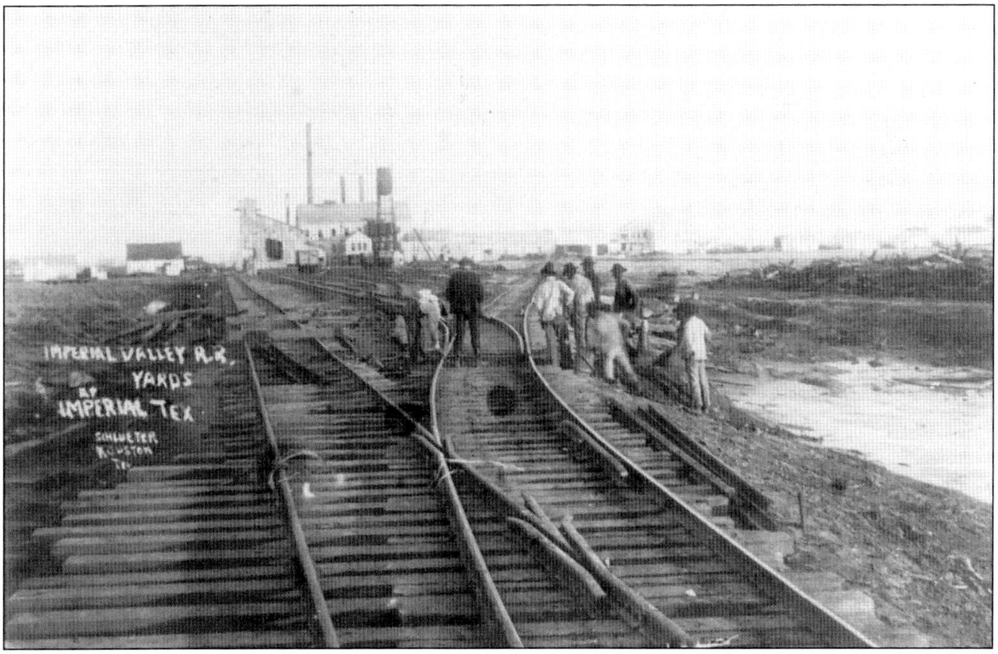

A track crew repairs a switch in the imperial rail yard located west of the imperial sugar refinery. Track maintenance is a never-ending necessity, even with modern-day railroading.

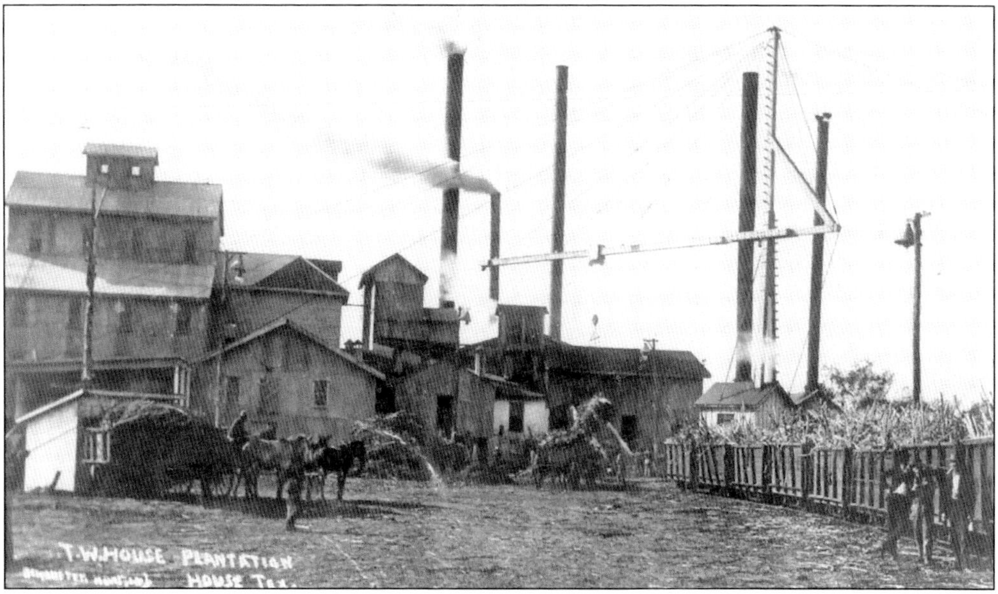

A train loaded with sugarcane has recently arrived from the cane fields and is being unloaded into mule-drawn wagons using a large crane at the T. W. House Sugar Plantation. The house plantation has its own sugar refinery for processing its raw sugarcane located southeast of Richmond, Texas. (Courtesy of the Ken E. Stavinoha Collection.)

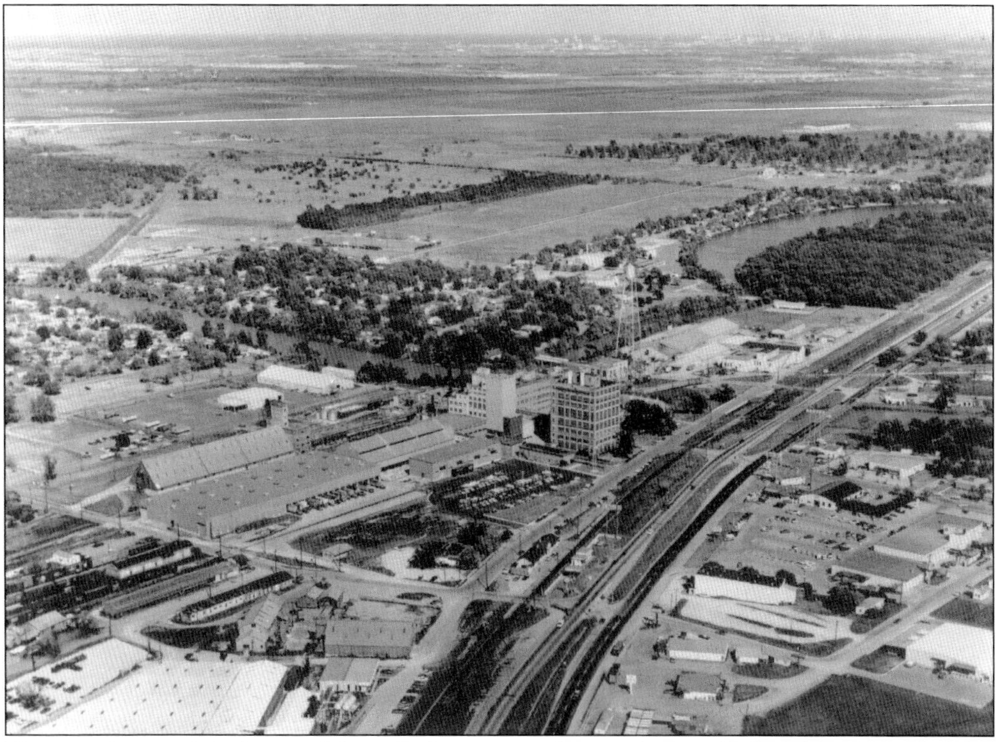

This aerial view of the Imperial Sugar Refinery was taken in the late 1950s. The GH&SA depot and rail yard facilities are in plain view in this photograph. Today many of the structures of this facility are still here; however, the refinery has been shut down since 2005.

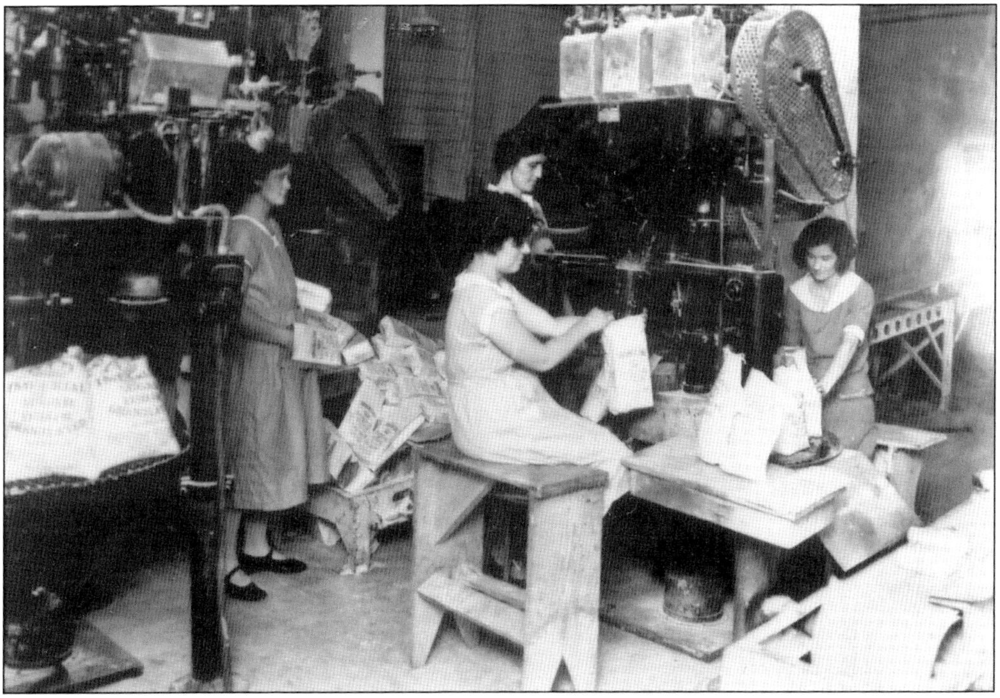

Young ladies are busy packaging extra-fine granulated sugar into sugar sacks for the Imperial Sugar Company. The granules are being fed into the loading hopper using a conveyor system to keep the sugar flowing.

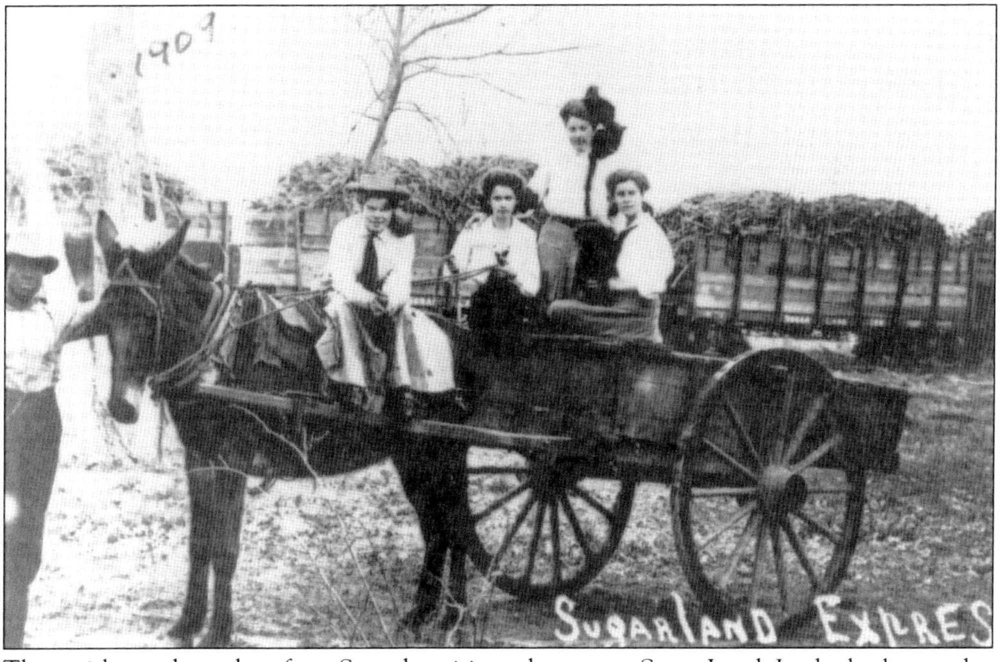

These girls are dressed up for a Saturday visit to downtown Sugar Land. In the background, a string of Sugar Land Railroad hopper cars loaded with sugarcane just arrived from the cane fields and wait their turn to be unloaded and processed at the refinery.

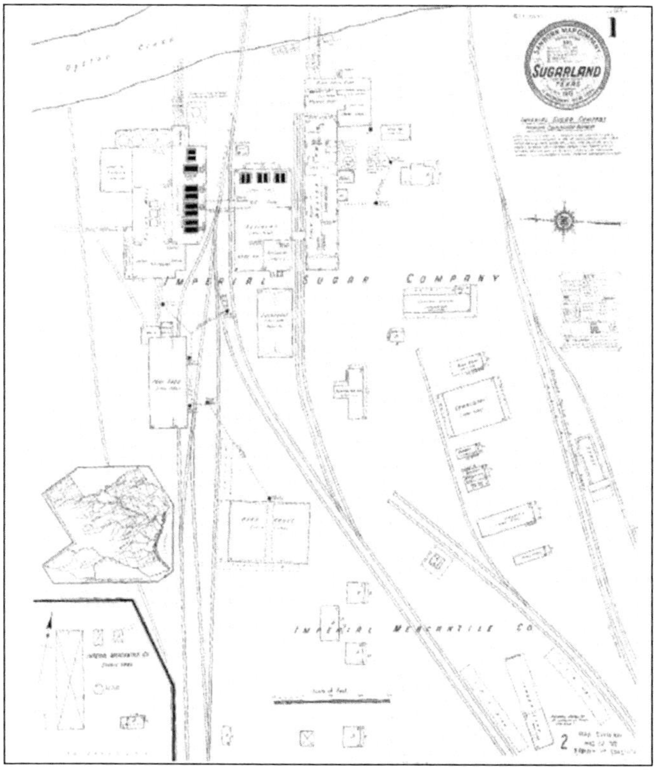

A 1913 Sanborn Fire Map of the Imperial Sugar Company shows the locations of the refinery and associated buildings used in the refinery process of manufacturing sugarcane into sugar. These early maps were used for assessing fire risk associated with specific properties for insurance purposes.

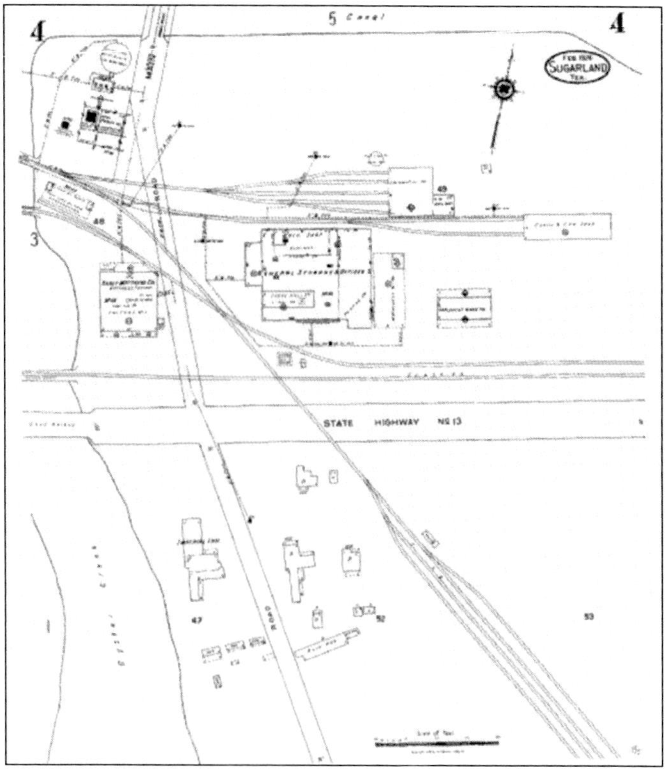

A 1926 Sanborn Map of the Imperial Sugar complex shows the location of interlocking tower 114 and the Sugar Land Railroad engine facility.

This 1926 Sanborn map shows the Sugar Land Railroad tracks throughout the Sugar Mill complex. The Galveston, Harrisburg, and San Antonio depot is shown along the main rail line.

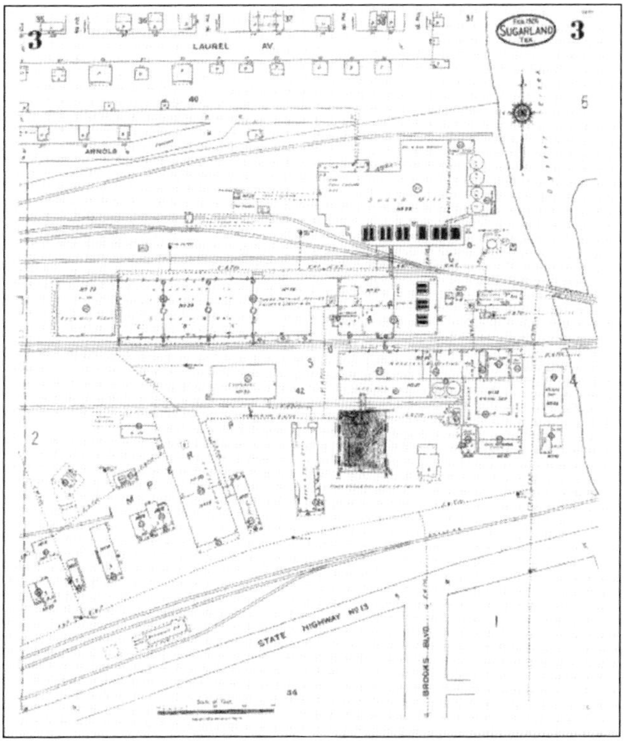

Seen here is the electrical substation building in front of the water tower. Also shown in the middle of the photograph is the location of the Sugar Land Railroad engine facility. Interlocking Tower 114 can be seen on the right-hand side of the photograph.

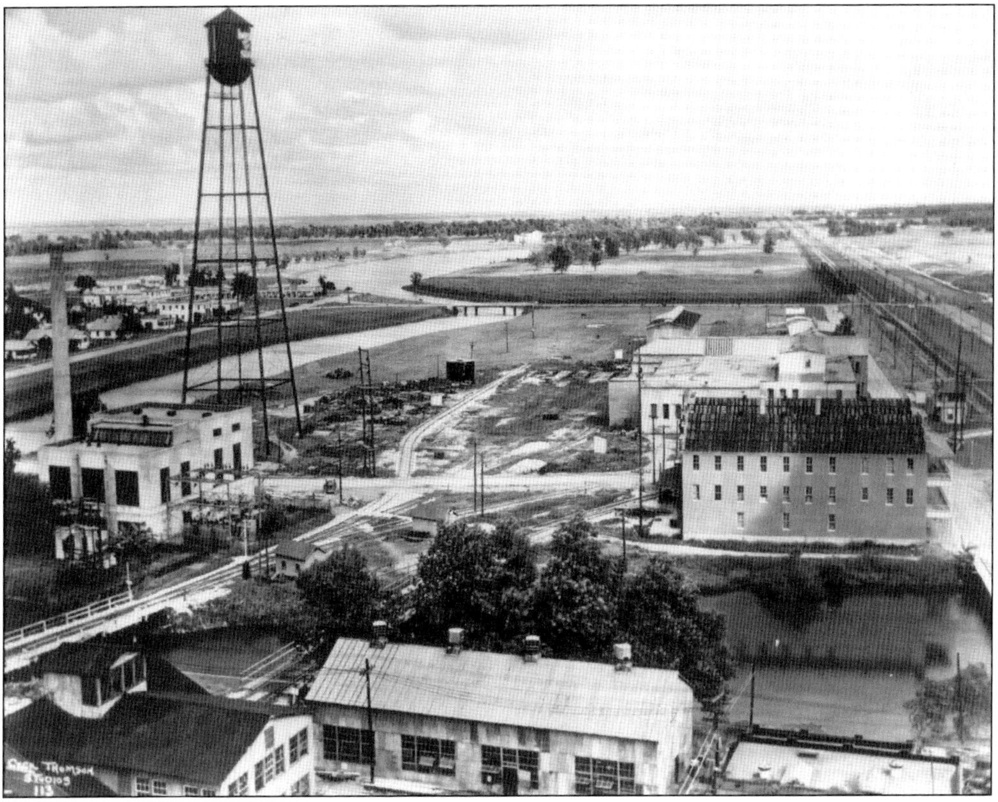

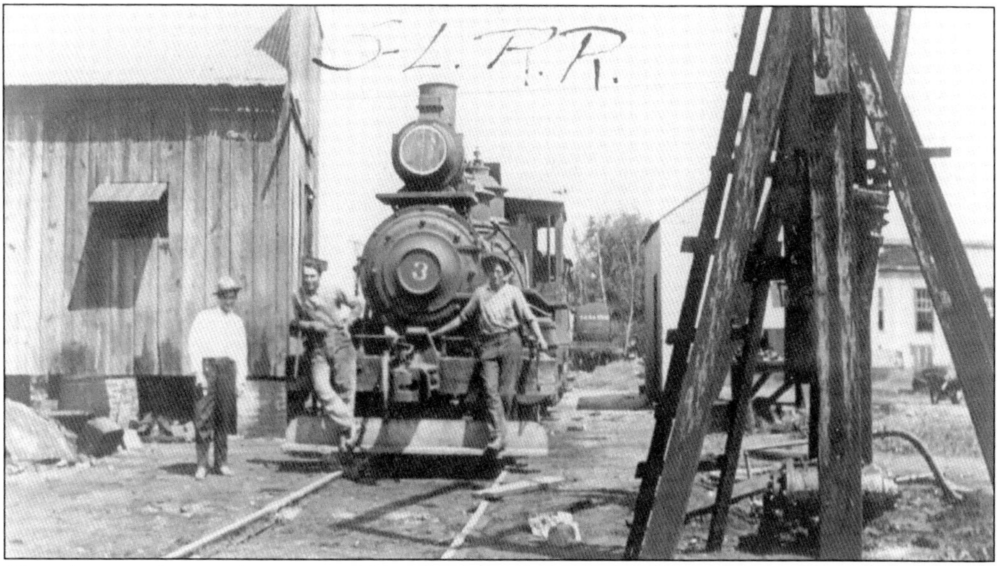

This photograph provides a view of Sugar Land Railroad Locomotive No. 3 in front of the engine house on the grounds of the Imperial Sugar Refinery complex. (Courtesy of the Rosenberg Railroad Museum Collection.)

SUGAR LAND DISTRICT—BETWEEN HICKEY AND ANCHOR

TRAINS—SOUTHWARD						TIME TABLE			TRAINS—NORTHWARD			
SECOND CLASS				Station Numbers	Distance from Hickey	No. 37	Distance from Anchor	Siding Capacity in Cars	THIRD CLASS			
			381 Mixed			Taking Effect DECEMBER 11, 1932			380 Mixed			
			Daily Except Sunday			STATIONS			Daily Except Sunday			
				850	0.0	HICKEY	50.3					
				838	11.8	11.8 CABELL	38.5					
			L 6.00PM	833	16.6	D 4.8 SUGAR LAND WOYS	33.7	Yard	A 10.55PM			
				827		0.0 S.P. INTERLOCKER						
			6.22		23.2	6.7 DEWALT	27.0	27	10.30			
			6.36	822	27.9	4.6 SUGAR LAND JUNCTION	22.4	Yard	10.10			
						0.0 G.C. & S.F. INTERLOCKER						
			6.45	820	30.0	2.1 HOUSE JUNCTION Y	20.3		9.55			
			A 6.50PM			1.9 HAWDON			L 9.45PM			
				820	30.0	1.9 HOUSE JUNCTION	20.3	Yard				
				818	32.1	2.1 TIGNER	18.2	10				
				86	43.7	11.6 OTEY	6.6	37				
					50.3	D 6.6 ANCHOR Y	0.0	Yard				
			Daily Except Sunday			50.3			Daily Except Sunday			
			0.50						1.10			

PALESTINE DIVISION

Sugar Land Railroad timetable No. 37, dated December 11, 1932, shows the station and major rail junctions of the Sugar Land Railroad. (Courtesy of the Ken E. Stavinoha Collection.)

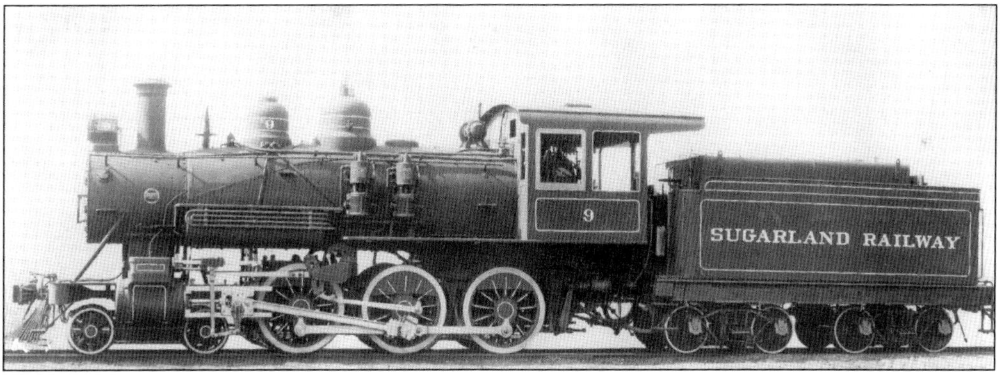

Sugar Land Railroad 2-6-0 Locomotive No. 9 poses in the manufacturer's photograph. (Courtesy of the Ken E. Stavinoha Collection.)

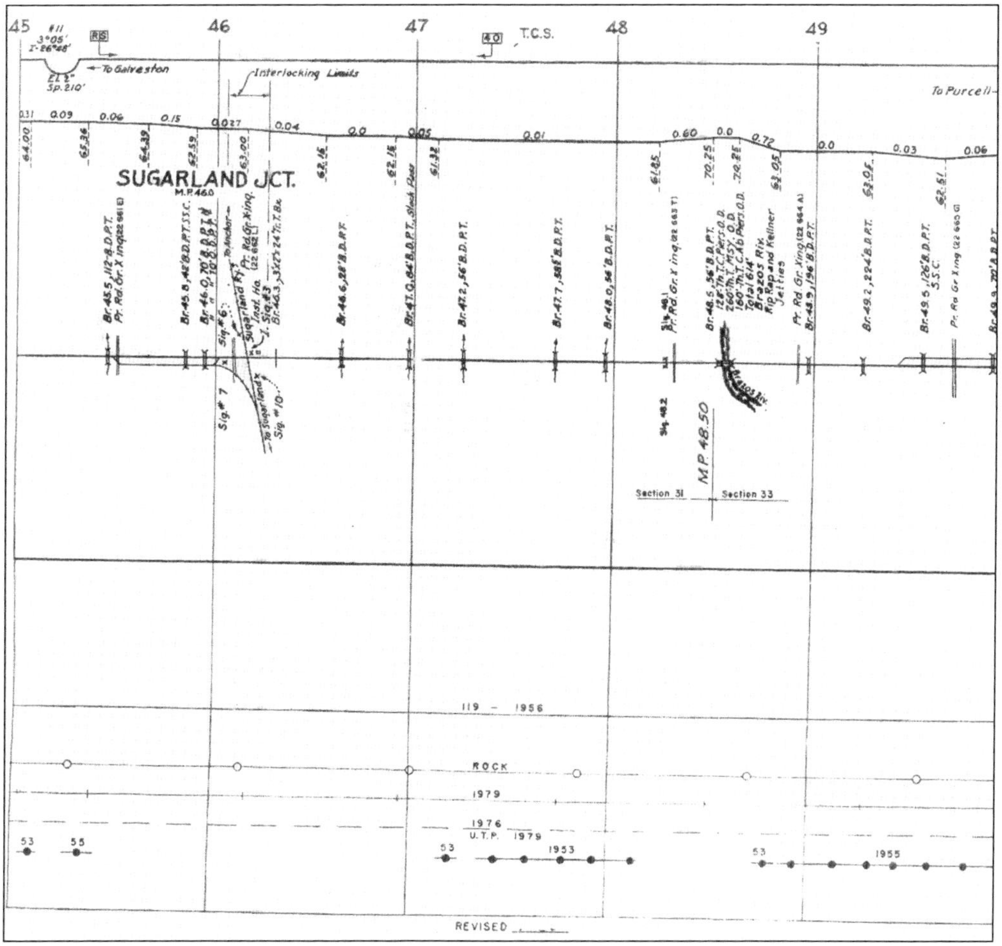

This track chart of the Gulf Colorado and Santa Fe Railroad shows the location and signals of Sugar Land Junction. The junction allows the Sugar Land Railroad to travel beyond the railroad's own limits. (Courtesy of the Rosenberg Railroad Museum Collection.)

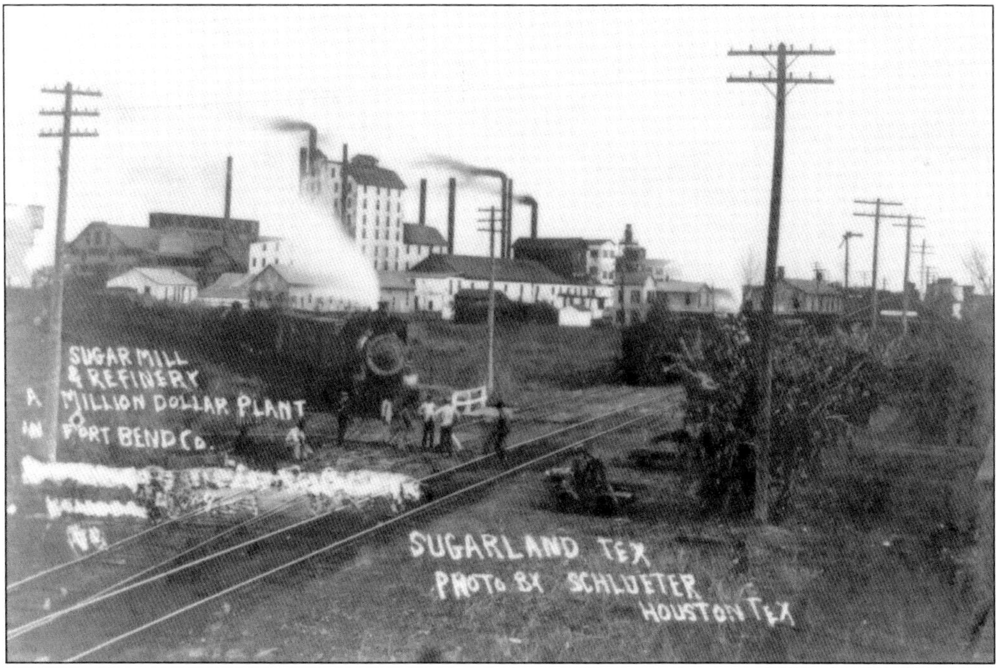

Switching crews are hard at work west of the Imperial Sugar Refinery and sugar mill complex. Setting out and spotting railcars throughout the network of tracks and buildings will keep this crew busy for quite a while.

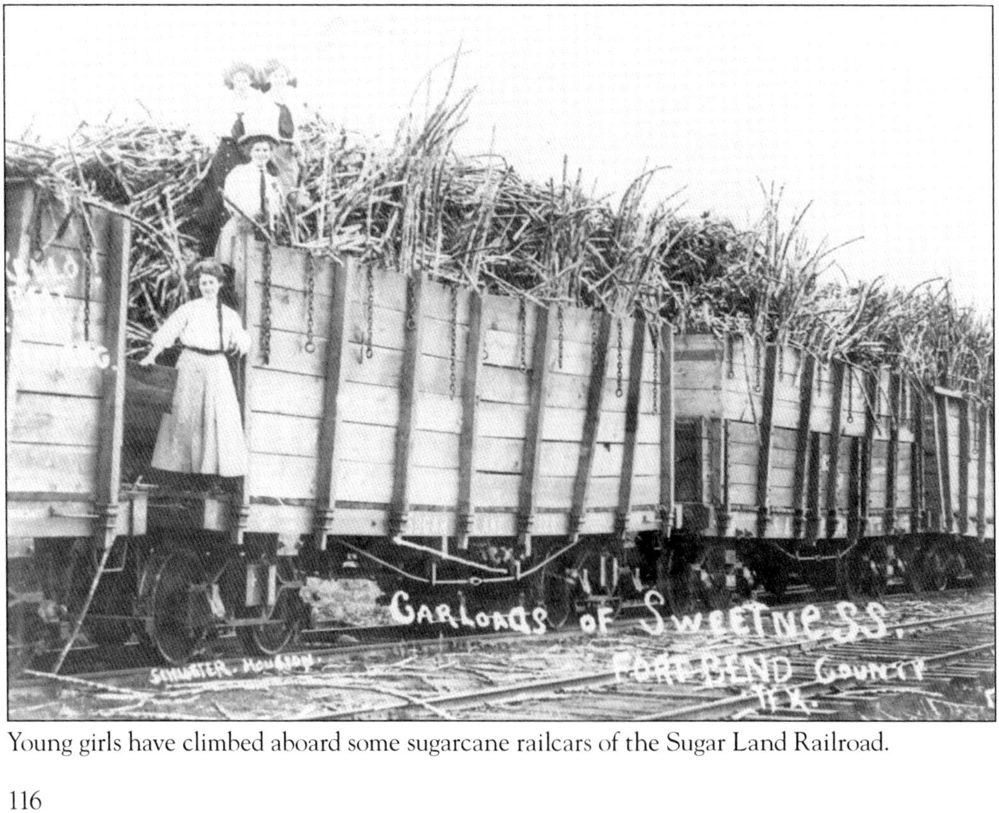

Young girls have climbed aboard some sugarcane railcars of the Sugar Land Railroad.

Eight

The Missouri-Kansas-Texas Railroad

The Missouri-Kansas-Texas Railroad Company (MK&T) was the first railroad to enter Texas from the north. The company began its corporate existence in 1865, when its earliest predecessor, the Union Pacific Railway Company southern branch, was chartered by the State of Kansas to build from Fort Riley, Kansas, to the state's southern boundary. The newly named railroad was intended to funnel business from Missouri and Kansas and the North and East to a new rail route across Native American territory to and through Texas. Nicknamed "the Katy," the MK&T was touted in advertisements as the "Gateway to Texas" and breached the Texas frontier near Denison. The company had no charter to build in Texas, but the one granted by Kansas was approved by the Texas Legislature on August 2, 1870. The Missouri-Kansas-Texas Railway Company did not become officially incorporated in Texas until 1891; until then, it operated in the state under its own name or through various subsidiary companies.

The railroad was built through the northern tip of Fort Bend County in 1893 to become the eighth railroad company in the county. The corporate name was changed to Missouri-Kansas-Texas "M-K-T" after reorganization in 1923. The Katy became a major player in the Texas railroad scene until after World War II, when it began a slow decline due to continued financial difficulties. The Union Pacific was given permission to acquire the M-K-T via its Missouri Pacific Railroad subsidiary, and on December 1, 1989, the Katy disappeared as a separate railroad company. The rail line east of the town of Katy, Texas, was abandoned and removed in 1998, and the right-of-way is now part of U.S. Interstate 10 into Houston. The rail line west of Katy, Texas, is still owned and operated by the Union Pacific Railroad.

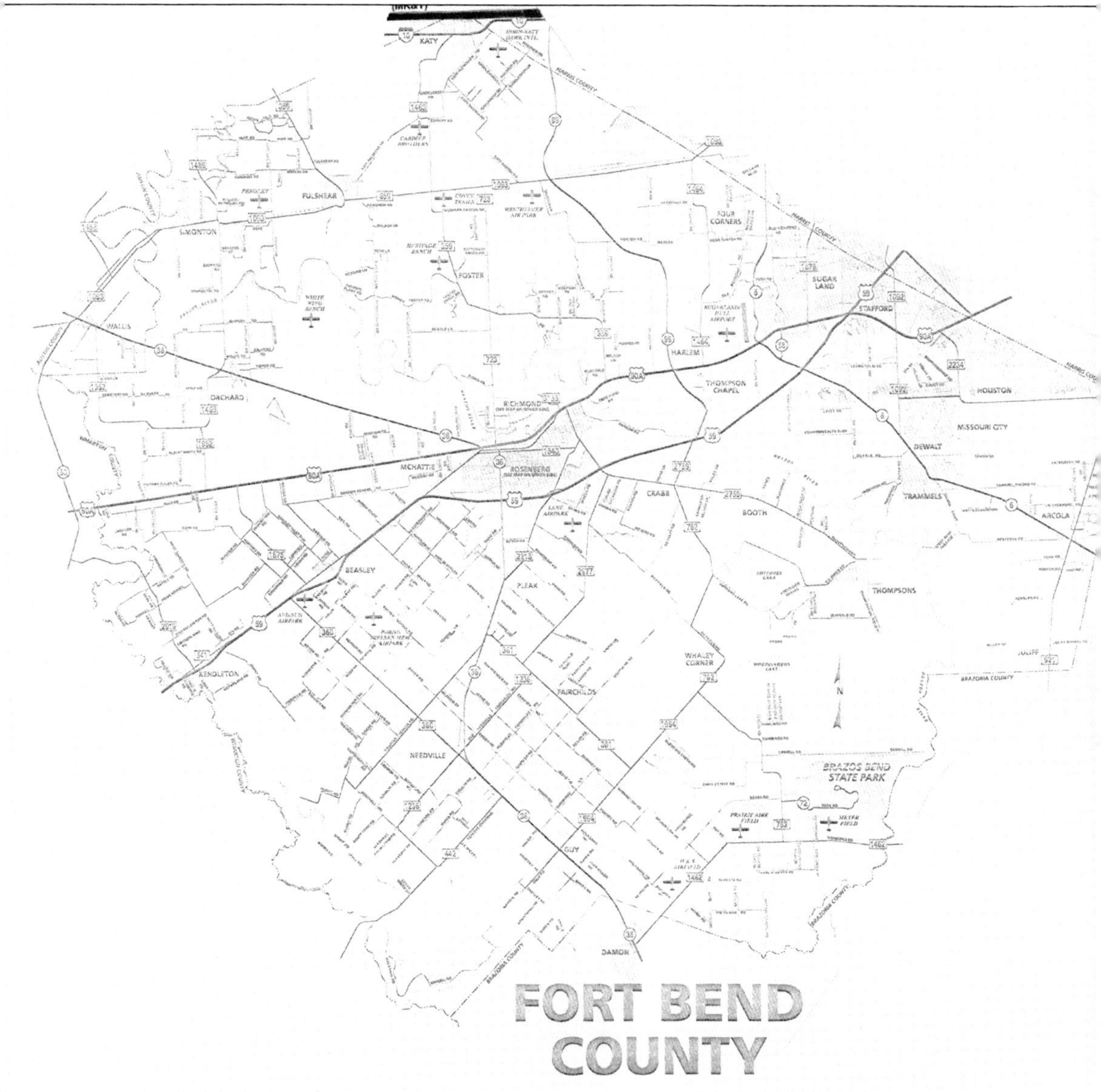

This map of Fort Bend County reflects the route of the Missouri, Kansas, and Texas Railroad along the northernmost portion of the county. Katy, Texas, is the only Fort Bend County town along this route. (Courtesy of the Rosenberg Railroad Museum.)

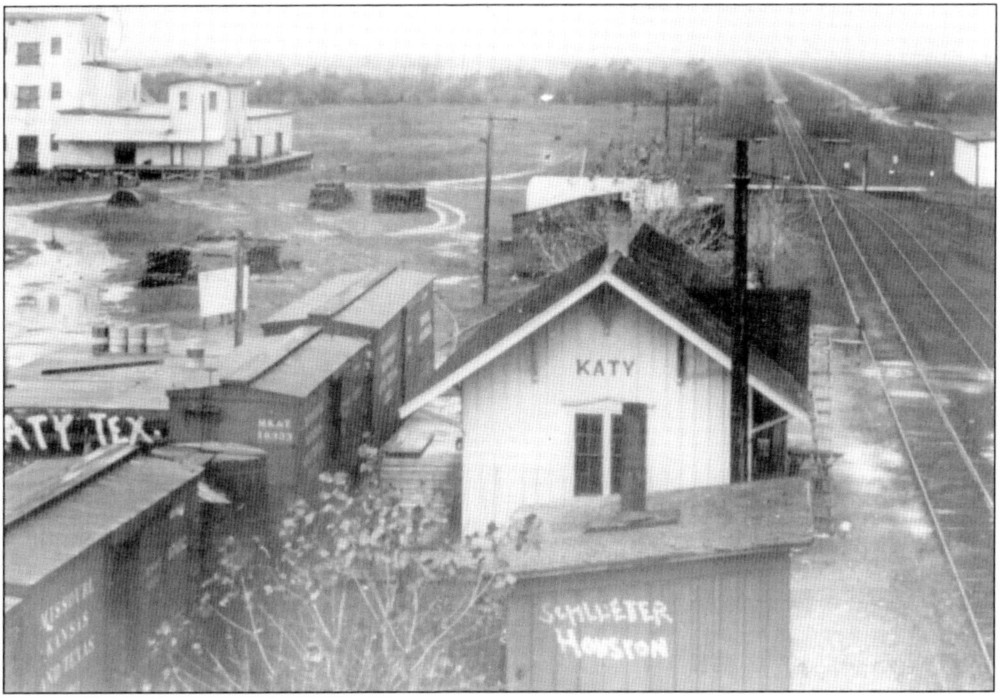

This photograph gives an eastward view of the Missouri, Kansas, and Texas depot, out structures, and mainline track around the late 1800s. (Courtesy of the Rosenberg Railroad Museum Collection.)

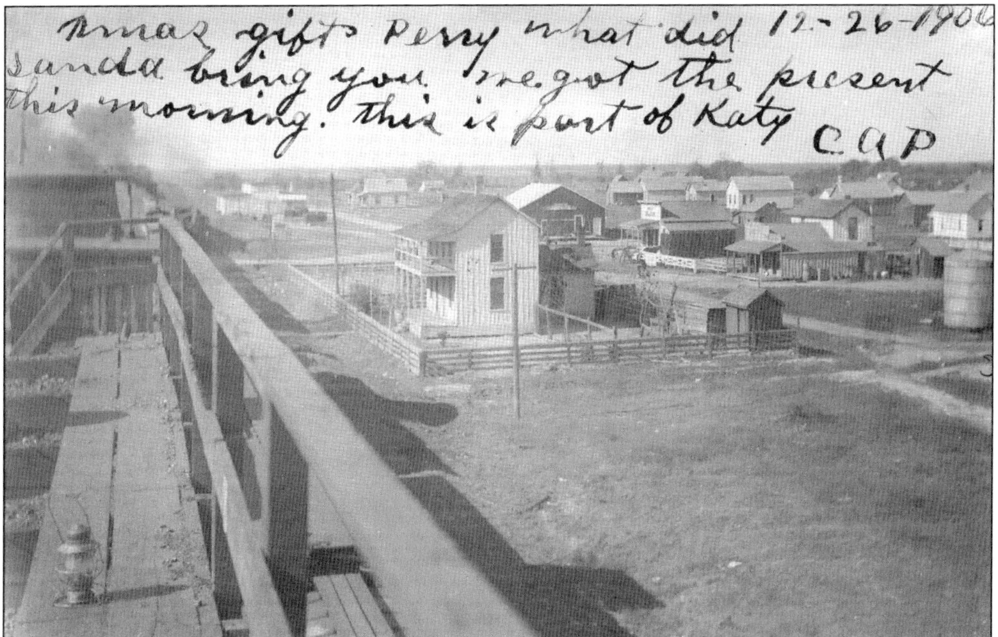

This photograph provides a view of Katy, Texas, from a railcar-loading platform on December 26, 1906. Two MT&T steam locomotives can be seen working the rail yard in the distance. (Courtesy of the Ken E. Stavinoha Collection.)

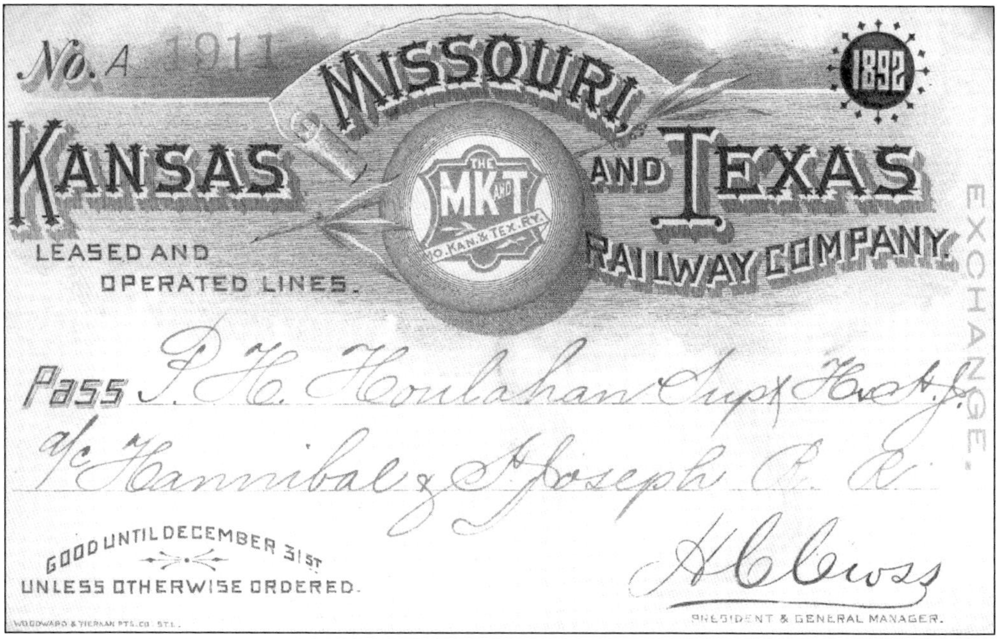

Pass No. A 1911, dated 1892 to P. H. Houlahan, superintendent of the Hannibal and Saint Joseph Railroad, was issued by H. Cross, president and general manager of the MK&T. (Courtesy of the Ken E. Stavinoha Collection.)

4 SOUTHWARD TRAINS							HOUSTON DIVISION		NORTHWARD TRAINS					
FOURTH CLASS		THIRD CLASS		FIRST CLASS			TIME TABLE NO. 23	Fuel, Water, Telephone, Turn Table, Track Scales, Wye and Car Capacity Siding	FIRST CLASS		THIRD CLASS		FOURTH CLASS	
95 Way	91 Way	71 Bullet	81 Katy Komet	11 Passenger	25 Katy Flyer	Distance from St. Louis	Effective 12:01 A. M. May 12, 1946		24 Katy Limited	26 Katy Flyer	72 Fast Freight	80 Katy Komet	90 Way	94 Way
Daily Except Sunday	Tuesday Thursday Saturday	Daily	Daily	Daily	Daily		STATIONS		Daily	Daily	Daily	Daily	Monday Wednesday Friday	Daily Except Sunday
	AM s11.00	PM 3.45	AM 12.30	PM s 2.45	AM 3.50	908.1	N GRANGER G	Yard 115 WYPO	PM s 3.45	AM 1.45	PM 4.40	AM 1.30	AM s11.30	
	11.15	4.00	12.41	2.55	3.59	915.2	7.1 EVANS	P 76	3.30	1.35	4.20	1.10	11.10	
	s11.40	4.10	12.47	s 2.59	s 4.04	918.9	3.7 N TAYLOR L-GN Interlocker JG	PYS 77 28 37	s 3.25	s 1.30	4.10	1.03	s11.00	
	11.50	4.20	12.54	3.10	4.16	923.9	5.0 HAYDEN	P 103	3.10	1.19	4.00	12.54	10.00	
	PM f12.01	4.25	1.15	s 3.14	4.20	926.7	2.8 D COUPLAND CD	P 41	s 3.06	1.15	3.50	12.45	f 9.50	
				s 3.25	s 4.33	934.8	3.1 N ELGIN T&NO Interlocker J	PY	s 2.56	f 1.05				
	s12.25	4.50	1.30	3.27	4.35	935.0	0.2 ELGIN YARD	PW 127	2.53	1.04	3.27	12.30	s 9.30	
	12.45	5.15	1.43	f 3.40	4.46	943.6	8.6 SAYERS	P 70	f 2.42	12.54	3.05	12.15	f 8.55	
	f12.55	5.25	1.50	f 3.48	f 4.52	947.0	3.4 DUNSTAN	PY 24	f 2.36	f12.49	2.55	12.08	f 8.45	
	f 1.00	5.30	1.53	3.51	4.54	948.9	1.9 PHELAN	P 99	2.33	12.46	2.50	12.05 AM	f 8.25	
	s 1.15	5.45	2.05	s 4.01	s 5.05	953.8	4.9 D BASTROP BA	FW 69	s 2.25	s12.39	2.40	11.55	s 8.15	
	f 1.25	5.55	2.13	f 4.08	5.12	958.4	4.6 LITTLE	P 93	f 2.17	12.31	2.30	11.47	f 8.00	
	f 1.35	6.05	2.20	4.15	5.18	962.4	4.0 UPTON	P 70	f 2.10	12.25	2.22	11.40	f 7.50	
PM 6.30	2.00 PM	6.30 7.30	2.30 2.40	s 4.25 4.35	s 5.30 5.35	969.4	7.0 N SMITHVILLE SM	OWPSTY Yard	s 2.00 1.50	s12.15 12.10	2.10 1.00	11.30 11.10	7.30 AM	PM 3.00
6.45		7.45	2.50	4.43	5.42	974.0	4.6 KIRTLEY	P 73	1.41	12.01 AM	12.35	10.48		f 2.45
7.05		8.00	2.59	s 4.51	5.49	978.3	4.3 T&NO Interlocker N WEST POINT WP	PY 110	s 1.33	11.55	12.20	10.39		s 2.35
7.20		8.15	3.07	s 5.00	5.56	982.9	4.6 PLUM	P 103	s 1.25	11.48	12.05 PM	10.31		f 2.20
				s 5.12	s 6.05	988.2	5.3 D LA GRANGE RA	P	s 1.16	s11.40				
7.50		8.30	3.19	5.14	6.07	989.0	0.8 LA GRANGE YARD	FW 38	1.12	11.36	11.50	10.19		s 2.00
8.05		8.45	3.30	f 5.23	6.14	994.2	5.2 HALSTED	P 65	f 1.05	11.29	11.35	10.10		f 1.15
8.35		9.05	3.46	s 5.35	6.25	1002.1	7.9 D FAYETTEVILLE VY	P 115	s12.53	11.19	11.15	9.55		s12.53
9.05		9.45	3.56	5.43	6.32	1007.1	5.0 NICHOLS	P 81	12.46	11.12	10.55	9.45		12.30
9.35		10.15	4.09	s 5.53	6.40	1013.6	6.5 D NEW ULM UM	TY 118	s12.37	11.04	10.35	9.33		s12.05 PM
10.05		10.52	4.30	s 6.08	6.52	1024.0	10.4 D CAT SPRING CS	P 115	s12.21	10.52	10.05	9.17		f11.40
11.10		11.30	4.52	s 6.23	f 7.05	1035.0	11.0 N SEALY GC&SF Interlocker SY	WPY 50 82	s12.05 PM	f10.39	9.35	9.00		s11.10
11.22		11.45	5.07	6.33	7.13	1041.9	6.9 ELLIS	P 56	11.53	10.30	9.15	8.44		9.30
11.44		AM 12.01	5.19	s 6.44	7.22	1047.8	5.9 D BROOKSHIRE BK	P 100	s11.44	10.22	9.00	8.33		s 9.00
PM 12.10		12.10	5.27	6.50	7.27	1051.7	3.9 JOHNSUE	P Yard	11.39	10.17	8.50	8.26		f 8.30
12.25		12.25	5.36	s 6.56	7.32	1056.0	4.3 D KATY RS	WP 92	s11.33	10.11	8.40	8.19		s 7.32
12.40		12.40	5.45	7.03	7.38	1060.4	4.4 CRING	P 98	11.25	10.05	8.25	8.10		7.10
12.55		12.55	6.00	s 7.12	7.46	1066.5	6.1 ADDICKS	P 181	f11.17	9.58	8.10	7.57		f 6.58
1.10		1.10	6.15	7.20	7.54	1072.9	6.4 HENNESSEY	P 119	11.08	9.51	7.54	7.45		6.45
1.25		1.30	6.30	7.29	8.02	1079.5	6.6 T&NO Interlocker N EUREKA KA	P 125	11.00	9.43	7.25	7.29		6.30
				f 7.34	f 8.06	1081.1	1.6 T&NO Interlocking Device HOUSTON HEIGHTS		f10.55	f 9.40				
						1082.5	1.4 SPRING STREET							

Timetable No. 23 for the Missouri, Kansas, and Texas Railroad gives the daily schedule of northbound and southbound train arrivals and departures on the MK&T. The Houston Division timetable was dated May 12, 1946. (Courtesy of the Ken E. Stavinoha Collection.)

Nine

Today's Railroads

Today Fort Bend County is served by four Class 1 railroad companies. The Union Pacific Railroad operates approximately 20 trains daily on the old Sunset Route through the county, which is now a part of the Glidden Subdivision. A local train operates out of Sugar Land, Texas, performing switching to local customers and providing interchange of freight with the Burlington Northern Santa Fe Railroad (BNSF) in Rosenberg, Texas.

The Burlington Northern Santa Fe Railroad operates approximately 30 trains daily on the Galveston Subdivision. The BNSF also operates a local train for customers in Fort Bend County and also performs freight interchange with the Union Pacific in Rosenberg. Originally stationed in Rosenberg, it operates out of Sealy, Texas, as of this writing. BNSF services the W. A. Parish Power Plant located in Thompson, Texas, with numerous unit coal trains originating from the Powder River Basin in Wyoming.

The Kansas City Southern Railroad (KCS) operates approximately six trains daily through Fort Bend County using trackage rights on the Union Pacific Glidden Subdivision to Tower 3 located in Flatonia, Texas, where the KCS turns south on its way to Mexico. The operation to Flatonia was abandoned in June 2009 when KCS reopened the historic Macaroni Line between Rosenberg and Victoria, Texas. It also opened and operates a new Intermodal container facility and automobile distribution center in Kendleton, Texas.

Amtrak passenger trains operate in and out of Houston, Texas. The Sunset Limited Trains 1 and 2 travel through Fort Bend County daily on the Union Pacific Glidden Subdivision. There have been no passenger trains servicing Fort Bend County since the 1970s, but discussions have been held about the possibility of future commuter rail service to the county.

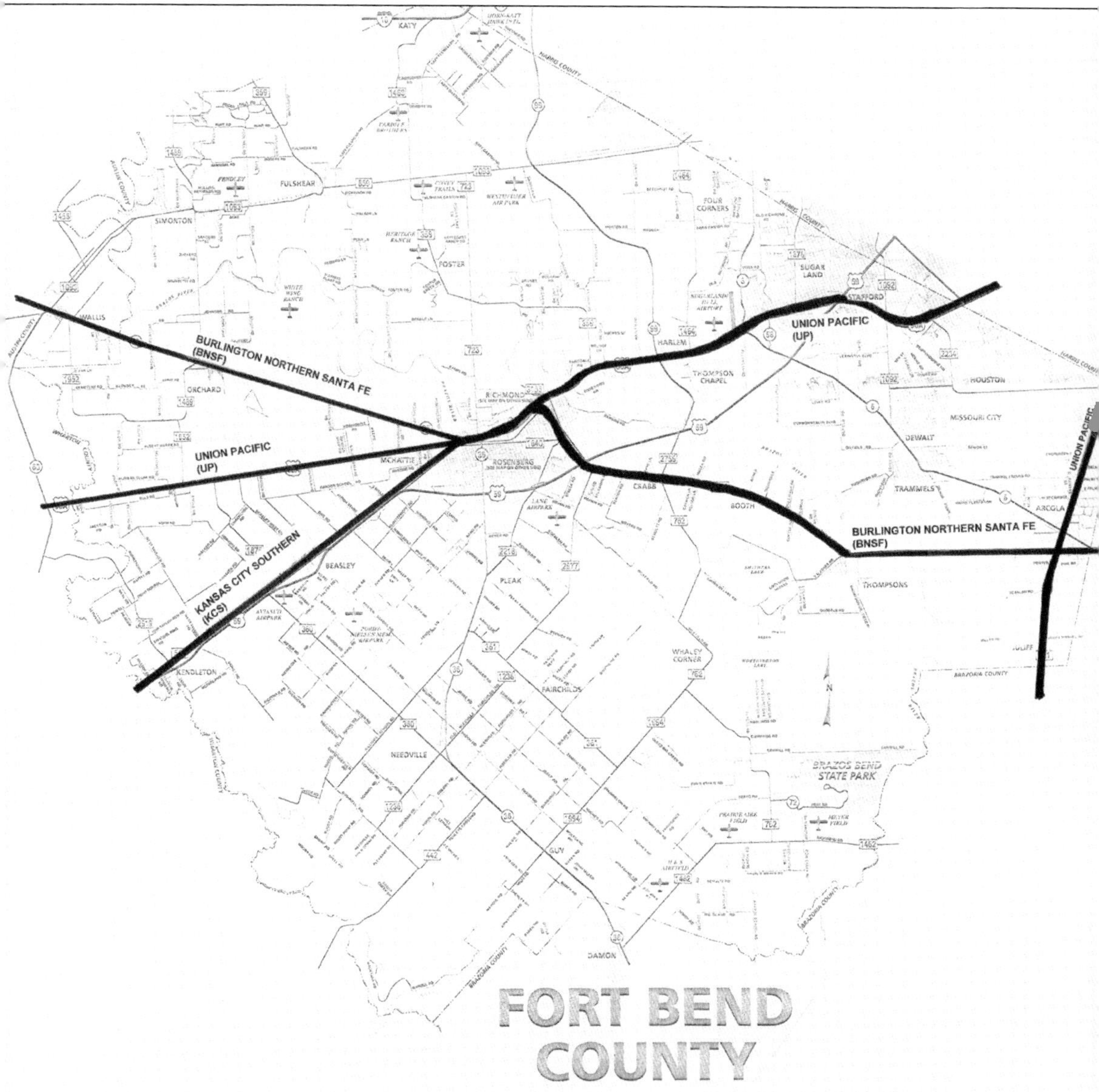

This map of Fort Bend County reflects modern-day railroading in Fort Bend County. Union Pacific, Burlington Northern Santa Fe, Kansas City Southern, and Amtrak make up today's railroads through Fort Bend County. (Author's collection.)

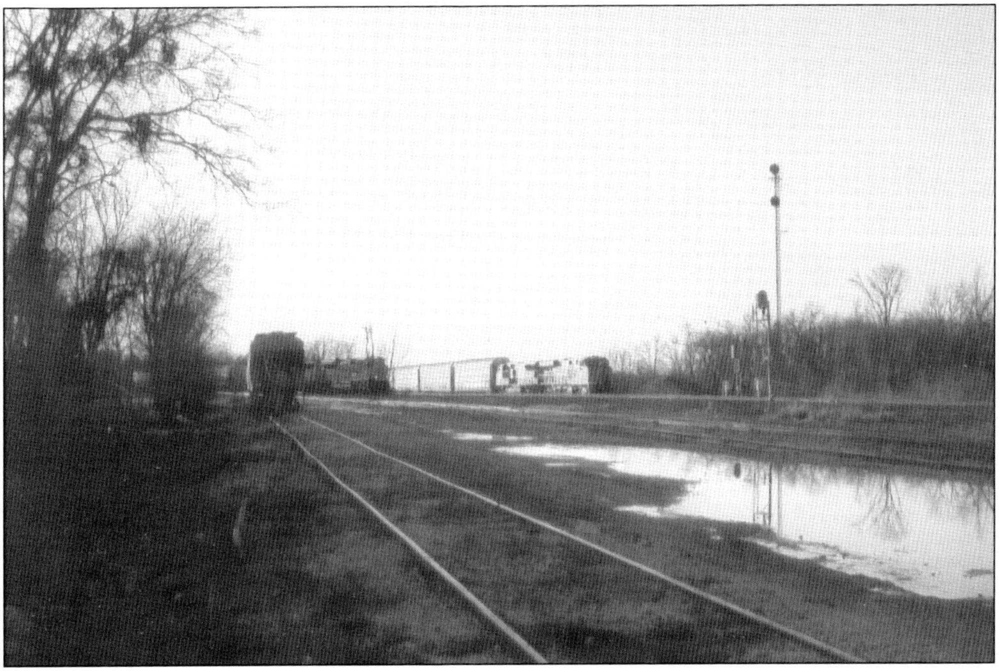

A Union Pacific stack train is holding in a siding, and a KCS unit grain train is ready to exit the KCS Rosenberg Division line to head east. Both trains had to hold their position while the Union Pacific dispatcher in Spring, Texas, allowed two BNSF trackage right trains to exit the UP Glidden Subdivision onto their own tracks at Tower 17 in Rosenberg. (Author's collection.)

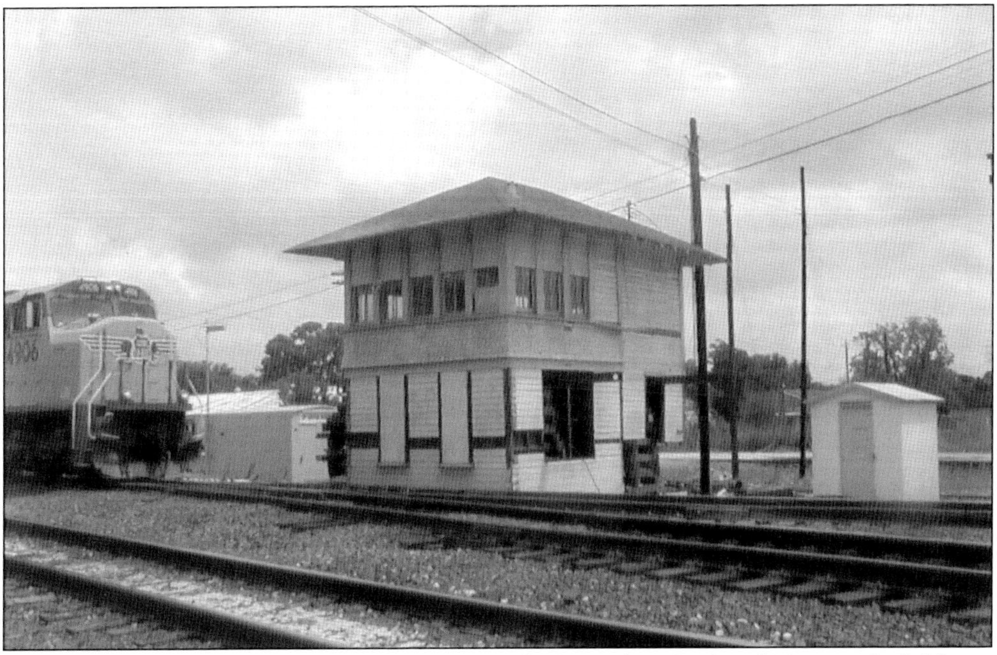

Day three of preparing Tower 17 for its move to the Rosenberg Railroad Museum finds Union Pacific 4906 leading a mixed manifest train westbound through the interlocker past Tower 17. (Author's collection.)

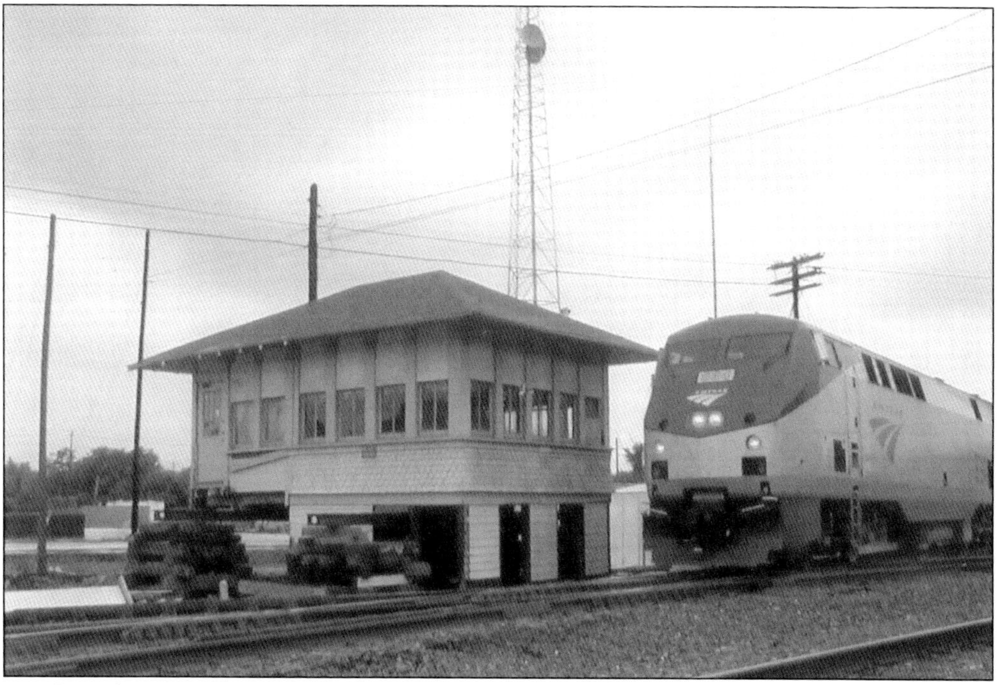

Day four of preparing Tower 17 for its move finds Amtrak's Sunset Limited Train No. 2 passing the tower. The first floor was removed from the tower in sections and moved to the Rosenberg Railroad Museum. The second floor was moved intact complete with the interlocker machine and metering still in place. (Author's collection.)

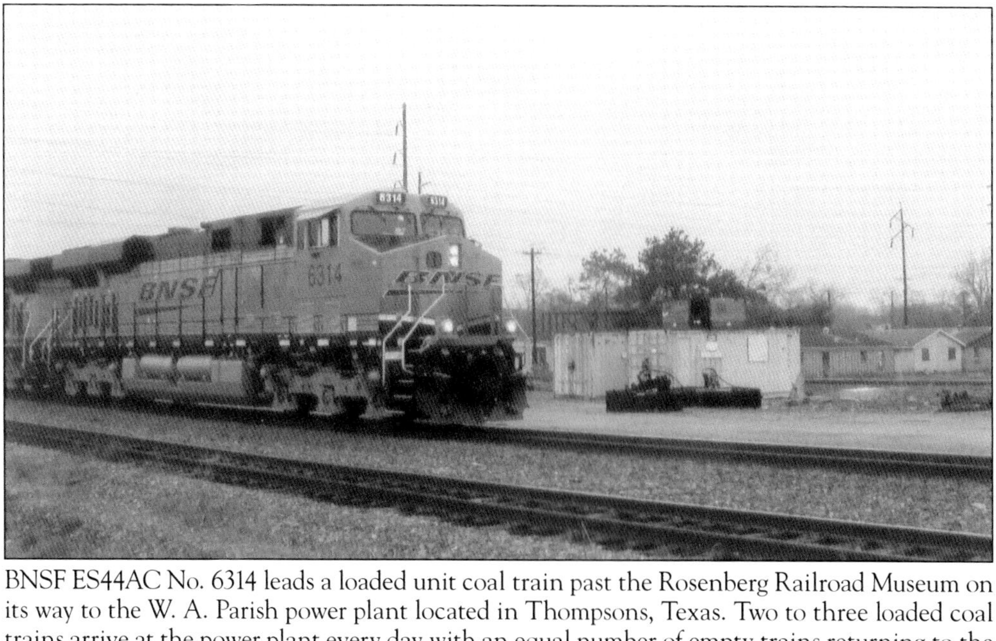

BNSF ES44AC No. 6314 leads a loaded unit coal train past the Rosenberg Railroad Museum on its way to the W. A. Parish power plant located in Thompsons, Texas. Two to three loaded coal trains arrive at the power plant every day with an equal number of empty trains returning to the Power River Basin for reloading. (Author's collection.)

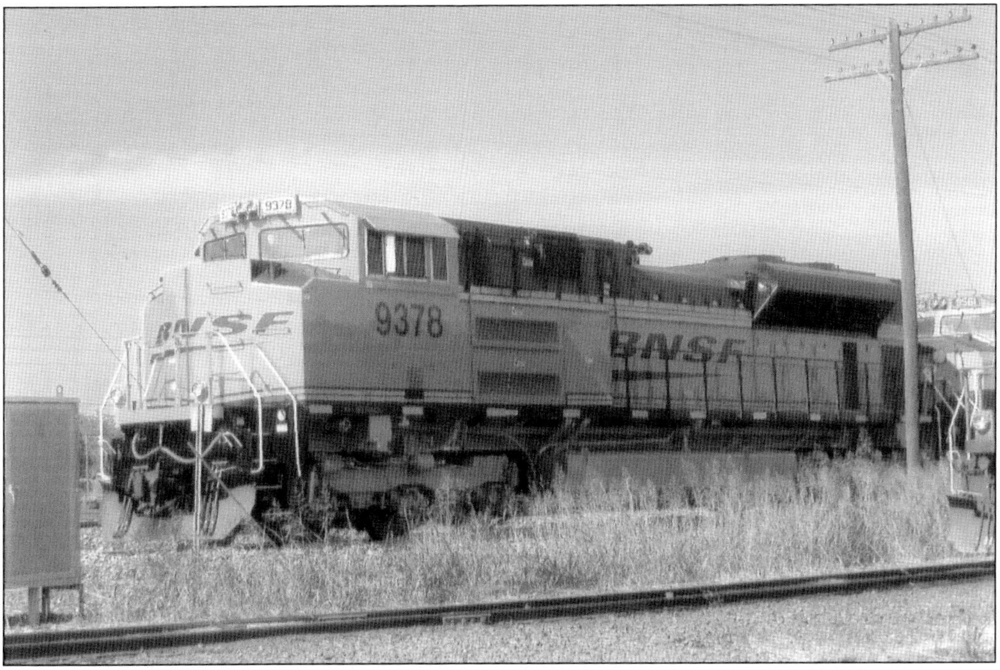

BNSF 9378 leads a northbound unit grain train through Rosenberg, Texas. This locomotive is one of BNSF's new SD70ACe environmentally friendly locomotives. (Author's collection.)

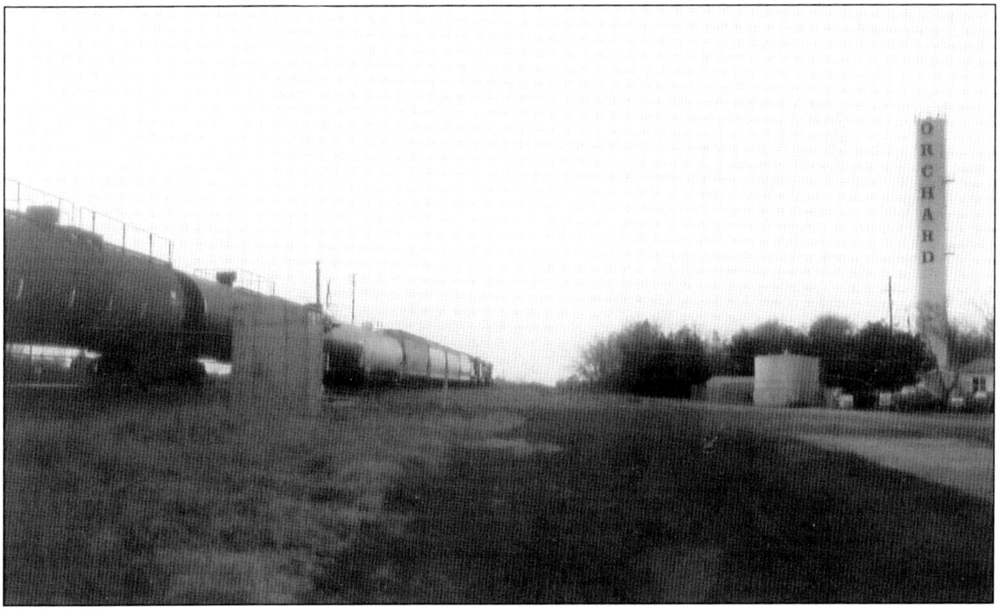

A northbound BNSF mixed manifest train passes through Orchard, Texas, at track speed. Orchard is located at the northernmost part of Fort Bend County on the BNSF Galveston Subdivision, formerly the Gulf, Colorado, and Santa Fe Railroad. (Author's collection.)

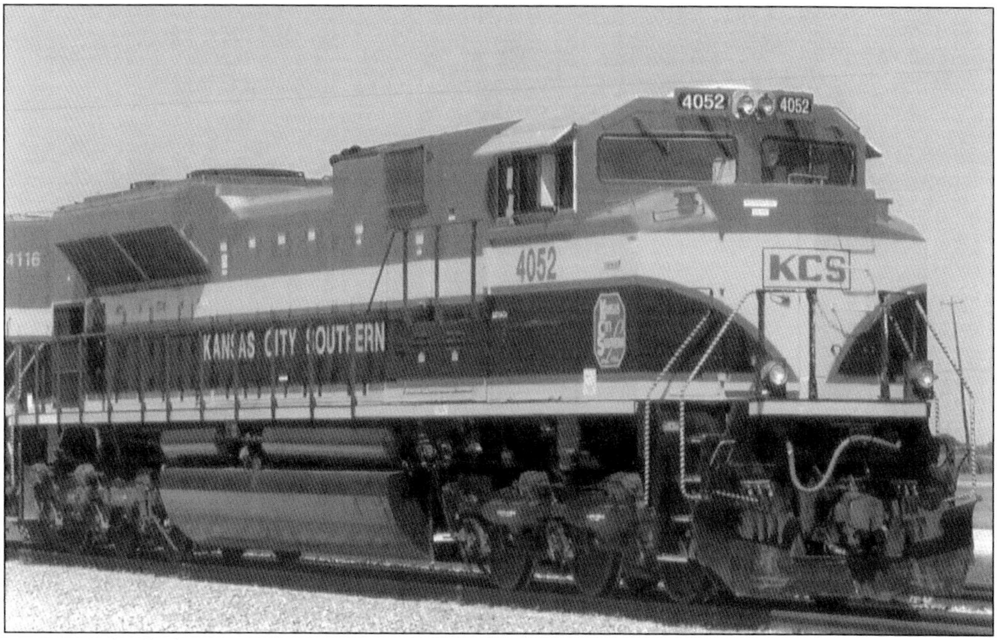

KCS 4052 leads the inaugural run on the former Macaroni Line now known as the KCS Rosenberg Subdivision. Starting at the new intermodal facility in Kendleton, Texas, this train was the first revenue run on the restored line. (Author's collection.)

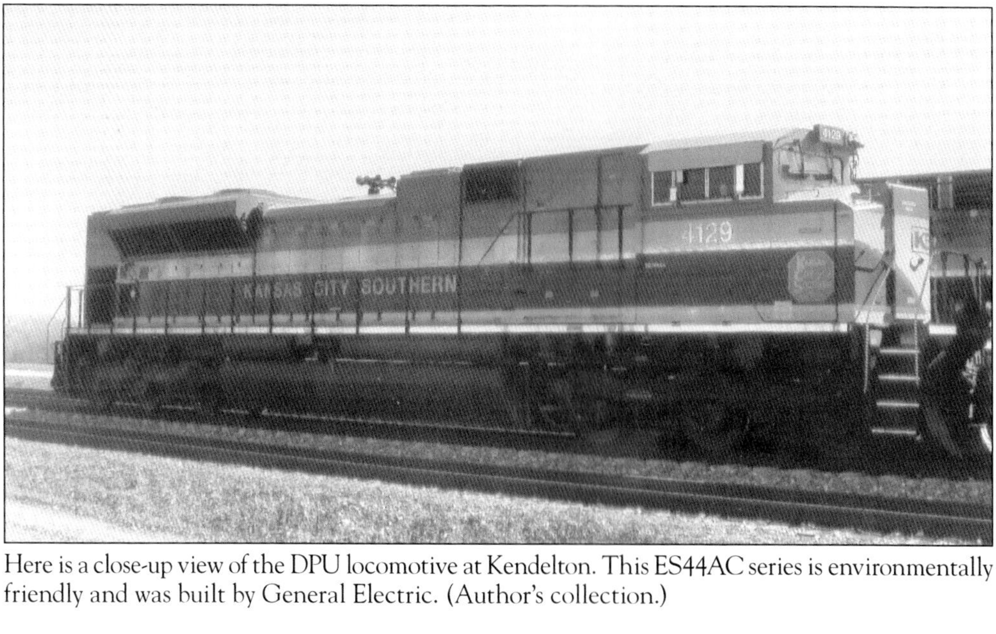

Here is a close-up view of the DPU locomotive at Kendelton. This ES44AC series is environmentally friendly and was built by General Electric. (Author's collection.)

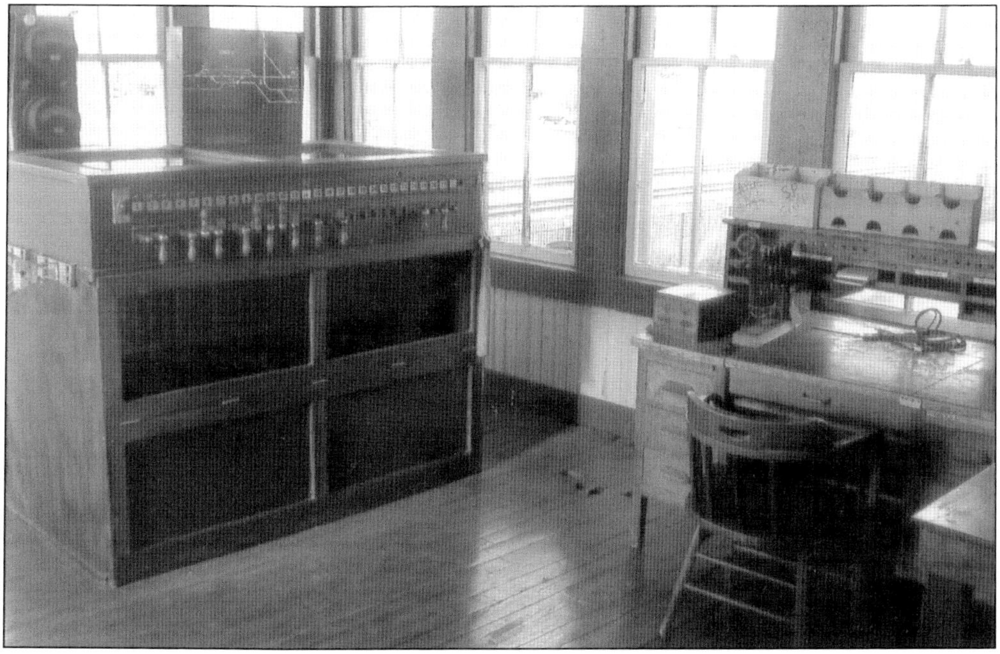

This photograph shows the original interlocker machine for Tower 17. The second floor of the tower was restored by the Rosenberg Railroad Museum to its precomputer days. It was researched and painted to the original railroad colors as an Eagle Scout project by Tyler Valentine of Richmond, Texas. (Author's collection.)

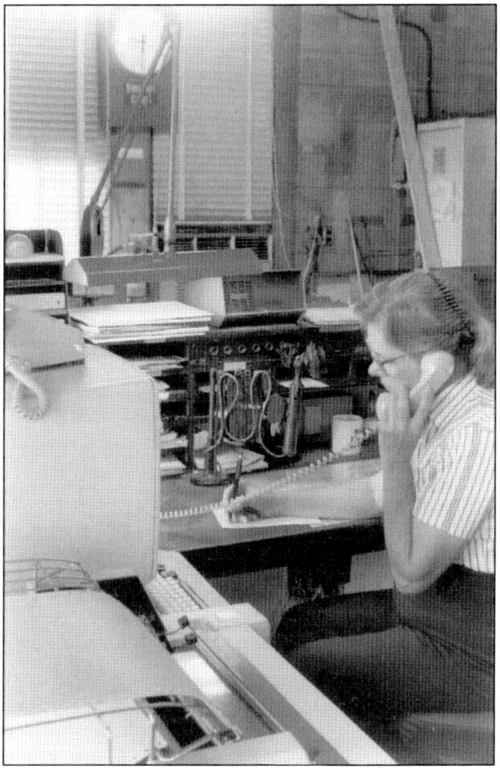

One of the first female tower operators for the Southern Pacific Railroad was Mary Meyers. Mary is seen here contacting the railroad dispatcher to confirm train movements through the Tower 17 interlocking plant in the mid-1980s. The scissor phone in the photograph is working as a microphone and continued operating until February 10, 2004, when Tower 17 closed and transferred its operation to the Union Pacific dispatcher located in Spring, Texas. This closure ended the tower's 101 years of continuous service. (Courtesy of the Ken E. Stavinoha Collection.)

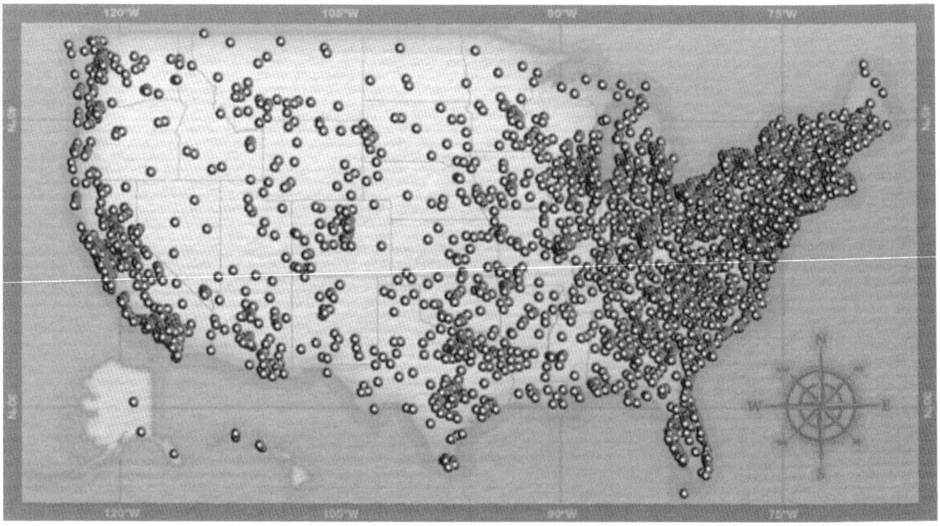